WOMEN VS CAPITALISM

VICKY PRYCE

Women vs Capitalism

*Why We Can't Have It All in a
Free Market Economy*

HURST & COMPANY, LONDON

First published in the United Kingdom in 2019 by
C. Hurst & Co. (Publishers) Ltd.,
41 Great Russell Street, London, WC1B 3PL
© Vicky Pryce, 2019
All rights reserved.

Distributed in the United States, Canada and Latin America by
Oxford University Press, 198 Madison Avenue, New York,
NY 10016, United States of America.

The right of Vicky Pryce to be identified as the author of
this publication is asserted by her in accordance with the
Copyright, Designs and Patents Act, 1988.

A Cataloguing-in-Publication data record for this book is
available from the British Library.

ISBN: 9781787381742

This book is printed using paper from registered sustainable
and managed sources.

www.hurstpublishers.com

Printed in Great Britain by Bell and Bain Ltd, Glasgow

CONTENTS

ACKNOWLEDGEMENTS

While preparing this book, I was conscious that evidence-gathering would be at the heart of it. There were times when I was fretting about the lack of controlled experiments I would have liked to quote in relation to women's work and status in the economy. Thankfully, a fair number do exist, but I was so convinced that all was not right in the use of women's resources that I ploughed on. I wish to thank particularly my old government colleagues Andy Ross and Mark Beatson, for pointing at sources and correcting my economics; Danae Kyriakopoulou for her revealing research into gender in the financial sector; Professor Danny Dorling, who encouraged me to carry on and who sent me his own findings and observations on the topic of gender equality; Simon Skovgaard for his comparative analysis, and Afroditi Argyropoulou for the insights of her master's thesis into organisational psychology and unconscious bias in hiring decisions.

In addition, I would also like to thank Jonny Gifford at CIPD, and Professor Peter Urwin, with whom I discussed my thoughts and who believed there was something new in my thinking. I am grateful to Gordon Stoker for his wisdom. Thanks go also to John

Kampfner and Helene von Bismarck for their brilliant insights into Germany's attitudes concerning a woman's place, at work and in society. I am particularly indebted to Beverley Nielsen, my colleague at Birmingham City University, for helping conduct interviews for this book with real live entrepreneurs, and to the women role models who answered our questions: Emma Bridgewater, Angela Burman, Sukhi Clark, Ann Bentley, Sara Page, Nicola Fleet-Milne, Katherine Jenner, Jeanie Falconer, Geeta and Reena Salhan, and Rebecca Struthers.

To these must be added Alex Marcham, Georgia Beesley, Alexandra Toogood, Laura MacShane, Kat Usita and Lydia Hajaj-Huhne, whose own experiences as young working women, sometimes with very small children, helped inform the book of whatever progress may have taken place in the workplace and in society more generally in the last few decades, both for them and for their partners. I wanted also to thank Nico Kourmouzis and Peter Huhne, archetypal young 'new men' who supported me throughout. I am also grateful to Pauline Neville-Jones, Belinda Phipps, Melanie Richards and Suzanne Franks, successful senior women who didn't shirk from telling it like it is.

But the book would not have been written without the encouragement of my agent, Toby Mundy, the tough editing of the current volume by Lara Weisweiller-Wu and Daisy Leitch at Hurst, and the support and enthusiasm of Alison Alexanian in promoting the idea of the book.

INTRODUCTION

It's time to tell a very uncomfortable truth: capitalism cannot bring about gender equality. Market forces alone just won't do it—they haven't, won't and can't. State intervention in the labour market is needed to achieve economic equality, and only with economic equality will there ever be wider social and cultural equality. This will require a large part of the population, currently largely excluded from decision-making, to become involved in shaping our economic system. This book is about why we haven't got there, and what we need to make it happen.

Of course, there are other explanations for global economic gender inequality, from evolutionary psychology, anthropology or elsewhere. But this book shows that, at root, it is a question of malfunctioning labour markets, which are failing to make the best use of the resources available in our societies, due to the short-termism ingrained in the capitalist system. Despite a substantial improvement across the world in women's education, women are still over-represented in lower-paid, lower-skilled occupations, in no small part due to ongoing

1

biases about what constitutes 'women's work', and this has been a contributory factor in the persistence of both the wage gap and wider gender inequality.

It has been said many times before, by Piketty and others, that capitalism does not automatically produce equality—and it is true. Adam Smith's 'invisible hand' doesn't quite do it, even when it's helped a bit by the more 'visible hand' of the state. The West has been operating for quite some time under a capitalist system of more or less free markets. If gender equality was going to happen under this system then it would have arrived by now. Sadly, I was born a woman in a man's world, and at this rate I will die a woman in a man's world. Yes, my own professional life has been 'successful'—despite some serious ups and downs on the way—and, believe me, I really do count my blessings for that. But, like so many women, I've found that, for just about everything a woman achieves, she has to work harder at it than a man does. Yes, we can open more doors today than we could in the past. Yet those doors are still heavier for us. That is not because we are the weaker sex, but because we so often have to haul men out of the way, all while tending to the many extra doors we are typically made responsible for.

So where exactly are we in 2019? There is some good news, and some very depressing news. The World Economic Forum (WEF) tracks a number of areas of women's involvement in the life of a country, such as economic participation and opportunity, educational attainment, health and survival, and political empowerment. According to the WEF, there has been an overall global improvement in the lot of women since 2006. But the depressing news is that this change has been at a 'glacial pace'. At the current rate, the WEF warns, it will take more than 100 years for the world's women to achieve equality with its men. Even in Europe, progress has been very poor, as shown by the EU's own Gender Equality Index. If we want proof, we need look no further than the near-straight lines in the graph below:

Trends in EU gender equality, 2005–15

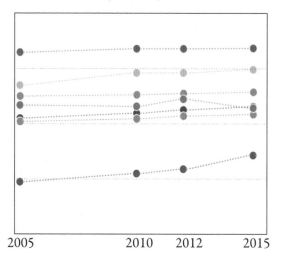

Source: European Institute for Gender Equality, 2017.
Notes: Measuring, from top to bottom at 2005: health, money, work, time, total, knowledge and power.

There has been some improvement in European women's pay and power in recent years, but the pace is still slow, and overall attitudes seem to have changed little. Although female representation in the European Parliament is improving, as recently as June 2019 Malta's EU affairs minister, Helena Dalli, bemoaned the lack of sufficient moves towards gender parity in EU institutions such as the Commission.

As the new Commission was being set up after the May 2019 European elections, the top roles—President of the Commission, President of the European Council, and chief of the European Central Bank—were being hotly disputed and finally allocated. Women were very much absent from the conversation and from the lists. Only one woman's name was really floated, though not very seriously: Christine Lagarde, a former French minister of finance and head of the International Monetary Fund (IMF) since 2011. As she toured European countries in early 2019, I was struck by the lone figure Lagarde often presented, sitting and being photographed with the cabinets of various EU states, surrounded mostly by men. Since the financial crisis, the fate of my home country, Greece, has been decided and controlled by the Eurogroup of Eurozone finance ministers, which has hardly ever featured a woman. Maybe that explains the lack of compassion towards the terrible plight of my compatriots, who have lost more than a quarter of their GDP since 2009.

To everyone's surprise, Christine Lagarde has been appointed the next President of the European Central Bank, and another woman, Ursula von der Leyen, is taking over as President of the European Commission. Time to rejoice? The only issue is that these two women were only nominated at the eleventh hour as compromise candidates, after the various countries and parties that dominate the newly elected European Parliament were unable to agree on their preferred candidates—all of whom were men. As a result, the two eminent women now appointed have come across as 'second best'. I sincerely hope they both prove those male parliamentarians wrong. Indeed, von der Leyen has asked early on that each member state present her with two candidates for Commissioner of the new European Commission, due to start operating from 1 November.

Of course in textbook economics, and according to most teachings in our universities today, market forces would quickly eliminate gender inequalities that are 'irrational'—that is, ones that do not fit with pursuit of profit. In other words, if, given the gender pay gap, women are equally as productive as men, but cheaper, firms that were neglecting such a resource would be competed out of business by firms that did not discriminate and reaped the rewards of cheaper labour. But the more these surviving firms take advantage of the cheaper resource, the more they will drive up its cost, until both resources have equal market value. In this naïve theory, competition and market forces are sufficient to eliminate the pay gap through a kind of business version of 'natural selection'. In reality, though, they haven't. I want to explain why, and what to do about it.

One reason why we haven't seen this self-correction to the labour market is that market mechanisms, usually portrayed as indifferent 'natural' forces, are in fact the outcomes of trillions of decisions made by real human beings. For domestic day-to-day life, those decisions are still usually made by a woman, while in the workplace the decisions still fall predominantly to a man. Even when women are in a position to make decisions at work, they are very often made to navigate gender expectations, by both main genders, and a workplace dominated by men. Moreover, the system of free market capitalism in which these women are employed is geared towards achieving short-term profit at the expense of longer-term sustainability that would benefit all. In most democracies, thanks to the political cycle, this short-term expediency also works against looking at the long-term value of business decisions. In free-market societies, the stock market requirements of quarterly profit reporting have the same short-termist effect. As the famous inter- and postwar UK economist John Maynard Keynes said, in the long term we are all dead. But that concept can be a very disturbing one for policy, as it shows clearly that people, both in private and in the public sphere, usually have a very high 'time discount rate'—in other words, they value short-term gain that is easily seen and enjoyed, more than they value waiting for longer-term satisfaction at some future date.

One possible conclusion from this conundrum—and it has often been expressed this way—is that feminism is simply not compatible with capitalism. Investing to achieve a long-term change (in perceptions of women's worth, for example) is inimical to short-term profit and the average political electoral cycle. Even if women did somehow achieve equality, this view goes, the system they inherited would still be a profoundly unequal one, unless we can be certain that women would make better and fairer decisions than men at every step of the way. Well, it is true that we can't be sure, as we haven't had very many female leaders in the past. But surely it is worth a try—and even if gender equality proved impossible, at least the economy would be more efficient, healthier and richer, thanks to the process of investing in women's talent and ensuring their labour force participation was not constrained artificially in any way. There is overwhelming evidence linking higher women's labour force participation with greater national development. I will cover this in later parts of the book.

Talking of constraints, in my mid-twenties, after university, I worked in the economics department of Williams & Glyn's Bank, later the Royal Bank of Scotland; I was also just about to have my first child. One day, late in my pregnancy, one of the assistants eyed my bump and told me that she wished me well, although she quickly stressed that she had never wanted children and that she and her trade unionist husband were perfectly happy as they were. A few years later, she confessed—to my great surprise—that she actually had a daughter, by then 14, but had been keeping her existence hidden, as she was worried that she wouldn't have been hired in the first place if she had disclosed that she was a mother. By the time she told me all this, in the late 1970s, the Equal Pay Act of 1970 had started having an impact, prohibiting different treatment of men and women in terms of pay and conditions of employment. So had the Sex Discrimination Act of 1975, intended to protect people from discrimination in employment, training, education and other activities on the grounds of sex or marital status. Nevertheless, my colleague had continued to keep her daughter a secret from most of her co-workers.

I was astounded. On reflection, however, it had made perfect sense for her to conceal her motherhood in the first place, and then of course it would have been difficult to reveal. Clearly circumstances had been very different then, I thought, and how good that things had changed. And yet, more than forty years later, a 2018 YouGov survey of small, medium and large firms in the UK found that fully one third of HR recruiters still asked women if they were pregnant or expected to have children anytime soon, even though this practice is now illegal. A majority of senior decision-makers in the UK private sector thought that a woman should have to disclose pregnancy at interview (59%), and only slightly fewer found it reasonable to ask women candidates if they had small children (46%). Two out of five firms thought that a woman with more than one child was a burden to other employees. The Chief Executive of the UK's Equality and Human Rights Commission, Rebecca Hilsenrath, called these findings 'depressing' evidence that British business was still 'in the dark ages'.[1]

In this environment, it's unsurprising that women still feel that motherhood could harm their career. A Fawcett Society survey looking at career prospects found that some 23% of women who had recently returned to work from maternity leave felt that their opportunities for promotion had worsened.[2] Around 55% of respondents felt that, in order to progress, they had to be working full-time. And of those, two in five felt that this was due to senior staff assuming that the returning women would no longer want or be capable of promotion. That is a very large percentage of people who feel, and in fact probably are, disadvantaged. Even in the UK civil service, which is an exemplar of good practice in this area, women working part-time say that not 'being there' all the time means that somehow, maybe even unconsciously, you get overlooked when there are especially interesting projects to do; in turn this means missing out on praise, recognition, rewards and advancement.

In April 2018, as larger firms started publishing their gender pay gap data, under government duress, there was more bad news. Many sectors and companies revealed substantial gaps between men's and women's median and average salaries, the worst being in the financial sector. I spent a lot of my early years as an economist sitting next to the foreign exchange trading floor, and yet at the time I did not quite comprehend what was setting them all apart from us. A number of traders I got to know—all men at the time, though things have changed a bit—retired early. This was partly because of burnout, as the job is very stressful and involves taking lots of risks—and partly because they had made enough to be able to give up work in favour of something more pleasurable and sedate. I, like most other women I know, have carried on working in the decades that have followed.

This pay gap is not just in the financial sector, although it was on average the worst offender in 2018. To give a few examples from other areas of the economy, the sportswear chain Sweaty Betty, where the staff are 99% women, had a median pay gap of 68%; at Phase Eight Fashion Design, women earned 51p for every £1 that men earned; the Universities of Liverpool and Manchester both had a massive bonus gap of 90% and 87% respectively. In 2019, *The Economist* Group remained the UK media company with the highest median pay gap, with women paid 29.2% less per hour than men. This is not only a UK problem: in the US, the women's national football team—winners of the 2019 Women's World Cup—have felt obliged to sue US Soccer over discrimination in rewards, despite their performance being superior to that of the men's team.

The gender pay gap is only partly the result of women being paid less for doing similar or effectively identical jobs. This is still sometimes the case, as recently made very publicly clear at the BBC, for instance; it is also demonstrated in the lower bonuses given to female managers in financial institutions. But the main reasons for the gap are gender differences in occupation and seniority. Women tend to be concentrated in lower-paid jobs, and are underrepresented in senior positions across most organisations.[3] We would be hard pressed to find many women pilots working for EasyJet and Ryanair, where men made up 89% and 97% of top earners in 2018. At JP Morgan, women held a meagre 9% of the senior jobs—better than Ryanair's 3%, but not by much.

Let's take management consultancy as a broader example. Top consultancy McKinsey UK reported an average pay gap of 23% that year, and the difference in overall pay also extended to bonuses, where the average gender gap stood at a whopping 75%.[4] These awful figures owe a great deal to the lack of female representation in the company's upper echelons: something like 60% of women at McKinsey appear in the lowest quartile of wages, despite its UK head being Vivian Hunt, made a dame in the 2018 honours list. Among the big four consulting groups (KPMG, EY, PwC and Deloitte), KPMG reported the worst gap in 2019, and was the only firm of the four that had failed to narrow its gap, which increased to 28%. Again, women account for less than 20% of KPMG's 635 partners. There have been reports of problems with promoting and retaining women in the sector, and the *Financial Times* quoted a former employee who said: 'When I returned after maternity leave my HR [representative] told me that consulting wasn't right for a woman with children and I should look for another job.' A partner at one of the 'big four' has said that certain major firms are 'basically an old boys' club'.

Even organisations with a clear social purpose—often disproportionately serving women—seem unable to oversee gender equality. Homes England, an executive non-departmental public body which replaced the Homes and Communities Agency in 2018, is sponsored by the UK Ministry of Housing, Communities and Local Government. The organisation is there to allocate funding and work with actors across the housing sector to improve housing affordability in England—a very worthy cause. Yet in March 2019 it admitted that its pay gap had barely narrowed over the past year, by 0.2%—it now stands at 18.1%—and the bonus gap was a high 62.7%. Looking at Homes England's management team, I could find only one woman, their Chief of Staff, which I am assuming means HR—a traditional woman's role in organisations.[5] That was a disappointment.

Across the housing associations working with Homes England, 34% of chief executives are women. They make up 36% of housing association boards and 39% of executive teams.[6] Nevertheless, there is a feeling in the sector itself that change isn't happening fast enough. Kelly Henderson is co-founder of the Domestic Abuse Housing Alliance and a board member at WISH North East, the network for women working in social housing. She has been quoted as saying that she wished there was an end to what she described as 'toxic masculinity' in the housing sector,[7] which has an impact on how both men and women behave, encouraging women to think they have to behave 'like men' to succeed. Alongside banking and technology, property has the biggest pay gap of any sector. In housebuilding, Berkeley actually saw a 1% rise in its second year of reporting. In 2019 British Land reported a gap of 40.6%, Landsec 37.9% and Barratt 30.7%. There were also some good performers. Taylor Wimpey reported no gap at all!

How can the system help correct some of these persistent inequities? It is true that a number of investment funds devote a certain percentage of their investments to backing firms that meet environmental, sustainability and governance standards (ESG), including ethical behaviour and non-discrimination in the treatment of staff. In theory at least, this should benefit women at all levels of such companies. But ESG investments still represent only a small part of overall purchase allocation—at the last count, just 2% of the global total. Though it may be increasing, the pressure coming from that side of the markets to do the right thing for women remains weak. I would argue that this surely isn't helped by the very small percentage of women in funds making that type of investment decision. In other words, lack of senior women is a self-perpetuating cycle in terms of the gender pay gap.

Another factor that explains both the pay gap and the lack of senior women is the disproportionately female burden of domestic responsibility. Economists can assign a value to most things. But if the average UK man were asked to guess how much it would cost him to replace his stay-at-home wife, he would probably be shocked to discover it's at least £29,000 on average—and that is just if one looks simply at the cost of hiring a full-time nanny (see Part 2). The figure would be much higher in London, of course, or if you added in all the extra costs of providing the activities a housewife is involved in—driving, tutoring children, household duties such as cooking, ironing and cleaning clothes. In fact, an Office of National Statistics analysis shows that women put in more than double the proportion of unpaid work that men do, when it comes to cooking, childcare and housework.[8] In 2014 *The Daily Telegraph* calculated, one assumes half-jokingly, what a housewife is worth, based on the general pay of all the different domestic and care professionals she replaces for free: washerwoman, private chef, driver, therapist, personal assistant, live-in nanny, tutor, cleaner and private nurse. The paper came to the conclusion that a housewife should be paid £159,137 a year.[9]

Of course, these figures are there to make a point. In truth it has become admirable rather than laughable to be a 'modern man', a caring kind of guy. Men pushing kids in buggies is a far more common sight than when I was a young mother in the 1970s, and even when I had my younger children in the '80s and early '90s. And, as one male friend describes with loving forbearance, he loves to cook. Usually at weekends, and not the slap-dash boiled eggs, beans on toast and frozen food meals his wife throws together during the week, but a major production: a full day of hunting down and preparing the finest ingredients, then an evening using every pan, pot and utensil in the house, discarded in a messy pile in the kitchen sink by the dishwasher, followed by a week of self-congratulation for his amazing culinary skills...! At least my friend, now of a certain age, knows he has had it easy. Many others now work harder at this and are truly 'born again men'. I hasten to add that my fantastic step-sons are absolutely at the forefront of what it means to be a new man, brilliant at cooking, and at washing up. But the overall statistics don't lie: women are being kept out of the paid workforce by unpaid labour they contribute in the home. Given this ongoing cultural imbalance, is it surprising that my former colleague felt the need to deny her child's existence in order to survive in her career?

Seeking gender equality in our economic life is not just a moral question—it is good economic sense. If women were freer, had more support and saw greater incentive to do paid work, to pursue a career or start a business that employed people (see Part 3), there would be more tax paid, and arguably less required for welfare and unemployment benefits. The economy would benefit from the greater availability of skills, and would expand, as there would be more labour and greater spending on goods and services, with more jobs created as a result. But it won't come easy. If there are constraints on women entering the labour market at a level that matches their skills—difficulties in advancing up the career ladder, social pressures that keep them at home, or a bias, conscious or unconscious, dictating what is 'women's work'—then the chances of women doing as well as men are reduced—for life. In the UK, for example, women earn on average 30% less than men per year throughout their working lifetime, with inevitable impacts on their wealth and wellbeing.

* * *

We know that one thing that helps women achieve equality is education. It is not enough by itself, but it is a necessary prerequisite. For one thing, educated women will tend to know much more about all sorts of issues, including sexism and women's inequality, which equips them to fight it; we will return to this towards the end of

Part Four. For another, education has clear impacts on life chances, as we'll see below. Women these days are much better educated across most of the globe than they were even in the late twentieth century, but this progress has not been universal, and legislation for equal access to education does not always guarantee equal uptake of education.

Depriving women of education—as happens and has happened in many parts of the world—is a great divider, with huge negative impacts on both individuals and, indirectly, on the economy. We know that there are correlations between poor education, and growing up and living in a 'disadvantaged area', and these affect all sorts of outcomes in life. Evidence from Scotland shows that, despite a fall in the gender pay gap between hourly wages of male and female employees (diminishing from 28% in 1993 to 23% in 2003), it was still a substantial 18% in 2016. With women earning a lot less on average, the difference in financial wellbeing was significant. From a social and economic perspective, this is bad news for the country. The study points out how perilous being less well-off is for, among other things, health outcomes. Here we start to see the relevance of women's education not just for individuals, but for national economies. People being poor and poorly educated has an impact on health provision, on costs and caring responsibilities by their relatives (which may take those people out of the workforce), and ultimately on the state—and hence public finances.[10]

We can also look at this link on a very broad scale. Economic growth through the twentieth century has been closely correlated with gains in female autonomy and numeracy, partly through the resultant increase in human capital.[11] A study that tracked European countries' development from 1500 to 1850 found a clear impact on economics of early age of marriage, which was used as a proxy for loss of women's autonomy.[12] Not only did girls who married very young drop out of the labour market, but the impact was felt more widely across the economy. Early-married women were less able to provide their own children with teaching and encouragement of self-learning, leaving not just the mother but the whole family and the next generation with fewer numeracy, literacy and other skills—to the detriment of the economy as a whole in the medium and longer term.

The study found 'a strong and positive relationship between average age at marriage and numeracy for the two half centuries following 1700 and 1800'. Lower age of marriage and lower women's numeracy appeared to harm a European country's chance of development and prosperity. Many of the countries of the Second Industrial Revolution, which took place in the late nineteenth century, had higher measured values for female autonomy and numeracy, and hence better human capital formation, which is crucial for growth—

Denmark, the Netherlands, Germany and Sweden, for example. Those that missed out on the Second Industrial Revolution—such as Russia, Poland, Slovakia, Italy, Spain, and Ireland—had lower values of women's autonomy and numeracy. This dynamic historical analysis offers an obvious conclusion: it was economies and regions where women's autonomy was more pronounced that did well in the age of industrialisation, because they had more and better human capital; others languished.

This evidence adds to a 2007 analysis in the US showing a substantial 'intragenerational return' on a mother's education: the more years on average a mother had been educated, the greater the benefit in terms of her child(ren)'s achievement, up to a certain age.[13] There are various factors behind this correlation. For one thing, higher-educated women are more likely to delay motherhood, which increases their chances of marrying a better-educated spouse—meaning a higher combined family income. Household income is also helped by mothers who are better able to help educate their children: each additional year of maternal teaching adds some 18% to household income. A family with higher income will invest more in books, musical instruments and so on, and the offspring will, on average, do better over the longer term. What is more, highly educated mothers who work spend just as much time reading to their children or taking them on educational outings as they would have done otherwise—an interesting finding that counters conservative fondness for stay-at-home motherhood. The conclusion: women's education is crucial for the wellbeing and prosperity of the nation as a whole, in the woman's own generation and in future generations.[14] In other words, the pay gap may still remain for higher-educated women in the US, but at least the individual, their households and their descendants, as well as the economy, are all better off than if they hadn't had those educational opportunities.

There have been similar findings from around the world. One study presented at the 2019 Royal Economic Society conference looked at evidence from rural Rajasthan in India, where a third of girls typically drop out of school by the time they reach 16, and the average bride's age is under 18. The study observed that, the longer parents in rural Rajasthan manage to keep their daughters in education, the larger the private and public benefit. This is because the longer they stay at school, the later they marry—and being more educated improves their chances of finding a richer husband. As in the US, then, the benefits to the individual, the household and the wider economy coincide. The study concluded that part of the answer is to remove barriers to girls staying at school, such as cost or distance from the school; another part is to delay the age of marriage and improve ways for girls to re-enter education if they have, for whatever reason, dropped out early.[15]

The evidence doesn't only suggest that longer education and autonomy is better—it has also definitively shown the inverse. Study after study from across the globe has demonstrated the negative impact of early child marriage, on women and nations. These are very useful, essentially randomised, controlled experiments where one can see in microcosm the impact of different policies on women's labour force participation. Take one bit of research from Tanzania. Lower educational attainment, as a direct result of early marriage, reduced girls' and women's opportunities for gainful employment and income generation, adversely affected household incomes and wider growth, and increased the chances of women and their families living in poverty.[16] Ending discrimination in the provision of education may not be enough to conquer the gender pay gap, but it seems certain that we can't achieve much for women's economic equality without it. This is a clear market failure that needs fixing.

* * *

We should be clear that the developed world has often upheld legal barriers to women's economic equality, too. Until 1985, Swiss women still had to get their husbands' permission to work or open a bank account; no wonder they have been on the streets as recently as June 2019 to demand equal pay.[17] There is also blatant evidence of discrimination in G7 countries below the state level.

There was widespread outrage in 2018 when it was revealed that Japanese medical schools were discriminating in favour of first-time male applicants. One school offered the excuse that men mature more slowly and lag behind women in communication skills, so they need an extra push! Another Japanese university was reported as saying that they did not favour women because they would leave at some stage to have children.[18] It appears that this discrimination has been going on for decades, keeping the pass rates for women medical students artificially low. The result is that women still make up only 21% of doctors in Japan, the lowest percentage in the G7—the UK is first at 47.2%, with Germany, France and Canada all following close behind.

In one medical school, discriminatory practice has now miraculously resulted in women's pass rates exceeding those of men for the first time in seven years. But this story demonstrates something deeper: another break in the market's ability to operate as a meritocracy, another failure of capitalism's supply-and-demand system to equate at the right balance for society. It is also my understanding that Japan has no ready availability of home-helpers or nannies, due to tight immigration rules that make it much more difficult for mothers to return to work. In any case, Japanese society apparently still frowns on mothers 'abandoning' their children to others. This is not just the case in Japan, of course. The historian Helene von Bismarck and the veteran journalist

John Kampfner, with whom I spoke recently in Berlin, bemoaned the fact that the culture in Germany also looks on mothers with opprobrium if they don't look after their preschool-aged children themselves, and restricts their representation in business.

These types of barriers, however, are much more pronounced in the developing world, and are perhaps relatively easy to track: early marriage, greater enforcement of gender norms, lack of legal rights, strong patriarchal societies. In more developed countries that have already legislated to get rid of gender discrimination in education and finance, there are still plenty of restrictions holding back women—they are just more subtle. Trying to navigate your way through prejudices that are often below the surface is not always easy. Women need help, and mentoring is one way to provide this. The experience of women who have made it to senior positions has been very useful in clarifying where the anomalies lie. It is encouraging, in fact, that women are now less afraid to ask for help. I for one belong to any women's network that will have me! This includes Women Corporate Directors, the International Women's Forum and the Senior Business Women Group, which is run by Melanie Richards, Vice-Chair of KPMG, UK. In my field of economics, we established what is known as the 'Women Economists Network', comprising UK economists in both the public and the private sector. It provides a forum for raising issues that are not just dealing with women's direct concerns, but also exploring their take on economics and what really matters in society.

It is welcome that, today, senior women are more than willing to help out those coming up behind them; in fact, they increasingly see it as their duty. One interviewee for this book, who is in a very senior role in a large manufacturing firm, told me: 'As a woman I believe that we must "lift as we climb". My team behind me are largely women—16 women and 3 men, as it happens. I look for talented women. No point in me continuing the work of women before me without having it better behind.' I hadn't realised quite how many successful women I know have had professional mentors, often paid for by their employer for a large part of their working lives. One very bright but rather physically tiny civil servant I know was bullied by her male colleagues when relatively junior; I suspect that it was her mentor's advice to dress flamboyantly and expensively, both to make it harder to overlook her, and also to exude the type of self-confidence that gets you places. She did become a permanent secretary, and a dame. Those were turbulent times, and I wish I had found her mentor earlier to guide me through all those years of shoes, hair, specially made dresses and poise. I can only dream of what could have been... But I must have achieved some gravitas just with the passing of time. Women whom I have never met before often start conversations with me as I travel on the train or bus, and by the time I reach my destination,

I find I've agreed to mentor yet another woman struggling with career and family, and against preconceived notions of where a woman's place should be!

All of which is to say that there is now an increasing understanding that networking among women matters. After all, it's worked for men for a very long time. Even if managers feel they are not exercising any bias at all in recruiting and promoting, their actions or the culture they oversee can inadvertently result in people who are different from them being excluded from activities that affect their career progression. In particular, it is clear that networks are important to combat what we refer to in economics as 'information asymmetries'—unequal access to knowledge that disadvantages women. Many of us know how constraining that is through personal experience. But it is sad that we are seeing friends and daughters struggling with it to this day, many decades after some of us first embarked on our careers.

Baroness Pauline Neville-Jones started her career in banking, and then moved to the civil service; she became the most senior woman in the Foreign Office during her time there, as a career diplomat. As a Conservative member of the House of Lords, she also served as a minister during the coalition government of 2010–15. But she is adamant that—certainly for most of her career in the City—the lack of a proper assessment process meant that there was no true meritocracy. There was, and she believes there still is, an invisible bar for women; those who got on were very loud self-promoters, usually men (or women who learnt to imitate them). But, in her view, the causes of the glass ceiling in the financial sector are deeper than just unconscious or conscious bias. Put simply, this is the way the market system works. It was clear that traders preserved their own high salaries by holding on to the information they had acquired. Men, of course, have traditionally had a number of outlets where such privileged information can be acquired or shared, in part or in whole, while women in banking were few in number, with restricted avenues for receiving or passing on valuable insights that would help them hunt for business. In other words, the few women traders were less able to compete for contracts against the men because of an information asymmetry—another market failure. This only served to reinforce (un)conscious bias in the firm, making it easy for men to conclude that women's worse performance proved they were unsuitable for promotion. In such an environment, a gender gap in salaries wasn't and still isn't a surprise.

Of course, information asymmetries between men and women are not only confined to the financial sector. In a 2014 interview with *The Times*, Dame Sally Davies, Chief Medical Officer for England and the first woman to hold that post in its 165-year history, said that 'she had missed out on networking in the pub with male colleagues' during her career. A study of social mobility in the cultural sector by the think tank Centre for London has highlighted up front that 'It's not about how talented you are, it's about who you know and how you know them'. This 2019 report finds that there is a glass ceiling related to gender as well as ethnicity and social class, due to lack of ability to network from an early age:

> Given the often informal approaches to recruitment, the benefits of knowing someone—a friend or relative—already working in the sector are considerable, illustrating the value of social capital and the challenges facing those students who have not accumulated it.

A US study has highlighted the need to address gender, ethnic, and social class inequalities in terms of access to college resources and post-graduation career trajectories. This inequality of access means that 'women are mainly in mid-to lower-skilled positions' in the arts and creative industries, which may come as a surprise to many.[19] Networking is not only important for the women employed within companies and sectors; it is also essential for the self-employed and for self-starting businesswomen. In its own response to the Alison Rose review on women entrepreneurs in the UK, which published its findings in spring 2019, the May government recognised the importance of networks that connect female entrepreneurs, such as the AllBright Academy, or the everywomanNetwork, which has 20,000 members.

Some might argue that the days of gentlemen's clubs are over, and that women are now free to network however and wherever men are. But that often means being prepared to stay late at work, to socialise in the pub afterwards, to play golf at the weekend. All this of course is inimical to having a family, or any kind of personal life. As we know, the household and caring burdens fall disproportionately on women, so this kind of 'extracurricular' commitment is of course more difficult for them. As Pryce, Ross and Urwin have outlined,[20] managers may believe that they are open and non-discriminatory because 'everybody gets invited down the pub after work, no matter what colour, sex, age, religion...' And yet that in itself can cause divisions, given that many, particularly women with caring responsibilities, may not be able to join in. They miss not just the banter, but also the networking that is so important for getting on and getting promoted: the casual mentions of opportunities coming up, the chance to get to know how your boss likes things done, the insider insights into what's happening across the industry, and so on.

Women find it hard to be taken seriously in many fields, but evidence in the financial sector is particularly stark, if we go by the gender pay gap alone. What if this is not a coincidence, but a result of actual barriers to their success within the industry? It is true that investment banking and the financial sector has now changed and is more sober, as the veteran financier Jon Moulton argued in a debate we did together in 2017.[21] But people are still expected to work anti-social hours. Women still enter only carefully, and not in vast numbers; pretty soon after, they opt out. As a result, there are few senior women role models. To keep the talent and the pipeline going, it seems to me that the financial sector needs a massive cultural shift to change the working environment in a way that ensures women stay. That means less of a long hours, macho culture and an end to the valuing of excessive 'presenteeism', which doesn't sit well with women's caring responsibilities; it also means better-managed maternity leave, so that women don't lose out in the promotions stakes while they are away; and easier part-time and job-share arrangements throughout their career. All these policies have worked successfully in the public sector, creating role models who now offer encouragement and inspiration to others coming up through the ranks.

The more information there is from the media and other outlets on the treatment of women (including women leaders), and about the sexism that exists in different sectors and the realities of what is required to 'make it' in various professions, the better. The *LSE Business Review* has deplored the silence around gender and the role it plays in influencing—and, often, hindering—aspirations; it reported on an initiative to include gender issues on business schools' curricula.[22] The clear implication is that women will have less chance of succeeding in their chosen career if they lack information about, and are unprepared for, the obstacles awaiting them as women, and sometimes also as mothers.

The power imbalances that emerge as a result of women's difficulties in networking and keeping up with long-hours culture can affect the choices that women make, as they often perpetuate this imbalance at every social level. One may then decide that the struggle isn't worth the effort. In my early book on women's quotas, I cited a marvellous passage from the King's College London professor Alison Wolf's book, *The XX Factor*, and make no apologies for doing so again:

> Imagine, for example, that you are offered an excellent new job. To take it you have to relocate ... but you are in a relationship ... Try another one ... you are offered the chance to join a small team working on a new, high-profile project. If it goes well, you have a real chance of promotion ... it also means working not just late, but every weekend in the future. It really is your choice ... Do you—did you—do it? Say yes to either of those choices and right there, if you are a woman, motherhood became significantly less likely.[23]

* * *

One thing we must tackle if we are to achieve economic equality for women is the inequality women face within economics itself. How can we have positive economic policy change if women's voices are hardly represented in policy-making?

As I'm writing in mid-2019, the Government Economic Service, of which I was the first female (co-) head in the late 2000s, now has two female joint heads.

Amazingly, the current chief economists of the IMF, the World Bank and the OECD are also all women, for the first time ever. The public sector does set an example, and there is further push and pressure than there was in decades past, with much more focus these days on activities surrounding the yearly International Women's Day for example. In April 2019 I went to Warwick University in the UK to speak at the Royal Economic Society's annual conference. At this event, Rachel Griffith, Economics Professor at the University of Manchester and the Institute of Fiscal Studies, became the Society's President for 2019/20, thus becoming only the second woman in its 129-year history to hold the post.[24] At the same time, Carol Propper, Professor of Economics at Imperial College London, became the President-Elect, due to succeed Rachel when her term is up. This means that, for the first time ever, the presidential triumvirate running the Society is two-thirds women; it's not beyond the bounds of possibility that all three members will be women in 2020/21, if the Society elects another woman as President-Elect in 2020.

But we shouldn't be too excited by progress in these individual, right-at-the-top positions. The overall progress of women economists in the private sector and in academia remains woeful. In June 2018 I was among a group of financial sector experts and practitioners attending a talk at the Guildhall, the political heart of the City of London. The occasion was the then Greek

Prime Minister's visit to London. A few hundred of us piled in to listen to Alexis Tsipras updating us on Greek politics and the economy, in English much improved since his radical-left party Syriza first came to power in the midst of the Greek crisis in January 2015. I follow developments in Greece, and write and talk about the country's fortunes on a regular basis, including in my book *Greekonomics*, so I had been doubly invited to this event, by both the Greek Embassy and the City of London, which had organised it. I was also asked to join them afterwards at a smaller, private session, to question Tsipras on his plans for Greece, and on which sectors would welcome potential investments from the UK. I looked around me as we sat round a large table. There were thirty men, and me. No different, really, from when I first started working for a bank four decades ago. The chair, a deputy head of the City of London, noticed it too. He seemed embarrassed, and I believe it was for that reason that I have now been co-opted for my sins onto the City of London's members' diversity working party.

I also sit on the advisory board of the central banking think tank OMFIF, which publishes a Gender Balance Index, tracking globally the presence of men and women in senior positions at public financial institutions. In 2019 it reported: 'Gender diversity in central banks has improved by six percentage points since 2018, but the overall picture remains heavily unbalanced. Our study, in its sixth year, is a call to action, drawing attention to this disappointing picture.'[25]

* * *

I could have been disheartened by all this, and given up. But, one sunny morning on an Easter bank holiday, reading the birthdays column in the *Times* (I've never featured, but one of my ex-husbands does regularly), I noticed that the first four names listed, as well as numbers six and seven, were all women. They were Professor Dame Anne Glover, biologist; Dame Geraldine Andrews, High Court judge; Gill Andrews, ex-President of the Society of Antiquaries of London; Sue Barker, former tennis player and sports broadcaster; Baroness (Jane) Campbell, ex-Commissioner of the Equality and Human Rights Commission and disability rights campaigner; and Dame Julia Cleverdon, formerly Chief Executive of Business in the Community and Chairwoman of the National Literacy Trust. Interestingly, out of some 28 names *The Times* decided to publish that day, the women dominated, including the well-known lawyer and campaigner Gina Miller, the Olympic gold medallist Dame Kelly Holmes, the theatre producer Sonia Friedman, the tennis pro Maria Sharapova, the fashion designer and businesswoman Paloma Picasso, the actress Kate Hudson, the comedian Ruby Wax and the academic Dr Bridget Towle.[26] Not bad going. Maybe 19 April is a good day to be born if you want to be a prominent woman! I was born in mid-July...

In seriousness, there's no doubt that the more powerful voices among feminists, the #MeToo movement and changing societal attitudes more generally—particularly a push from the younger generation—are all increasingly focusing minds on the need for gender equality in society as a whole. It is true that, despite the economic advances of some women, we are still faced by all sorts of harassment and bullying, particularly but far from exclusively in industry cultures such as accounting, law and finance, which are still considerably male-dominated in their leadership. The #MeToo movement, in other words, has highlighted an aspect of inequality going beyond economics and into culture: the uneven power balance between men and women, which is detrimental to society. The historian Mary Beard has written eloquently about this, tracing that lack of female power back through ancient times and showing that nothing much has changed.[27]

Whether you look at Beard's very long view or your own short view, it's hard to feel that much real progress has been made in recent years. In July 2019, *The Guardian* discovered that the number of rapes reported in the UK has risen sharply since 2015, likely prompted by the #MeToo movement, but that the percentage of rape reports resulting in a charge or summons has plummeted over the same period—from 14% to 1.5%.[28] And, despite the UK forcing publication of gender pay gaps, which has sparked a conversation about representation and seniority in working life, women are still absent from many public conversations. At an infrastructure dinner in London in early July 2019, I was the only woman around a table of 14 men. I'm not necessarily suggesting that this is typical across all sectors, but it has reinforced my view: that, however urgent and worthwhile the #MeToo movement and other initiatives like 'Time's Up' are, contemporary feminists should be focused like laser beams on economic empowerment. How can we be empowered in our individual relationships, particularly at work, when we are systematically disempowered by the capitalist structures within which we all live?

This is not only the case in the Western economies where the recent movements have received most attention. Global female economic disempowerment was highlighted by the Commonwealth Secretariat in 2016, in a piece bemoaning the very slow progress made in political representation; only 22% of all legislative seats across the Commonwealth were held by women, and the figure was worse in local government. The main impediments cited were a patriarchal society, lack of education, poverty and illiteracy. The piece argued that a prerequisite for advancing women's participation in politics, and hence in decision-making at all levels of government, was promoting economic empowerment, via quota systems. These needed to be continued where they were already operating and expanded to other Commonwealth jurisdictions where they were not yet in place.[29]

In other words, improving representation of women in power—let alone equality—is very unlikely to happen on its own, without a lot of extra help. And this was not the case only in emerging markets. A European Parliament survey on women's democratic participation found in 2007 that, even in the more developed world, 'women lack financial and power resources and time to engage in traditional politics.'[30]

* * *

However we achieve greater women's involvement in decision-making, in economics and beyond, the possible consequences of more equal participation are not well understood. They usually centre on the likelihood of 'women's issues' rising up the agenda and being dealt with by more sympathetic (female) eyes. For instance, having more women in government and politics could make a difference to domestic policies such as childcare provision, the costs of which are still crippling women's career chances in many countries. In business, more women decision-makers could be instrumental in better supporting women's retention and progress. It is true, though, that this is as yet untested, given the continuing dismal representation of senior executive women, as the political philosopher Lorna Finlayson argued in a *London Review of Books* piece on feminist writing.[31] We haven't had the chance of controlled experiments about what would happen if women were in charge. And although women's role at the micro level is well researched, if not yet proven, what tends to be missing is an understanding of the impact on the wider economy if more women were decision-makers.

The literature suggests, for example, that women on corporate boards are found to be more conservative than the men, and more risk-averse in their decisions. That seems to carry through across other areas of activity. Most research studies find a positive connection between the presence of women in executive positions and the profitability of the firms involved. Some studies have suggested that, because women are not as over-optimistic about their own abilities as men—making them less confident that they can 'beat' the market—their increased presence on trading floors would balance that male exuberance, and end up with better trading results overall. Sukhi Clark, former Head of Engineering & Operations at Jaguar Land Rover, argues from her experience that women 'tend to be more cautious. They need more answers, more detail and probably don't jump as high as quickly.' It is not always, therefore, simply a question of needing more 'women brains', but of needing more types of brains in general. Danae Kyriakopoulou, Chief Economist and Director of Research at the central banking think tank OMFIF, has pointed me to analysis by the International Finance Corporation showing that venture capital funds with gender-balanced senior investment teams have returns on private equity that are some 10–20% higher than those of funds that are either mostly male-run or mostly female-run. This confirms that the diversity in decision-making avoids 'groupthink' which can be detrimental to alternative thinking—and therefore negatively affect performance.[32]

My view is that, for private firms, diversity in board composition is much less significant than diversity on the executive committee, when it comes to changing the culture of an organisation. But for central banks and supervisory bodies where major decisions are taken that will affect the whole economy—and often the global economy too—diversity on boards is now believed to matter hugely. For one thing, if central banks and other institutions don't reflect the balance of society in their leadership, then trust in a country's public institutions suffers too.[33] For another, it seems to result in better, or more balanced, decision-making. A 2018 study found that if there were more senior women in central bank bodies, which make interest rate decisions, then rates would be higher at every inflation level—in other words, women would make more hawkish decisions.[34] That may be hard to swallow for those who, like me, have been advocating continued loose monetary policies since the financial crisis. But maybe, if women had been at the helm back then, we never would have had the huge and reckless deregulation that led to an unsustainable boom and the ultimate bust of the 2008 crash! In a podcast for OMFIF, Ed Sibley, Deputy Governor of the Central Bank of

Ireland and chair of the bank's diversity and inclusion steering group, spoke about the 'groupthink' that comes from lack of diversity in an organisation, and the problems this creates for our economy—particularly, the unchallenged assumptions in central banks at the time of the financial crisis, which led to poor risk management and decision-making, and so contributed to the depth of the crisis and recession that followed.[35]

So diversity in itself is better for business and the economy, but there are also specific benefits to having women leaders in greater numbers. A paper co-written in 2018 by Christine Lagarde, Managing Director of the IMF, and Jonathan Ostry, IMF Deputy Director of Research, argues that having women on the boards of banking supervision entities improves the financial stability of the system as a whole.[36] In their view, what is often missing is the appreciation that women bring complementary—that is, different and particular—skills that would disproportionately raise productivity and economic welfare, if put to proper use. Their analysis goes further than monetary institutions alone. They found that it is precisely because women and men are not perfect substitutes that diversity is actually a bonus for innovation, productivity and growth. Arguing that the impact of this 'gender complementarity' has been ignored in many models, they estimate that increased female labour force participation can have a much greater impact on the economy than has been suggested by other studies. In the sample of countries that the IMF looked at, it found that those ranked in the bottom half for gender equality would see an average rise in GDP of 35% by closing their initial labour force participation gap. What is more, while four fifths of this increase could simply be put down to more women at work, a full fifth would be due to the increase in productivity as a specific result of the ensuing gender diversity (see Appendix).

So we are back where we started. Even in the face of clear evidence that women's equality in the labour market is good for the economy and good for business, organisations in both the public and the private sector are still failing to make the necessary steps—starting with improving the number of women in senior, decision-making roles. There are many impressively successful women and some excellent organisations and companies. But they are the exception and by no means the rule—not by a long shot. Progress for women has been both patchy and painfully slow.

Before we begin looking at why this is the case, a brief note on terms and definitions. There is a question currently being asked, certainly in the Western world, over who can rightly call themselves a 'woman'. The intensity of this debate has increased in the 2010s. Clearly, gender is much more than simple biology and the 'right' chromosomes. But, with no wish to offend anyone, this rightly sensitive area is not a focus for this book, and gender socialisation, important though it is, will only be touched upon. Although economic and gender roles clearly interact, my argument is that economic empowerment for all should be the priority. We can respect those who do not consider themselves to fall within one of the two main genders (men and women), but we can't take that respect so far as to refrain from discussing the gendered problems of economic inequality. Even if gender or the 'gender binary' is a social construct, it is one that has a real impact on us all, from birth onwards. For this reason, the problem of gender inequality has been measured and researched overwhelmingly in terms of men and women. There is simply no other meaningful way to talk about it in this book.

On the same note, a word about 'gender diversity'. The term occasionally comes up in this book where it has been used in the research of others, but we are not really talking about 'diversity' when we talk about women's equality. It is not right to call a board more 'diverse' because it has some women on it, given that women in most countries represent the majority of the population. Diversity, which must most definitely be the aim, is to ensure that there is no prejudice and discrimination against representative inclusion of people of any colour, ethnicity, religion or sexual orientation. An important aim in itself, but at present more than 50% of the population is largely losing out in terms of economic recognition. That is something more clear-cut than a spectrum or a multitude of identities, and—bearing in mind what

I've just said about the necessity of using binary terms to discuss gender inequality in this book—'gender diversity' can be a misleading term, since (unlike religions, ethnicities and so on) gender equality and fair gender representation amount to the same thing, 50:50. In any case, if we manage to sort out gender equality, I would be astonished if our economic and workplace culture didn't change so drastically in the process that we also end up dealing with the other manifestations of conscious and unconscious bias that currently act against greater diversity.

In this book, I draw on personal experiences, ideas of economics, and plain old data, to try and explain why women still suffer from economic (and so wider) inequality. More than that, I show why this lack of progress is intrinsic to capitalism itself. This doesn't mean that we have to give up capitalism in order to achieve gender equality; but it does mean that we will need forceful and substantial state intervention to correct the inherently unequal forces of capitalism. The system that develops may still, by its very nature, be called 'capitalist' or even 'free-market', but it will be more inclusive, more equal and more prosperous. One small step at a time for womankind must surely be better than no step at all, and, put together, the steps outlined in this book could add up to a radical change in the way people think about women's contribution to society.

PART ONE

WOMEN UNDER CAPITALISM

1

WOMEN UNDER CAPITALISM

The term 'capitalism' is potentially a problematic one. Types of capitalism and thoughts on capitalism differ widely. A standard definition is not very helpful for this book's purpose, such as 'An economic and political system in which a country's trade and industry are controlled by private owners, rather than by the state'. But, not to embrace Marxism, it's useful to note that Karl Marx identified a phenomenon unique to capitalism that is vital for understanding women's position in a capitalist system: the 'commodification' of labour. In other words, unlike other socioeconomic models, capitalism requires labour time, i.e. work, to be bought and sold in the market, much like any other physical commodity, such as bread or Coca-Cola. In pre-capital feudal times, for example, people were born a serf under the 'obligations' of a fiefdom, or, if they were luckier, a lord 'entitled' to their serfs' allegiance and service. In tribal societies, gender roles are generally determined by tradition and basic biology, such as physical strength. But in capitalism, gender roles and status have been shaped and adapted around market forces, particularly after industrialisation in the pursuit of profit. Free market capitalism is unique in that it rewards the production of commodities, but neglects the wider social contributions that make this production possible, or the wider societal and economic costs involved in that production.

Gender roles, attitudes and expectations have been shaped, established and embedded over the centuries. As the requirements of reproduction, household production and the workplace have developed, the gender inequalities inherent to our system have become a major source of economic inefficiency and substantial loss of economic growth. The waste of economic potential is easy to see in the fundamentally short-termist model of a slave society, where people themselves, and not just their labour, are commodities to be bought and sold: imagine if America's Deep South had quickly developed into a system whereby talented black people were channelled and encouraged into positions where they could reach their economic potential—in that meritocracy, there would have been many more white-skinned cotton-pickers, but Africans and African Americans would have added much higher value as free and diversified workers than they would ever do as slaves. Overall output and progress would have been far greater, even if some plantation owners would have lost out. Now take that example and apply it to the centuries-old under-valuing of what economists call 'household produc-tion'—the domestic work and care for dependents that enables an industrial workforce in the first place, but which is systematically unrecognised, and so unpaid.

Of course, depending on their social status, women have always worked for money if they could—in the days of the Industrial Revolution, in the cruelly 'dark satanic mills', or as servants for the upper and upper-middle classes, and also outside formal work, in home-based piecework, taking in boarders, and caring for others' children. It was also women who were hired in large numbers for the production of low-cost 'commodi-ties' products, and women again who have been dis-placed in the era of globalisation, when new countries with even cheaper labour forces started to compete with the West, attracting increased investment and spelling the end of much of what women had previously been engaged in doing. Most studies now suggest that tech-nology will bring a further upheaval in women's work in the twenty-first century, as it is women, concentrated in lower-paid and routine jobs, who are most likely to be at risk from further automation and AI. But the depend-ency of capitalism on short-term results makes it all the more important that we protect women now against the precarity to come.

Failure or refusal to optimise the use of female labour, for all sorts of less-than-rational reasons, is exemplified by two important problems already explored in the Introduction: the gender pay gap, and gendered job segregation. Put together, these phenomena leave women less economically empowered, less able to influence the course of events, and over-represented in weaker labour market areas where pay tends to be lower and where robots are likely to come first. Economists have a term for describing situations like this, in which the allocation of goods and services by a free market is not efficient. They are called 'market failures'. And when such market failures occur, intervention is often needed to correct them. We seem to have forgotten in the neoliberal age that this is the case. It is revealing to remember that, for centuries, children were expected to work, often for very long hours and in dangerous conditions. But child labour—much like slavery—was not ended in the West by inexorable market forces. Instead, it required powerful social movements, extensive health and safety and child protection acts, and their strong enforcement. Many capitalists complained at the time that child labour was an economic necessity, but today we no longer see compulsory schooling for children as 'political correctness gone mad'. Today, it is not at all controversial, because we all understand the wider social and economic benefits of this policy, despite its direct fiscal cost, which is huge.

Likewise, we will only accomplish economic empowerment for women, and hence wider gender equality, with the help of powerful leadership, social movements and the state. We can't wait for a culture shift in favour of gender equality and the change needed to make it happen—it comes the other way around. This market failure must be corrected by inducement and, if necessary, force, and only then will the broader benefits of equality be felt and universally appreciated. Patterns of gender inequality today are far more subtle than they used to be, and it is not always easy to detect, let alone correct for, conscious and unconscious gender bias in society. But we don't have much choice about trying. Beyond the obvious morality of gender equality in terms of fairness and women's wellbeing, there is another justification for women's economic empowerment that should concern even the most hard-nosed money-counter. It is about economic efficiency, productivity and growth, and the vast amounts of wasted female potential—for the individual, the household and the wider economy. Instead of worrying about the cost of equality, we should be worrying about the cost of inequality.

So that is the message of this book. Sally Spear, Vice-Chair of the Women's Advisory Council at pro-UN charity UNA, has put it simply: 'gender equality is not an optional extra, it is a necessity'. If nothing else, it is justified by narrow economic productivity criteria alone, moving our economies nearer to optimal equilibrium. But this equilibrium does not arise naturally in our free-market system, so more forceful intervention in shaping markets is now desperately needed to deal with that inequality—one big market failure. Capitalist systems, left to themselves, cannot easily produce equality, let alone gender equality. It is not their nature or their aim.

What does the world need?

This fact brings us to an obvious question. If capitalism consistently fails to deliver gender equality when left to its own devices, perhaps the problem is with capitalism itself? It seems that more socialist states have got considerably closer to equality for women in the past. For much of the postwar period, a large percentage of Soviet women, particularly in Russia, were able (and expected) to work; they had access to free childcare; and they received good education and training. They were treated as legal equals in marriage and did better financially after a divorce than their Western female counterparts.[1] In Warsaw Pact countries, male chauvinism was widely seen as a remnant of the pre-socialist era.[1] The Eastern Bloc countries seemed to recognise the market failure that gender inequality would represent; and this has left a legacy. Although wage disparities were certainly prevalent during the Cold War, larger numbers of women east of the Iron Curtain were in leadership positions than their Western counterparts. I saw this with my own eyes when working in former Eastern Europe and Russia shortly after the Berlin Wall came down. I was there to produce privatisation strategies for state-owned firms, and I was pleasantly surprised to find that many of the senior people I dealt with were women.

But the answer is not to advocate communism—to be sure, women in the Soviet Union, in addition to working hard, had to struggle every day for food and basic necessities. They did not necessarily enjoy a better life than their sisters in the West. And in practice, of course, women were often paid less than men, and were simply expected to do their salaried job as well as, not instead of, performing the household duties. There were particular periods in the twentieth century when patriarchy aggressively reasserted itself. Rainer Zitelmann's book *The Power of Capitalism* argues that, in fact, the evidence of the last 70 years shows that 'more capitalism means greater prosperity'. This was certainly adopted in post-communist Eastern Europe, and there is no doubt that the move towards liberalising the economy in China since the Deng Xiaoping era has lifted hundreds of millions out of poverty.

That said, it has also brought huge inequality. We have seen the rise of oligarchs in a number of former Eastern Bloc countries, and inequality has risen hugely in China. Across the capitalist world, top CEO rewards, often not connected to performance, have been discrediting the system. The huge salaries of CEOs of large companies have been augmented by bonuses and share options, whose value has been rising as companies increasingly use their resources to buy back their own shares, rather than investing in the company in a way that shapes its future. As John Kay notes in *Other People's Money* (2016), people are less concerned about the take-home pay of footballers or Bill Gates, as they believe that exceptional talent should be exceptionally rewarded. But many CEOs have average talent and, as Kay says, 'inequality which seems unconnected to deserts is particularly corrosive'.[2] As we will see, this is so for the underpaid (women) just as much as for the overpaid (men). So capitalism, yes, but there is more than one kind of capitalism. We know that socialised capitalism has proven more than capable in the past of correcting market failures for the benefit of society and the economy, and there is no reason why it should not do so again. We just need to wake up to the reality that such course correction will not necessarily be automatic; it will, in most cases, require substantial, sustained and sincere extra efforts at intervention.

We saw in the Introduction that the World Economic Forum has predicted it will take a century to achieve gender equality, based on current or recent trends of progress. But it seems the WEF is now worried that even this depressing estimate is too optimistic. Its 2017 report found that the preceding twelve months had actually seen some reversal in previous gains for women. The top places in the WEF ranking for gender equality were occupied by Scandinavian countries: Iceland came first, followed by Norway and Finland. Sweden came 5th. Among the larger European countries, France was 11th and Germany 12th. The UK ranked 15th. The United States did not appear in the top 20.[3] Targets for gender equality were of course part of the Millennium Development Goals, a set of international goals agreed upon at the UN in 2000, to be achieved by 2015. Goal 3, to 'promote gender equality and empower women', was aimed at reducing the gender disparity in access to primary and secondary education; improving the disadvantageous situation of women in waged employment outside the agricultural sector; and addressing the poor representation of women in power. But as Marianne Haslegrave, Director of the Commonwealth Medical Trust, pointed out in a letter to *The Economist* in April 2015, these did not go far enough. The new Sustainable Development Goals, agreed in 2015 for achievement by 2030, go further. Goal 5 'will cover discrimination against women, violence against women and girls, child, early and forced marriage, unpaid care and domestic work, women's participation in decision-making; and their sexual and reproductive health and reproductive rights.'[4] As Haslegrave put it:

> This new development agenda is universal; it is to apply to all countries and all people. It is not a bureaucratic process that is 'out of control'. Women and girls make up more than half the world's population and have a right to this agenda for the achievement of gender

equality in the next 15 years. These targets truly aim to 'leave no one behind'.

Of course, many of the other Millennium and Global Sustainable goals will hopefully also contribute to achieving gender equality, in the economy and beyond. But the omens are not good in relation to pay. Just before its January 2019 meeting in Davos, the World Economic Forum worried that it would take some 202 years to close the global pay gap between men and women, because the gap is so vast and the pace of change so slow. Although the pay gap had narrowed slightly, the overall concern was that the improvement appeared to be stalling. Saadia Zahidi, the WEF's Head of Education, Gender and Work, cautioned that 'The future of our labour market may not be as equal as the trajectory we thought we were on.' The research suggested that women across the world were paid on average just 63% of what men earn, with no country paying women more. Intriguingly, Laos, in south-east Asia, appeared to be the closest to men and women having achieved pay equality—the gap there is just 9%. But this may in fact be more of a relic of its socialist/communist past than a sign of hope for today's undisputed capitalism.

Capitalism in its current form can go unchallenged no longer. For those filled with horror at the idea of us taking up socialism in order to achieve Sustainable Development Goal 5, the responsibility and challenge is on them to show that such a step is unnecessary, because instead socialised capitalism can and will do more.

What exactly is the 'gender pay gap'? And why does it matter?

There has been much conversation—and rightful outrage—in recent years about the pay gap, but how many of us know off the top of our heads what it actually represents? The gender pay gap is measured by the difference between representative measures of male and female earnings from employment, usually expressed as a proportion of male employment earnings. But it is not a perfect comparison. The pay gap relates to hourly wages, but the gap in overall earnings is actually about twice as big as the gap in hourly earnings, because women are more likely to work part time. For reasons we'll explore in Part 2 of this book, 41% of women in the UK work part time, compared with just 13% of men. Similarly, pension contributions are smaller and fewer for those whose paid work time is shorter, again impacting women's prosperity in later life, due to their over-representation in part-time work. Moreover, the gender pay gap looks only at pay, but household income and household chores are not evenly split—the evidence shows that both are on average in favour of men. All of which is to say that the overall real 'earnings to work' gender gap is much, much bigger than the pay gap can show.

What the gender pay gap looks like depends on which kind of average you use to measure it. The more commonly used measure is the median, which is calculated by laying out all the hourly wages earned by women working full time, from the lowest to the highest, and then selecting the hourly wage right in the middle: the median figure. It then does the same for men, and finds the median figure for them. The median pay gap is the difference between the two numbers, as a percentage of median gross hourly earnings (excluding overtime) for men. By this measure, which excludes non-paid work, Britain's median pay gap has fallen from just over 17% in 1997 to slightly under 9% in 2018.[5] On the face of it, this is very good news—but it isn't the full story. The other way of measuring the pay gap is by establishing a mean, or average, gap, adding together the wages of all employees, then dividing the total by the number of workers in each group. Using the mean, the UK's pay gap, for example, is at around 14% for the fully employed, and has been stuck there for a number of years.[6]

The reason why the mean gap is bigger than the median gap is that it tells us a great deal more about the distribution of wages, and specifically the greater number of men in senior positions, dwarfing that of women on high salaries. And even on median pay, women (according to the ONS) earn less than men in all major occupational areas, despite overall progress. What is more, women are over-represented in part-time work, which is generally lower-paid, and men are over-represented in overtime work, which is paid at a higher rate than contracted hours. If we include overtime hours, the median full-time pay gap rises to 19%. Even if we exclude overtime, the median difference in hourly wages between all workers (both male and female, full-time and part-time) is about 18%.[7] If we separate part- and full-time work, the median gap between hourly pay for the two types of work is a shocking 35%.[8] In 2018 the average hourly rate for part-time work was £9.36, compared with £14.31 for full-time jobs excluding overtime.

Looking at OECD figures for 2017 (see Appendix, Fig. 1), we find that in Europe the greatest median salary gaps in 2017 were in Estonia (almost 27%), the Czech Republic (23%), Germany (22%), and the UK and Austria (both 21%). Analysis by Market Inspector concluded that the UK figure reflected the fact that very few women work in the higher-paid science, technology, engineering and mathematics (STEM) sectors, and many more work in part-time jobs.[9] The gender pay gap is much smaller in low-paid occupations such as clerical support work, services and sales. The situation for women in management and senior management positions across Europe is also worrying: in 2017 female hourly wages at those levels were on average 23% lower.

As the French newspaper *Le Figaro* points out, although the gap has narrowed on average—from 17.7%

in 2000 to 14.5% in 2010 across the OECD—in recent years it has barely moved. In 2016, six years later, it had only further reduced by 0.7%, to 13.8%.[10] Data for 2017 suggests that in many countries the task of bringing this gap down has stalled. In the US and UK, the pay gap halved from the 1970s to the 2000s, but has been more or less static since. This grinding to a halt has not been specific to any one region. In 2017 South Korea remained at the top, or rather the bottom, of the OECD's league table, with a median pay gap of 34.6%, falling from just 36.7% the previous year. Estonia had the second-worst gap (28.3%), followed by Japan (24.5%), Chile and Latvia (21.1%), Israel (19.3%) and then Canada and the US (18.2%). But EU countries that were worst hit by the global financial crisis, and which have seen huge job losses, are showing some of the smallest pay gaps (4.5% in Greece and 5.6% in Italy). There the pain was shared by all.

As we know, though, there is more to it than just the overall pay gap. The World Economic Forum has addressed this by creating an index that augments the wage gap using wage data, level of education, economic participation and opportunity, health and political empowerment. The highest possible score is 1 (equality) and the lowest score 0 (inequality). No country passed the 0.9 mark, and only five countries scored 0.8 or better (Iceland, Finland, Norway and Sweden were the top four). The UK was 20th and the US 45th; right at the bottom came Iran, Chad, Saudi Arabia, Syria, Pakistan, and Yemen in last place with a score of 0.516. As *Business Insider* commented, 'If nothing else, it's a reminder that the wage gap is just one aspect of gender-based inequality, and there's still a lot of work to be done in terms of gender equality.'[11] Even if we focus specifically on economic inequality, there are plenty of things going on beyond the basic pay gap.

For example, French women in 2015 were collecting some 18.6% less in average salary than men—but in managerial positions the gap widened to 20%. Across the OECD, women are much more likely to end up in poverty, because on average they do more work part-time. In France, 30% of women work part-time, as against just 8% of men. There are similar trends in many countries. A study using the US National Longitudinal Survey finds that part-time work and lesser work experience, because of motherhood or other caring responsibilities, accounts for some 40% of the wage gap. In short, on average, women end up doing low-paid jobs and are less likely to progress professionally than men with similar skills.[12]

Again, what you measure matters. The French statistics office (INSEE) looks separately at developments in the private sector—something not done with such precision in most countries, which tend to lump it all together. France therefore offers an interesting example of firms' attitudes towards women when not under the watchful eye of public-sector administrators, who generally have to pursue more stringent targets or quotas. INSEE's latest figures covered the period 1995 to 2015, and are rather worrying. In 2015 the private-sector gap in salaries, irrespective of industry and number of hours worked, was at 23.7%. The gap in earnings for men and women working full time was 18.7%. Of course, that does not differentiate between skill levels. The gap between men and women working the same hours and with similar skills was smaller, at 9%. But the gap was also wider the higher up a woman was in an organisation. For administrators, the gap in monthly salary was 20%.[13]

The gap also increases the more educated a French woman is. At the top of education—that is, among people in France with a Baccalaureate and at least 3 more years' education (e.g. a bachelor's degree)—INSEE found that the average annual salary for women was over 30% less than the average for men. This is because motherhood intervenes, and for highly qualified and senior women, the loss in salary is highest, and difficult to recover when they eventually go back to work, often at a level below their skills or only part-time. When women have children, their average take-home pay goes down, and stays down—whereas that of a man continually improves, regardless of parenthood. By the age of 45, the hourly wage gap between French mothers and fathers increases to 25%.

It is not difficult to understand why. According to figures published in *Le Figaro*, after children are born, eight times more mothers than fathers in France work part-time, with the obvious consequences for their earnings.[14] And that does not take into account the resulting pensions inequality. Again, using France as proxy of what happens in the Eurozone, on average women retire from work one year later than men, yet their pension is a whopping 42% lower—presumably as a result of having worked thousands fewer hours, due to childcare or other responsibilities deemed to be 'women's work'.

It is not very different in the UK. Paul Johnson of the Institute for Fiscal Studies has identified the effects on earnings of the disruption caused by motherhood. He calculates the average weekly earnings gap throughout a woman's career as 30%. This translates to a shocking fact: according to a 2018 report by the Chartered Insurance Institute, the average pension wealth of a woman aged 62 to 65 was £35,700, which is just 20% the average worth of a man's pension at the same age.[15] The state pension at least tries to balance this out a bit, but private-sector occupational pension schemes, on which many depend, only work on the basis of contributions—so women lose out if they take time off or are working in lower-paid occupations. In these circumstances, it is understandable that women's groups in the UK are taking action against the government for having increased the female state pension age to 65, retrospectively and with very little warning. In effect this is forcing many women to carry on working for longer than they would wish (and longer than men), as their occupational schemes alone wouldn't provide them with a large enough income to prevent them from sinking into poverty on retirement.

The value of 'women's work'

A large part of the problem is that women work more hours than men, across both the developed and the developing world. If this confuses you, after our exploration of women's loss of earnings due to maternity leave and part-time work, the explanation is simple: women do more work, but a lot of that work is either grossly undervalued or entirely unpaid. The following chart uses data from UN Women, the UN entity dedicated to gender equality and women's empowerment, as well as national surveys from 1998 to 2013.[16] It shows that, in every part of the world, women do more work than men, both paid and unpaid.

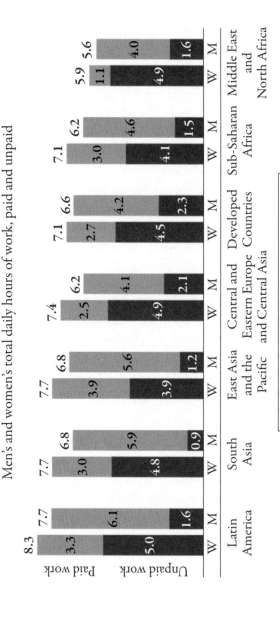

Men's and women's total daily hours of work, paid and unpaid

Source: MenCare Advocacy, *State of the World's Fathers* report, 2017.

We know that the more time one spends on unpaid work, the more difficult it is to move nearer to the pay of those who are gathering skills and experience in the workplace. That is disproportionately the men, while the women nurture, look after the house or children or elderly parents, get involved in worthy but unpaid charity work to make up for the state's deficiencies, or engage in low-paid part-time work that is easier to fit in with the rest of their obligations. A recent study in Australia showed that women undertake 72% of all unpaid work—mostly childcare and care for elderly relatives. In Sydney alone, 40% of women work as unpaid carers. The Australian Bureau of Statistics calculated in 2006 that the replacement cost of this unpaid labour would be some 43.5% of GDP, a staggering figure. Looking at the wider opportunity cost, for individuals and for the country, the amount came to an even greater 57.1% of GDP.

The ONS reports that, each week, UK women do 60% more unpaid hours of work than men.[17] The OECD[18] has calculated that, across the G7 countries, using a number of methods that arrive at more or less the same broad numbers, the imputed monetary value of household chores is significant. Under one such measure, the replacement cost—what you would have to pay someone to do the same household chores—would vary from 11.5% of GDP in Canada to 23.7% in Italy. If we look at the opportunity cost—extra money that could be earned by those freed from such chores—the impact on GDP would be 41.1% in Canada and as high as

66.4% in Germany. In most countries, as in the UK, this work is mostly done by women.

Men's and women's average weekly hours of unpaid work (UK)

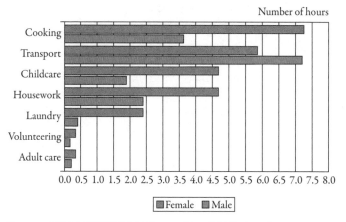

Source: UK HETUS 2015, cited by ONS, 2016.

In a 2019 BBC radio programme, Mary Ann Sieghart explored the issue of this 'real pay gap', looking at the real cost and value of unpaid work.[19] The programme referred to 2017 ONS data, which measured total unpaid work—but the ONS does not include this data in official GDP estimates. GDP, as calculated every-where, overwhelmingly only allows for production and consumption for which a price is paid. It registers zero when no payment takes place. As a result, GDP fig-ures—by which we measure a national economy—do not include the output of those outside the official labour force, or the opportunity cost of unpaid work—what women could be doing, and being paid for, if they were not so burdened by so-called 'women's work'. The ONS calculation in 2016 was that such unpaid work in the UK is equivalent to over £1 trillion.[20]

It was a fascinating programme. As soon as it finished Belinda Phipps, ex-Chair of the Fawcett Society, sent me this text:

> They must have had a microphone in my house listening to the many times I have tried to explain to children and man that there is actual domestic work, there is planning the work and there is keeping the emotions sorted. NONE OF WHICH IS NOTICED OR PAID (yes shouting) and is not counted in GDP and the vast majority of it falls to the female in a heterosexual partnership.
>
> It means your brain is full so to do a paid job you have to be superwoman (✔), you have to be able to manage on little sleep (✔) and you have to be very very determined (✔) and despite the ball and chain fastened around the legs of most women they still do fabulous things at work too even though they are heavily discriminated against there and paid less too!!!!
>
> Where were the women when the GDP rules were drawn up .... yep .... absent I bet ... that's why women need to be there when decisions are taken.
>
> Let's play it over the loudspeaker on every train, at every football match etc until all those of the male persuasion get it.

> The gender stereotype of the weak and incapable woman is absolute nonsense designed to keep us in that free work second class citizen place.

The opportunity cost for women is not just in terms of careers and promotions. As we've seen, it affects pensions, and forces women on average into a life of greater hardship than for men. It would be different, of course, if they were properly recompensed for all the work they do at home for free and for their caring activities in the community. The problem is that the value to society of childcare provision and care for dependents is not properly weighted by market mechanisms. I would also argue that, when women do get paid to provide social and other care on behalf of the state, the remuneration for that work is well below its true value to society. Again, feminists have highlighted this anomaly.

The pay that women generally receive for delivering state social and other care services (and it is mainly women working in that sector) does not accurately reflect the value society really needs to be attaching to these services. This is hardly surprising if women's pay in such areas is dictated by big, powerful monopsonies (dominant employers of a certain type of labour, like the UK's National Health Service), which are tasked by the state with keeping costs down—particularly in a period of austerity, which the UK was only just hesitantly coming out of at the end of the 2010s. Why are these caring jobs, by dint of the fact that they are done mostly by women, relatively low-paid? Why are UK nurses, for example—paid for by the state—or cleaners for local councils valued less than, say, rubbish collectors? In 2015, women cleaners in Birmingham won a pay discrimination case against the local authority; the mostly male rubbish collectors were being paid more than twice as much.

Women's lack of seniority

Many UK firms have defended their pay gap since 2018 on the basis that it is due to women's under-representation at senior levels, and they are not wrong about that. When you look at corporate board representation, the picture is stark, even in previously socialist countries: in 2017, just 7% of board members in publicly listed Russian companies were women. In the same year the Czech Republic was at 8.2%, Estonia at 7.4%, Lithuania at 14.3%, Hungary at 14.5% and Slovakia at 15.1%. There were slightly better figures for Poland (20.1%), Slovenia (22.6%) and Latvia (28.8%), and even better in Finland (32.2%) and France (43.4%), both countries where much effort is being made to increase women's board representation. But the former Eastern Bloc looks to be doing very well when contrasted with other countries where women's progress is really lagging behind, for cultural and other reasons. Just 5.3% of board members in Japan were women, and South Korea was even worse at 2.1%.[21] Nevertheless, progress has been far from good enough in Europe's formerly communist states.

Women's UK board representation, showing women non-executive directors at a record 'high'

FTSE 100 boards

0%	25	50	75	100

100% have at least one female director

35.4% of non-executive directors are women

32% have at least one third women directors

29% of directorship are held by women

22% have executive directors who are women

9.7 % of executive directors are women

Source: Cranfield University/Guardian Graphic, 2018.

Further down than board level, however, the picture is better. It seems that the old regime's expectation that women should have equal rights may have survived the transition to free-market economies. Rankings for 2018 by Grant Thornton suggest that these countries are actually ahead of the game, with 87% of the businesses it surveyed reporting at least one woman in senior management, compared with 73% in the EU as a whole. Some 36% of all senior roles in business were held by women in the former Eastern Bloc, against the EU-wide figure of 27%. Again we can compare this with Japan, where, despite targets to improve gender balance, just 5% of senior positions were held by women.[22]

Of course, much depends on your definition of 'seniority'. The number of senior executive posts held by women on UK boards was still only just above 9% in 2017, up by just 3% from ten years ago, even though a wider definition of 'director' within companies makes that figure a more respectable 29% for FTSE 100 companies.[23]

At least on boards concerted action has resulted in some progress, with lots of government push and partnerships with the private sector. The UK's 2015 Davies Review encouraged firms in the FTSE 100 to achieve 33% representation by 2020. On current progress, the target may well be met early. By 2017, the percentage of women on UK boards had already risen to 28% and is now hovering around 30%, mostly due to the appointment of women non-executive directors, many of whom hold multiple board positions across various companies, rather than the positions of executive chairs, CEOs or finance directors. But other European countries are doing better. By 2015, Norway already had 47% women's representation on boards, France and Sweden were at 34%, and even Italy had 31%; the UK was then at 21%.[24] In any case, the trend is upwards.

But boards are not the only story, and not the most important one. It is really what happens further down that matters. In 2016, a Credit Suisse 'Gender 3000' report, looking at gender diversity across the 3,000 firms the bank analyses globally, found that women were severely lacking in top management positions overall.[25] Credit Suisse found no clear correlation between the numbers of women on boards and the numbers of women in management positions. If anything, the appointment of women on boards may be draining female talent away from senior management. We certainly see this phenomenon in the UK: senior women become serial non-executive directors, reducing the availability of women for senior management positions.

We know that globally only 3.6% of CEOs are women. We also know that in 2018 some 24% of global firms had no women in senior management roles, a fall from 25% the year before, according to research by Grant Thornton.[26] So board representation has probably been the wrong thing to tackle. No surprise, therefore, that even in Norway—where a quota system for boards has long been in place, with penalties for non-compliance—only 7% of top company bosses are women. In France, where a quota system had also been introduced, the figure is just 2%. Even though Norway's representation is higher, both countries have made slower progress than the quota-free US (now 5%) and Germany (6%), where, as in Spain and the Netherlands, there are quotas but no sanctions.[27] Other countries such as Italy and Belgium also have quotas for boards of between 30% and 40%, and companies can be fined, dissolved or have payments to existing board directors frozen—yet when we look at the different roles on boards, women make up a poor percentage of senior executives in management, rather than external non-executive directors.

This reinforces an argument I have already made in a previous book: that there should be quotas not for boards, but for senior executive positions instead.[28] Indeed, the Credit Suisse analysis that linked companies' performance with their management structure pointed out:

> gender diversity on both boards and *particularly* senior management is a tremendous benefit to companies and their shareholders. Management manages companies, while boards supervise them ... To understand the full impact of gender diversity, we need to focus on management ... The data shows that there is a strong correlation between companies with high levels of diversity in management and their performance.

In 2016, for example, the UK could boast just seven female CEOs of FTSE 100 companies, and only ten women CFOs (chief financial officers); two years later, analysis by the Cranfield School of Management found little progress in top companies and a worrying drop in women's participation on company boards in the FTSE 250—from 38 women occupying full-time executive positions to just 30. In the FTSE 250, there were just 6 women CEOs and 19 CFOs, just 6.4% of the total. It found no progress over a four-year period in the number of women executive directors on boards.[29] This matters especially because women in these roles are perceived to be providing the pipeline for senior roles in larger firms. Without quotas, it seems, these executive roles are not opening up for women. Germany has just achieved 39% female representation on supervisory boards of DAX companies, through quota enforcement, but if you look one level below—at the executive boards, where quotas do not apply—suddenly women make up less than 10% of the total.

There is clearly a great deal to be done to improve women's pathways to senior executive positions. The presence of one or two female board members, though undoubtedly a positive sign, is unlikely to achieve much in terms of fundamentally changing internal organisational culture and bias. Not all agree with this view: Melanie Richards of KPMG believes that boards and senior director female representation can help to reinforce a message. Maybe this is so. In one sign of progress, the government-commissioned Hampton-Alexander Review was set up in 2016 to look at ways to improve British women's representation in both senior executive and board positions. The prompt for this step was the evidence, accepted by the government and incorporated into its modern 'Industrial Strategy', that bridging the UK's gender pay gap could add some £150 billion to the economy by 2025. But the Review's 2018 interim report revealed dangerous complacency in Britain's boardrooms.

Despite all the positive noise coming from businesses following the first annual publication of pay gaps in

April that year, the Review found a continuous bias against appointing female board members. Some of the reactions of organisations responding to the Review's authors were astounding and included statements like:

1. 'I don't think women fit comfortably into the board environment'
2. 'There aren't that many women with the right credentials and depth of experience to sit on the board—the issues covered are extremely complex'
3. 'Most women don't want the hassle or pressure of sitting on a board'
4. 'Shareholders just aren't interested in the make-up of the board, so why should we be?'
5. 'My other board colleagues wouldn't want to appoint a woman on our board'
6. 'All the "good" women have already been snapped up.'

Worryingly, a number of the people interviewed believed that the existence of one female board member meant that they had done their bit and could carry on with business as usual.[30]

It is certainly not the case that women are less ambitious, or that they can't handle complex issues, as some male chairmen obviously still believe. But their conditioning as they grow up, in terms of how they are perceived and what is expected of them, plays a big part in how women strive for success in later life. By contrast, a recent study compared the attitudes of Chinese women who grew up under the 'properly' communist regime, which emphasised gender equality, with those who grew up during the post-1978 reform era or in capitalist Taiwan. It found that the women who had been exposed to strong messages of gender equality, even for a short period, were generally more determined to progress and more competitive in their dealings with others.[31] The conclusion? Cultures and institutions that support women's endeavours and women's equality strongly influence women's willingness or ability to compete with men—and with each other!

Why has the capitalist system produced so few senior women? Why has it left so many others in lower-paid jobs? In part it is because, as we've already seen, the system encourages short-termism. The need for quick returns and the rush to produce as cheaply as possible to beat the competition mitigates against investors and managers worrying about the long-term sustainability of their business. All too often they fail to undertake the type of long-term investment in the working environment that would be required to render a place attractive and accommodating for women to work in the longer term—particularly, an environment that supports talented women who want to return to work after having children, by offering them the potential to travel as far up an organisation as their capabilities will take them. But this is not serving the aims and principles of capitalism: it is undermining them. It amounts to an enormous market failure.

What exactly is a market failure?

Capitalism works on a basis of demand and supply. This is as opposed to communism, for example, whereby the state decides the demand and controls the supply accordingly. A demand and supply system depends on the price mechanism to best allocate resources to produce a good or service. This means that capitalism will fail to end up with an optimal equilibrium if there are failures in the system that disrupt flow of information to producers, or failures that disrupt or impede the inputs that go into the production process. For instance, if women are obstructed from returning to work after giving birth, then this is obstructing optimal production. This means markets are not functioning as they should.

Often, market failures arise because there are broader values or costs involved in production, which would need to be considered to allow proper reflection of these factors in market outcomes. The problem is that they are external to the price mechanism that drives market decisions, which means that their positive or negative value does not factor into the market's equation. These are known as 'externalities'—factors beyond 'pure economy' that nevertheless have an economic impact. They can be positive or negative. One example of an important externality is the harm done to the environment and human health by pollution and climate change, but the price of fossil fuels tends not to reflect this negative impact, because it is difficult to capture via market mechanisms. Thus government intervention is needed to sort it out.

Gender inequality is also a market failure, resulting from inability to take into account the externalities (the broader impacts) of women's unequal participation in the labour market. Women are a valuable resource, whose true value is not understood or reflected in market prices, resulting in inefficiency. In fact, economists have a very precise definition of this type of inefficiency, called 'Pareto inefficiency'. Named after the Italian economist Vilfredo Pareto, Pareto inefficiency describes a situation where there is potential to improve overall welfare without anyone losing out, but it is not acted on. A 'free gift' of potential extra welfare is left as no more than that— potential. For example, by ensuring that people move to their most productive use, not only are their incomes increased but they can now pay more taxes to ensure that others can be made better-off. When the gift is not taken, this is called a 'deadweight loss' in economics.

The opposite, naturally, is Pareto efficiency: an optimal situation of resource allocation where nobody can be made better-off without somebody else losing out. All potential benefits have been extracted, and any further individual gains can only be made at the expense of others. Market failure decreases the total benefit gained, and so the economy in question would no longer be operating at optimal efficiency. But these externalities—the true short- and long-term costs of further production to other individuals, the environment or the wider economy—can be obscured. Thus the positive externalities of improving women's economic inequality, and the negative externalities of failing to do so, are not taken into account by decision-makers. Gender equality is on a par with corporate social responsibility or sustainability: there is a big consensus that acting in accordance with these principles makes excellent long-term business sense, but the majority of firms simply won't do it unless they are pushed. This is because the market signals that exist do not encourage them to act, failing to fully correct the imbalance that exists. There is a woeful societal and policy blind spot about the enormous gains in efficiency and growth that would result from full or even better gender equality.

How women's work is valued and remunerated (or not) is just one part of this market failure. The persistence of a gender pay gap and of unequal access to the labour market can be called the 'proxy indicators' of the market failure—the ways it manifests, with substantially suboptimal outcomes across a wide range of areas for society as a whole. In many aspects of women's lives, the way they are perceived acts against them, made worse by widespread bias, both conscious and unconscious. There is only one way to fix this, and it is not trying to persuade businesses or individuals to change their attitudes: market failures, by their nature, usually require intervention to be corrected. If a free-market economy could make such corrections 'by itself' with the mystical power of 'market forces', then restrictions on women's labour supply—or withdrawal of women's labour due to caring commitments, for example—would cause women's overall wages to go up, due to a scarcity of resources. Or, from the opposite end of the spectrum, if women are indeed commanding a lower wage than the men for similar work in the same sector, then surely this would lead them to leave their current work in order to seek employment in higher-paid areas or sectors—this would also provoke a wage rise for women over time in the sectors they have been exiting.

But Adam Smith's 'invisible hand' seems not to operate here. Pay gaps remain, as we have seen, because of the persistence of obstacles to women's labour force participation. Across a wide variety of roles and professions, the odds are stacked against women, who do not compete like-with-like. This is another market failure: imperfect competition, allowing rents ('windfall gains') to be earned by men in a disproportionate or suboptimal allocation of resources. For the men who worry about women competing with them and taking their jobs, one can look as far back as the splendid Sidney Webb, who looked at the alleged differences between men's and women's wages in 1881. He found that even when women were competing with lower wages in a particular sector, then men tended to leave that sector and find plenty of new employment elsewhere.[32] This misconception that there is a fixed and finite amount of work available in an economy is known as the lump of labour fallacy, and it was exposed as a fallacy from an early age. Doesn't this mean that women, too, are free to seek a better deal elsewhere? Sadly not—even in the late nineteenth century, Webb's analysis suggested that women stay in those low-paid jobs for longer than men, who tend to be more mobile—something that has changed little through the ages, for all of the reasons outlined above. Norms, unconscious biases and all sorts of other restrictions affect women's work, and the added value of their contributions is not fully recognised. And so we're stuck with Pareto inefficiency, unless and until there is intervention to fix it.

Of course, there are vociferous people on the right of economic and political thinking who believe that market failures don't exist—except when the government intervenes and distorts the market, so-called 'government failures'. There are also more centre-left economists like Mariana Mazzucato, who believe that we go too far in teaching civil servants to focus on market failure as the only reason for intervening, when in fact there is so much more to do to shape the economy.[33] We all know, after all, that governments can have a powerful role in reshaping markets where such market failures arise. In other words, we needn't just stand by while the market failures develop in the first place. Government action should lead by example, by taking into account the externalities which the markets aren't capturing. It should weigh properly the considerable fiscal costs of current gender inequality, which makes unpaid domestic labourers of potential tax-payers. This can be seen in other fields too; for example, in the externalities of damage to the environment caused by our extraction and consumption of fossil fuels, and the inability of markets to weigh in those externalities in the price we currently pay for energy.

All the evidence suggests that a better use of women's skills should improve productivity in the workplace and add to a country's GDP. This is true across the globe and applies equally to the developed and developing worlds. In India, for example, only 14% of women are in top management positions. In his paper for the *International Research Journal of Interdisciplinary & Multidisciplinary Studies*, Dr Shankar argues that women leaders 'have an enormous potential to influence the way people live and work by promoting better management practices and a better balance between work and family life'. In Europe, work done during the Swedish presidency of the European Union as far back as 2009 calculated that GDP would be some 27% higher across the EU if the region achieved true gender equality.[34] Below the state level, numerous studies since have shown the benefits for firms, such as better brand value, improved productivity, better retention, higher workplace innovation and better returns on investment.

Faster growth and a more prosperous society overall would of course allow lots of money to be recycled towards better pay for those who perform the 'lowly' services of domestic and caring work, and to cover the costs of childcare. Childcare is one of the main ways in which the costs of motherhood alter and cripple women's career paths. This denies to the economy women's full potential as human capital, due to their loss of investment in knowledge and skills and of paid work experience. Without corrective intervention, the pricing mechanism works against women, which values highly those 'years of service'. It deprives the economy of growth that would provide benefits over and above the costs of paying for greater economic equality. And it deprives women of the empowerment to earn well, reach top positions and make their voices heard. So long as that is the case, there will be a market failure in need of correction, not just for the sake of individual women or even womankind, but for the economy to become more productive and for better decisions to be made.

And yet the advocates of capitalism are not asking for more interference; they are asking for less. While accepting that the current system in much of the developed world is a mixed one, where the state has an important role, they still believe that the pendulum has swung too far in favour of 'big government'. This reluctance to let the state make real change, whether to address gender inequality or for any other reason, does not follow the 'rules' of how market capitalism was designed to work. In the case of women's inequality, it also seems to fly in the face of practical economic sense, as we will see in the next section.

Women's equality and economic growth: can we see a clear link?

Many studies have tried to link women's empowerment and economic development. Earlier analysis had not found direct causalities one way or another, but had agreed that there is a circularity and interdependence. In other words, economic development tends on balance to bring with it greater women's empowerment, but economic empowerment resulting in more women making decisions also has a direct impact on economic development.[35] More recent dynamic empirical studies, conducted in the twenty-first century, have come to the same conclusion more forcefully: that economic empowerment makes a direct difference to economic development.[36] Anything that prevents women from contributing their economic potential restricts growth—and so anything enabling them to reach that potential will enhance growth.

A 2018 working paper by the IMF found that the welfare and GDP costs of restricting women's labour force participation are greater than was originally thought—increasing the urgency of change—and that the benefits of reducing these costs are substantial. Barriers to women's participation at present were estimated as equivalent to something like an average 4%

extra tax on female labour in Europe and Central Asia. High, but nothing like the staggering 53% average in the Middle East and North Africa. Removing those barriers would lead to huge improvements in welfare through higher production and consumption—more than 20% gains in the Middle East and South Asia, for example, which are regions with lower starting incomes from which these improvements would occur. The marketable output gain from closing the pay gap would be over 60% in the Middle East and North Africa, and about a third in South Asia.[37]

Let me focus on the difference that legal intervention can make. As the World Bank's 2019 study on sexist discrimination points out, despite considerable improvement over the past decade, with many countries having removed discriminatory laws or enacted anti-discrimination legislation, the average score among the 187 countries studied is 74.71—up from a decade earlier, but still indicating that women typically have only three quarters of the rights enjoyed by men in relation to work.[38] It is having equal rights to work that empowers women financially, and this is the means through which one can at least facilitate empowerment in every other way. Of course, equal rights are still a long way off from guaranteeing equal treatment—it is not a sufficient condition, but an essential one.

Women's potential is not used and developed to the full in free-market capitalism, a waste of resource and productivity. In an environment where globalisation is probably irreversible and where competitiveness is key, a society that is neglectful of a powerful resource will lose out. Women represent more than 50% of the population and deserve better. While those in higher-skilled professions have done relatively well so far in the age of globalisation, and will continue to do so, women's jobs are mostly bunched in the intermediate and lower-skilled areas at greatest risk in the high-tech future, which could worsen inequality further. As Thomas Piketty has argued, the resulting social division and impact on growth is significant.[39] Taking his analysis to its logical conclusion for women, if you start with lower wealth—as women generally do—then you move further and further away from those that have more of it—typically men. Paul Krugman argues in turn that, over time, persistent inequality leads to social unrest and less investment, which then reduces productivity and growth.[40] What I am arguing in this book is that the persistent inequality of women may well have similar negative impacts on growth, though through different routes.

But with inequality now an increasing focus of attention, I would argue that women's issues have risen up the agenda partly for that reason. Worryingly, though, research from the US has found that the recent improvements in labour force participation and gender equality now seem to have stalled. The problem seems to be a lack of anticipation of the difficulties faced by women when motherhood hits, in terms of both the direct costs and also the difficulties associated with caring for children.[41] I will look at motherhood in more detail in the next part of the book, but having one's first child acts as an information shock that causes women to rethink their family/work balance and reconsider whether they are able to maintain both commitments. As we saw in the case of France, this issue seems to affect better educated women worse, which may be a surprise to many.

The EU's draft Joint Employment Report for 2019 points out that, despite a 5% increase in women's employment since the financial crisis, gender inequality persists, and progress is very uneven among EU member states.[42] In the UK, for instance, according to HMRC data, five times more men than women earn over £150,000; ten times more earn over £1 million. Ann Francke, Chief Executive of the Chartered Management Institute, has referred to men still having 'a stranglehold on the best-paid jobs', while Sam Smethers, who runs the Fawcett Society, has bemoaned the fact that in 2019 '61 per cent of low paid workers are women'.[43] With less purchasing power, women do remain the 'weaker sex' economically, and this reduces their overall impact on decision-making across all levels of society's choices. Their influence on the domestic and global agenda is reduced. However crude or incomplete a measure of women's equality, earnings matter.

* * *

One unambiguous finding, reinforced by IMF analysis, is that the impact on GDP of removing gender barriers is substantial. We've already seen several examples of this from across the globe. Just to remind ourselves of the scale we're talking about: in an interview to mark International Women's Day 2019, Christine Lagarde, Managing Director of the IMF, argued that some countries, particularly those in the bottom half of the league tables for gender equality, could achieve a huge boost to their GDP if they abandoned laws that discriminate against women and allowed women's skills to be utilised properly in the economy.[44]

Talking of league tables, everyone has been bending backwards lately to ensure that gender equality now features in the rankings measuring social wellbeing and economic development. These league tables show that, when the legal environment in a country does not afford women equal opportunity in the jobs market or legally enshrined rights, the impact on the economy is significant. As the World Bank argues, 'lack of freedom to legally pursue a profession has been found to have a negative association with female employment'.[45]

Yet, according to the IMF, some 88% of countries still have restrictions against women working, and as recently as 2015 there were 18 countries where women needed their husbands' permission to work, including Bahrain, Iran and Cameroon.[46] The World Bank has also highlighted the fact that, even today, only six countries in the world have equal legal rights to work: Belgium, Denmark, France, Latvia, Luxembourg and Sweden.[47] It concluded that reducing discrimination would have a positive impact on women's labour force participation, particularly in paid employment and earnings across the world.[48]

When a country moves to allow equal rights, for example, to property and inheritance, there is a clear positive association with women's labour force participation.[49] Many developing countries still restrict married women's ability to enter paid employment, particularly in the Middle East and North Africa. In a study of various regions in Ethiopia, for example, the increase in female participation of even limited reform—such as removing one spouse's ability to stop the other from working outside the home, establishing joint property rights or introducing a minimum wage—resulted in women's labour force participation rising by some 15–24%.[50] More broadly, a study looking in detail at the development of legislation in 100 countries over the past 50 years found that 57 of them had introduced reforms strengthening women's legal rights, and 28 of these had actually abolished the legal restrictions.[51] The results were clear: removing obstacles to gender rights led to an increased move of women to paid employment.

It also had important by-products for national development: higher educational attainment for women, and improvements in health for them and their children. To go back to our economist's dictionary, this again reinforces the point that gender inequality is a market failure in need of correction; the benefits of women's economic empowerment do not just apply to the individual, but have significant additional externalities, in terms of the wider positive impact on the wellbeing of both a woman's family—her being richer—and the economy—her spending more, paying taxes, being more productive in the paid economy, and reducing burdens on the state by improving health outcomes for the family.

Are we right to focus on market failures? What if people are simply exercising choice?

Of course some women choose to stay at home, looking after children and engaging in traditional 'women's work' in the house, and would do so even if the costs were the same as those of being in paid employment—but there are many more who want to work and to pursue rewarding careers. A substantial percentage of these women end up working less or below their skills level, or give up exhausted and disillusioned. Not really what they had anticipated through years of schooling and, for a good number of them, university. Women are often more highly educated than men these days and have spent time, effort and often money to get that education. A 1997 paper in *The Review of Economics and Statistics* revealed that, even allowing for wage differences, there is a strong positive correlation among women between higher education levels and greater willingness to supply more labour, because of 'the desire of a woman to recoup the investment she has made in her education'.[52] This is even more the case in the UK today than in 1997, given the introduction of tuition fees a year after that paper was written, currently costing undergraduates almost £10,000 a year. Wage levels matter, of course, and they also matter for less highly educated women—but less so in terms of return on investment.

This makes perfect economic sense. But the market, unaided, finds it hard to recognise and price in the negative economic externalities of childcare costs or wasted investment in education if highly educated women disappear from the system, while also ignoring and failing to price in the positive externalities of both women's paid work and the added value of their unpaid or low-paid work. The short-termism of the capitalist system does not allow for those failures to be properly dealt with. They require long-term investment, which simply won't be forthcoming unless the state intervenes and the supply side responds to new incentives. While these constraints remain, economic equality will not happen for women.

Over the course of this first part of the book, we have seen numerous market failures that prevent women from developing their potential and making their human capital available at the right level and the right price to ensure gender equality is achieved. The list could be much longer. And, when you look around the world, some of these market failures are more important than others in different countries or regions. But they will come up again and again in the parts that follow, as I look at a number of obstacles in achieving economic equality. All have been touched on in the Introduction and here in Part 1, and all will require corrective intervention to be overcome. These market failures are:

– *Unequal access.* Women do not have equal opportunity to participate in the labour market, due to information asymmetry, unequal access to education and other factors. If we want to know why this is so, we need only look at the rest of this list.
– *Insufficient support for motherhood.* In the next part of the book, we will look in more detail at the costs of childcare and the continued unnecessary prevalence in today's economy of inflexible working, and at the consequent relegation of mothers to certain sectors and, often, to part-time work.
– *Conscious and unconscious bias.* Workplace culture has an enormous impact on women's chances, including in recruitment and promotion cultures that are weighted against women. This leads to lack of women in senior positions, which in turn reinforces the bias that they aren't natural leaders, and relegation of women to certain industries, which reinforces the bias that there is

certain work that is more 'natural' for men or for women. We will look at this in Part 3.

– *Failure to weigh the future.* This concerns both the general short-termism of public- and private-sector thinking under free-market capitalism, and one specific, pressing issue: the looming, gendered threat of further automation, which will hit women (who dominate the service and care sectors) hardest. We'll turn to this in detail in Part 4.

The common theme running through all of these market failures related to women's inequality is the most important failure of all: rationality failure. It is blindness to the well-evidenced truth that gender equality is economically beneficial. We've seen plenty of proof already, and we will see plenty more as we explore the negative impact of different barriers to equal participation. But the far more damaging result of the rationality failure is policy failure. This is not about what certain right-wing economists term 'government failure' (the state intervening and 'messing up' a market that it should have left alone), but about how governments have actually failed women in free-market capitalism: with insufficient policy intervention and lack of appropriate regulation.

As we're starting to see, much more can be done, from quotas, to naming and shaming, to transparency laws. Part 4 of this book therefore focuses on policy proposals that would put governments on the right path, and perhaps nowhere could the state be more powerful in lifting women up than when it comes to the questions of motherhood and care work.

PART TWO

MOTHERHOOD AND CARING

2

MOTHERHOOD AND CARING

When women first enter the UK labour force, the gender pay gap is virtually non-existent. By their late 20s, the gap has risen to 10% and it rises steadily thereafter. A recent study looking at the pay gap for women aged 22–29 found that, if that gap persisted on that basis alone, women who carried on working would ultimately earn £223,000 less in their lifetimes than men.[1] For some it's all blindingly obvious: women have babies and men do not. Our roles are set by God/Nature and our sex. Take this quote from a blog piece by James Knight for the free-market Institute of Economic Affairs, entitled 'The "gender pay gap" is a non-issue':

> In fact, if you just look at males and females in their 20s and 30s, females earn slightly more. Obviously this tails off in the late 30s and 40s as motherhood becomes the primary driving force in the re-introduction of a wage gap—but it's not to do with discrimination, it is to do with biology and life choices.[2]

The data doesn't quite agree with that assertion. Birth and even breastfeeding are only a small part of total parenthood, and parenting should not fall to one section of society, given that it is necessary to reproduce the labour required for production and social stability, which benefits us all. But, as we saw from the ONS, and as we all know from casual observation, the direct parenting burden falls disproportionately on women. Because of this, motherhood acts as a barrier to equal access to paid work and career progression.

What does the evidence tell us about this? According to the Institute for Fiscal Studies, when women take time off work to have children, however they may structure their maternity leave and subsequent professional life, they will have difficulty recovering their previous wage path. For mothers in the UK, the IFS finds that the gap continues increasing, to 33% by year 12 after the arrival of the first child.[3] This is as striking as it is revealing.

We know why this is the case. Those mothers miss out on critical workplace skills and experience and therefore promotion prospects, even when they come back to work quickly after the child's arrival, on a part-time basis. Part-time workers tend to not get asked to do important tasks as they are not there all the time and often miss out on training opportunities, even if they only take a short time off with each child. There is also evidence that women returnees who downgrade from full-time to part-time within their organisation will then be working at least one

Gender pay gap in the years before and after arrival of a woman's first child

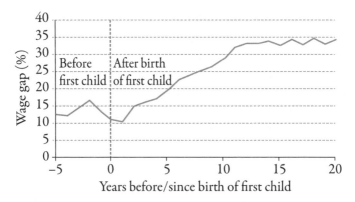

Source: IFS, 2016.

step below their skill level. Monica Costa Dias, Associate Director at the IFS, says: 'It is remarkable that periods spent in part-time work lead to virtually no wage progression at all ... It should be a priority for governments and others to understand the reasons for this. Addressing it would have the potential to narrow the gender wage gap significantly.'[4] Paul Johnson, Director of the IFS and my former colleague at the UK Government Economic Service, wrote in *The Times*:

> The part-time problem arises from the fact that, once you start to work part time, you lose out on the wage progression that full-timers enjoy. You might start off on the same hourly wage as you would have done if you'd stayed full time, but the wage increases grind to a

halt. That's a big part of why the wage gap grows inexorably in the years after childbirth. Women lose out not only from taking time out of the labour market but also from reducing hours of work, and these effects cumulate over time.

What all this suggests is that we may have a big problem in the way in which we organise work in the UK. Training, progression, promotion are much harder to come by if you work part time. We can all think of reasons why this might be true, from cultures of presenteeism to losing out on informal interactions down the pub. What is clear is that there is still an awfully long way to go to make workplaces work effectively for half the population.[5]

Despite impressive advances in support for mothers in some countries, at best including better support for fathers, overall progress has been painfully slow. Appallingly, in the UK, research from as recently as 2016 shows that three in four working mothers report having faced discrimination at work, and a majority feel that having children has been bad for their career.[6] While I was writing this book, news came out in early June 2019 that Sarah Morris, equality champion and Aviva's award-winning 'Chief People Officer' (HR Director), was fired while on maternity leave. She had said in the news a few months earlier that she intended to come back to her role, but wasn't sure how exactly or for how many days a week. She had sounded optimistic about restructuring her work in the future: 'I think you can have a brilliant career and love what you do and have a family'. The news item covering Morris's sacking also quoted Ann Francke of the Chartered Management Institute, suggesting that maybe Aviva wasn't walking the walk and worrying about the impact of this incident: 'What sort of signal does this send to employees? To women—and men—who want children? And what does this say for the next generation?' As I myself wrote in a 2017 article for the public finance think tank OMFIF, 'the message to our daughters is clear, if sad: take as little time off when you have a baby—and when you go back, assuming your job is still there, avoid taking on part-time roles'.

We don't know the exact details of what went on here and there may be many other factors we are not aware of. But that life is still tough for new mothers seems to be confirmed by a 2015 survey by the UK Equality and Human Rights Commission, which found that some 54,000 women lose their jobs each year in the UK as a result of having a child.[7] Its findings suggested that one in nine new mothers 'had been dismissed, made compulsorily redundant [when others were not] or treated so poorly they had to quit their job'. Ten percent said they were treated worse and 7% said they had been put under pressure to hand in their notice.[8] Before things even reach that stage in a woman's career—the return to work—a 2014 survey of hiring managers revealed that a third of them would hire a man in their 20s or 30s over a woman of the same age, in order to avoid any future problems around maternity leave.[9]

The EU has taken steps to address the problem, but is still falling short of fully empowering mothers to return to work. In 2001 the Barcelona Agreement set a target for formal childcare to be available by 2010 to at least 90% of preschool children aged 3 and over, and to at least 33% of under-3s. Preschool childcare availability has increased considerably as a result and, in many countries, it is heavily subsidised with the aim of encouraging female employment. Nevertheless, by 2010, only nine EU countries had reached the first target, and only seven the second. And by 2013, according to OECD data, it was still the case that women with children in developed nations found it more difficult to work than those without.

Even these figures often hide an underlying situation that is even worse. Participation rates obscure the fact that a large percentage of women, certainly in most countries a vastly larger percentage than men, work part-time—including a majority of women in the Netherlands. That is fine if it represents a woman's free choice to stay at home and care for dependents, to further improve her training or education, to engage in leisure or charitable activities, or to step away from a strenuous job to spend more time with family. But that cannot be the case for all of those women. We know that in many cases women feel forced to opt out because their workplace is unwelcoming to women and mothers, inflexible to their needs, or both, or because the costs of childcare are too great. What's more, this situation perpetuates the gender pay gap, which tends to remain higher in countries with higher female part-time employment rates.

As the UK's Institute for Fiscal Studies and other studies have shown, being at work and getting experience is crucial. With equal pay legislation in many countries, it is difficult to pay women and men differently for doing exactly the same job, but we know that age and accumulated experience still matter in promotion—and that it is disproportionately men who get these promotions. It is the longer-serving and older members of the BBC's Today programme, for instance, who are paid more—much more—than newer members. Of course, this preference for more long-established staff doubly prejudices against women, not only because they're likely to have lost out on promotion due to motherhood, but also because historically there have been fewer of them in the workplace, creating an automatic advantage for the men who've been around in greater numbers for longer.

Evidence from other countries also confirms this. In France, a survey of 3,100 hospital doctors and pharmacists published in early March 2019 by the trade union Action, which represents hospital practitioners, found that the barriers to women progressing were still serious. One in three women respondents said that their pregnancies had adversely affected their careers and three quarters said that their career path would have been different if they had been men. There was a clear sign that the hours they were expected to work were putting a huge strain on them, particularly as the survey results showed they were also required to do the majority of the housework and meal preparation.[10] We will look more later in the book at how this burden, and the bias connected to it, contribute to the pay gap.

Many studies in the 2010s have linked higher childcare costs with increased incidence of women exiting the labour force. As the non-profit Washington Center for Equitable Growth reported in 2016, as much as a third of the reduction in US women's labour force participation between 1995 and 2011 can be directly explained by lack of family-friendly policies in the country, according to researchers at Cornell University.[11] Follow-up research by the then-Princeton PhD student So Kubota looked at the impact of the staggering 32% rise in US childcare costs between 1990 and 2010, during a period when wages across the economy were more or less stagnant. Not surprisingly, Kubota found that this cost hike acted as a disincentive, and women's labour force participation declined, at a time when it was rising in most European countries, which had friendlier pro-family policies. According to Kubota, rising childcare costs resulted directly in total employment for women falling by 5% over the period; employment of working mothers with children under 5 fell by 13%. OECD stats show that women's labour force participation continued to fall in the US up to 2015, whereas in other countries such as Germany, Japan and Australia it rose (Appendix, Fig. 7).

You might point out that women's increased participation in the US since the 1970s has been described by the Harvard economics professor Claudia Goldin as 'revolutionary'—coming after three earlier 'evolutionary' phases in the last century.[12] As far as I can see, this change—probably helped by the pill, a rise in divorce rates, more single parenthood, women's liberation movements and the rise of feminism, and improvements in education—was down to women starting to see their labour force involvement as a 'career', rather than just as a job, secondary to husbands and children. But despite the 'revolution', Goldin's later work (some ten years on), using US census data from 2000, found that the gender pay gap still existed, and widened for college graduates between the ages of 26 and 39.[13] That was particularly pronounced between the ages of 26 and 32; the main reason seemed to be getting married and having children. Despite wider acceptance, by both men and women, of women having a career, and despite women's willingness to invest more in their education to achieve those aims, the evidence is very clear: the gap between men's and women's career achievements grows as women's family responsibilities grow. The inescapable conclusion, as Goldin says, is that 'Having children imposes differentially higher costs on women than men'.

In many developing regions, women have to work very hard to feed their families. As incomes increase, they can reduce that manual supply for a while.[14] But it is worrying when the same story is happening in Western market economies, due to rising costs of childcare coupled with low maternity pay. A Warwick University (CAGE) paper studied the impact of maternity leave and pay on women academics in the UK, collecting data from 10,000 academics and looking at issues of productivity, child-rearing and individual career paths. The conclusions, perhaps not surprisingly, were that there is an unambiguously strong relationship across all academic disciplines between the generosity of maternity pay and the share of professors who are women—in other words, the number of women who manage to stick around, despite their motherhood, long enough to be promoted against the odds.[15]

The impact of children on careers can also clearly be seen in the shared experiences of senior women, several of whom were happy to be interviewed for this book. Sukhi Clark, a past Head of Engineering and Operations at Jaguar Land Rover, said:

> If you're a woman, and get into a senior position in your 30s and take a break to have children, then effectively you start your management role again on your return. When I had my first management role at 30, I had male peers in the same position. I had my first child at 34 and my next at 35. I lost 6 years of management experi-

ence because, when I came back, I had to prove myself all over again. So I did not get a Senior Management position until my 40s, whereas my male peers hit senior management earlier than me. That's probably where the unconscious bias comes in.

Beverley Nielsen, Associate Professor and Director of Studies at Birmingham City University, recalls an interesting encounter over dinner with a senior partner from an accounting firm, back in the 1990s when she was working for the Confederation of British Industry in Birmingham. The man started enquiring about whether she had any children. What followed was quite extraordinary. 'He asked their ages. I responded. He seemed to get a little agitated, asking, why was I back at work. I said I needed to work and was blessed with great support from my family. He became angry, asking did I even know my children's names, at which point he stormed out of the room!'

Well, what can one say!

A final example illustrates the full range of issues facing mothers that we will explore in this part of the book, from poor maternity pay and career prospects lost through time off to inflexible workplaces. A family friend of mine, a British-French dual national who studied in Canada, has returned to the UK with her Canadian husband. Now nearing 30, she has begun to think about a good time to have children. But she has no idea how she will be able to afford it. She is of course enthusiastic about the chances of free childcare, but she knows that it will still harm her career having to take time off work till the child is three, when free nursery hours could be available. While she frets about this, her husband is unwilling to discuss timing and other related plans with her. She feels the burden of parenthood will be on her—not financially, but for her time and career choices. She has started rating the firms she may apply to join next by the generosity of their maternity leave. Outside the public sector and charities, the best seem to be financial-sector companies. I was intrigued to see that Goldman Sachs in London, for example, has started offering super-generous maternity leave, a creche in the building and a breastfeeding room! Perhaps things are finally changing.

Not so fast, though. Women at Goldman Sachs can probably afford nannies. What about the rest? And it is understandable that the financial sector is finally moving ahead, since it has been exposed as the worst offender when it comes to pay and bonus gaps. I also sense that banks and insurance companies probably feel under pressure to increase their female intake and improve their pipeline of female talent—they wouldn't, one guesses, want to continue receiving bad publicity. Nor would they want to become targets for extra regulation and compliance. So, yes, pressure has helped. But it is simple economics: the system will never produce an optimal outcome, because it is not designed to do so. The UK civil service has been assiduous in its attempts to achieve diversity targets, as have pockets of the creative economy, where more women are evident. But this is far from typical and doesn't seem to have achieved equality even in those sectors, as we'll see in Part 3.[16]

If we can remove the circumstances of parenthood that cause women to lose out on accumulating skills and experience, then we will remove much of the current justifications or defences of the gender pay gap. It can't be differences in education, for example, accounting for the gap, given that women's educational achievements actually exceed those of men in many countries, including the UK. Motherhood is too often pointed to as a circumstance beyond the employer's control, as if women are choosing to hamstring their own careers—but this is not a real choice, and there is plenty that can be done about it. We need state intervention to ensure the best use of resources—which means ensuring that mothers, and women more generally, can work as easily as fathers and the majority of men.

Redressing the balance: parental leave

There are of course economists like Catherine Hakim, now at Essex University, who would argue that women freely choose to stay with their children, to spend more time with them and less time at work; they are prepared to surrender power for the pleasure that being home carers gives them. This is true for some women, of course.

But all the evidence from research literature suggests that the willingness to do so has been diminishing steadily over the decades, and that the provision of both free or subsidised childcare and paid parental leave, including paternity leave, has a big influence on women's willingness to work—and their achievements.

There is no reason why the economy should not be adapted to allow for greater flexibility, so that both women and men can spend more time with their children. And, in fact, the evidence suggests that, when fathers take paternal leave and see their new-borns more, mothers return to work quicker and do better in their later career. But there is a problem getting in the way of this 'everybody-wins' solution. Children are not a commodity—not something produced, bought and sold for profit—and so capitalism finds it difficult to measure the value of parenthood. For this reason, national policies vary wildly. In some Western nations, like France, there are incentives to produce children and rewards for large families; in others, like the US, there are none. In China, of course, the opposite was the case under the One-Child Policy (1979–2015), with specific financial and societal disincentives to having multiple children. The PRC was worried about population explosion and wished to make it clear that women were expected to work, even in the generally harsh conditions prevalent when the policy was first introduced.

Nevertheless, the global trend was for a general improvement in maternity leave and paid leave in the

1990s and 2000s, as well as moves towards an additional offer of paternity leave—sometimes paid, sometimes shared with the mother, and sometimes non-transferable. In much of the West, there have been tentative signs that perhaps society is finally putting some monetary value on motherhood, while also sending a signal that parents are valued by the company/organisation they work for: 'Take time off, be comfortable during your leave, share it with your partner if you wish, but then please come back!' This makes business sense, as firms should not wish to lose resources they have invested in. I have experienced it myself. In the mid-80s I was working for an oil company in London, and expecting child number 5. I was offered 2 months' extra salary if I returned to work within a couple of months! Of course, I did so. But when I say this to friends now, it is clear that such practice was rare then, and is still rare now.

Because the burden of parenthood falls disproportionately on women, the balance of economic power between men and women is distorted. It is usually mothers who feel the strain of this life-changing event, much more than fathers. A 2006 survey by the social geographer Danny Dorling found that men who had just become fathers were much less likely than new mothers to list that new arrival as an 'important event' in their life![17] What is more, surveys suggest that this unequal impact on women is often unforeseen: it comes as a shock, as women are unprepared and uninformed of what lies ahead for them in their economic life. This is particularly so for highly educated women, who lose more in terms of career progress and pay projection as a result of any interruption that motherhood brings. Another factor is that this category of women tends to have more children, because their family unit is better able to afford them.

It is generally women who are expected to adapt their life the most to becoming a parent; if left unaided, they typically take up the historic norm for women: either withdrawing from work for a while and becoming home carers, or returning to work (usually after an interval) in a less productive, worse-paid role that offers greater flexibility in days and hours. In purely economic terms, the effects of this are twofold. In terms of human capital, these women's return on their educational investment and skills falls relative to that of men and of women who have been in continuous full-time work. In terms of opportunity cost, they lose more potential every year they spend at home looking after children, as less experience and fewer skills are accumulated. Because of this, women suffer more than men from what economists call 'hysteresis'. The skills you once had are lost or forgotten if they don't get applied for a while, particularly if they don't get reinforced or renewed through continuous training, both formal and on-the-job. As a result, women see their earnings trajectory flatten considerably compared with that of men.

The UK lags behind many other developed nations in tackling this problem. In 2015 it finally introduced shared parental leave of up to 50 weeks, with up to 37 of them paid at the statutory rate (as of April 2019, £148.68 per week or 90% of average weekly earnings, whichever is lower). But women on Statutory Maternity Pay, rather than Shared Parental Pay, are also entitled to 90% of their average weekly earnings before tax for the first 6 weeks, and sometimes also enhanced maternity pay from their employer. It is not surprising, therefore, that only 2% of couples have taken up the shared leave. This has prompted the government to start an information campaign targeting men, under the slogan 'Share the Joy'. But the sad truth is that, in practice, women get paid less on average, so in most heterosexual households it makes much more sense for the woman to take the time off than the man. There had also been provision in UK legislation for paid paternal leave introduced six years earlier, but the majority of firms still only offer the miserly two weeks of full-pay paternity leave. Stronger intervention is needed to force employers to offer meaningful paid leave to men. Norway and Sweden, for instance, offer separate parental leave, as well as heavily subsidised childcare provision from a much earlier age than in the UK. This is part of the Scandinavian 'social contract'. It's hardly surprising, then, that these countries come top in terms of gender equality.

Evidence presented by the European Commission in 2019 shows clearly that generous paternal leave helps ensure a higher take-up by fathers, and that this increases the rate of employment of women.[18] But before understanding this, the UK has some catching up to do if it even wants to match most OECD nations on maternity pay—in 2013 it was the seventh least generous, behind Chile, Cyprus and Costa Rica, among many others. The US paid mothers least of all. The ten most generous countries were overwhelmingly Scandinavian social democracies or former socialist states, with Austria a rare outlier in a sea of ex-Eastern Bloc and Nordic nations. There is a similar pattern in public expenditure on overall parental leave. The UK spend in 2013 was just half the OECD average; the most generous nations were again, though in different order, the former Eastern Bloc countries and the Scandinavians. In any case, of course, a lot of the leave on offer is unpaid or at a low, flat rate of statutory pay, unless one works for a generous employer—in the UK, that means the public sector!

Paternity leave was initially promoted mainly by Nordic countries, which instituted in law a non-transferable right for each parent to take leave in the first year of a child's birth. Norway was the first to pioneer a socalled father's quota in 1992, and it is believed that this has contributed to gender equality. Although it is not universal across the Nordic countries, this non-transferable paternity leave has been regarded as a very important measure toward not only better gender equality, but also improved father–child relationships. By the mid-

2000s, a number of countries had instituted paid paternity leave, but, as with general parental leave, the length of this paternity leave varied greatly from country to country, and continues to differ to this day.[19] The longest back then was in Iceland (13 weeks), while Greece, Ireland, Luxembourg, the Netherlands, Spain and Austria each awarded less than one week of paid paternal leave. The EU average for fathers was 1.9 weeks of available paid paternity leave; for the OECD as a whole the average was slightly higher, at 2.8 weeks.

In 2009 the UK also moved to grant paternity leave as a right for the first time. The new act meant that the male partner of a woman on maternity leave, or the biological father of an unborn child, could claim statutory paternity leave at the flat weekly rate in the child's first year,[20] on condition that the leave was taken within the first 8 weeks of the birth, or thereafter in blocks of one or two weeks. But again, unless the employer also paid paternity leave at a rate that would compensate men for the loss of their generally higher salary, the prospect would not seem that attractive.[21] Take-up of paternity leave in the UK has been particularly poor in its first decade. But we know that if it is done properly it can lead to a substantial improvement in gender equality. The Prime Minister of Iceland, Katrín Jakobsdóttir, reported at the LSE equality conference in early May 2019 that, in her country, the introduction of universal childcare and properly shared parental leave with a 'use-it-or-lose-it' portion has had the biggest impact so far on boosting gender equality.

This is an important finding, and it has been confirmed more than anecdotally. A study in Spain found that the introduction of paid, non-transferable paternity leave did result in women going back to work earlier and taking less unpaid leave, with a 400% increase in fathers' uptake of leave.[22] For the broader picture, a 2013 study looking at practices across the OECD concluded that well-established paid parental leave in Western countries meant that, on average, more women were to be found in senior positions than in countries without those arrangements.[23] Interestingly, it was not the length of leave that determined the presence of senior women. While France, for example, had one of the longest statutory periods of paid leave, and an above-average share of top women in companies, the US had no statutory maternity pay, but a greater percentage of women in senior positions than France, Germany and Denmark, which offer a year's paid maternity leave. Nor did the generosity of the pay correlate with the numbers of senior women: Australia, with the second-lowest level of paid leave, topped the table for women high up in organisations. Japan was average in its leave policies, but had the lowest percentage of senior women. What the study did find was a much closer correlation between women in senior positions and paid paternity leave.

Things are changing—employers are now much more generous, and legislation is encouraging this while also getting tougher on enforcement. The EU in particular is now moving strongly ahead. Promoting equality between men and women was enshrined in the 1992 Maastricht Treaty, while Article 23 of the EU's Charter of Fundamental Rights—which entered into force with the 2009 Treaty of Lisbon—explicitly requires this equality to be across all areas, including employment, work and pay. In April 2019, an earlier EU directive entitling each parent to at least four months of leave was substituted by one setting new minimum requirements for parental leave across the EU, including a minimum of 10 working days' paid leave for fathers—or what they called 'equivalent second parents'. The directive also made it harder for men to transfer their paternity leave to women, thus encouraging them to take it or lose it.[24] Finally, it reinforced the right of working parents, both mothers and fathers, to ask for flexible working throughout the EU, using IT and long-distance options or changing their mode of working to suit their commitments.[25]

It remains to be seen how the paternity leave requirement will be enforced in countries that have so far been far less enthusiastic than the Nordic models emulated in this new EU directive. What's more, even where paternity leave is well provided, take-up of the entitlement tends to need time before it becomes fully utilised. It seems that, beyond legal entitlement, there is a further barrier: men are concerned about the impact on their career of absenting themselves from work, requiring reassurance before they take the leave that their promotion prospects won't be harmed. But a recent Aviva survey suggested that those who do take the leave seem to come back refreshed and reinvigorated after the break, so perhaps they'll get the hang of it eventually.[26] And the trend has now been established. There is an increasing acceptance that further state intervention is required to force laggard countries to improve the terms and realities of maternity leave. Firms, even though many studies have shown that this is in their long-term interest, will not do it if left to their own devices.

The EU is clear that paternity leave or flexible work arrangements for fathers impacts on how much unpaid family work women undertake, at the expense of paid employment. The EU's steps in this area absolutely reflect the general belief that the way to mitigate the cost of parenthood is through better maternity and, increasingly now, longer paternity leave. Many of the studies done so far have focused on the impact of better paternity leave on developed nations, where labour force participation is already high. Some of the results suggest that some leave is good, but too much leave is detrimental. The reason for the latter could well be that women then lose many of the skills that made them employable in the first instance, which is a drawback in terms of their ability to earn a wage that can cover their childcare costs. The economic evidence suggests that measures to alleviate the costs incurred as a new mother—such as subsidies, vouchers for childcare or tax credits—seem to be particularly effective in increasing mothers' labour supply and improving their purchasing power, including their ability to buy more of the goods their children need.[27] But mothers will never have equal access to the labour market while the burden of childcare falls mainly on them.

Childcare: can free or near-free provision ultimately pay for itself?

A French survey of medical professionals in 2019 threw up suggestions from healthcare staff with children that they needed the ability to be more flexible in their work patterns, without this having consequences for their careers. But this went hand in hand with another recommendation: having a creche in the hospital for staff use. In the UK, the average family spends some £10,000 a year on childcare. The state system is quite complicated, with differing hours of free childcare for qualifying under-2s versus the standard provision for 3- and 4-year-olds (15 hours); the free hours go up to 30 hours per week for qualifying working parents of preschool 3- and 4-year-olds. Overall, subsidising early-years education is costing the UK taxpayer some £6 billion a year.[28] Other countries start subsidising childcare a lot earlier in a child's life. But big differences still exist across the OECD: in Canada childcare takes up about 45% of a single parent's net income, while in France, Germany, Sweden and the UK it is under 10%. For dual-parent households, British parents are spending about a third of their income on childcare, while in Spain it's less than 10%.[29]

Childcare costs after state support relative to household income in developed nations

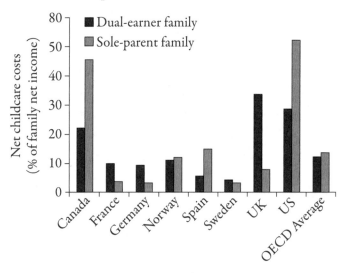

Source: OECD, *Society at a Glance 2016: OECD Social Indicators.*

For those paying for nursery education, free availability surely would help with individual economic freedom, as do childcare vouchers in the UK and elsewhere. But that system is by no means perfect. As free preschool care has been expanded in the UK, childcare vouchers provided by the employer (which can be worth as much as £55 per week) are being phased out. Tax-free childcare from approved organisations, worth up to £2,000 per child annually, is still available for all children up to the age of 12, with the government effectively adding £2 to every £8 paid by parents; for those on benefits like universal credit, between 70% and 85% of childcare costs can be covered for a maximum of a month. But getting one's head round these overlapping systems is exhausting, not to mention the bureaucracy costs of administering them. And the system seems to be crumbling.

The hourly rate paid to private and state UK nurseries to cover the extra cost of the move from 15 to 30 free preschool hours has been so low that many are either closing, refusing to take more kids, or making paying parents contribute more. That has led to choice being restricted, with lesser availability of nursery places near people's homes—contributing no doubt to stress and adding a new barrier for women, paying or otherwise, to much-needed childcare for the under-5s. It also creates an additional barrier to working for mothers, who must contend not only with getting between work and home, but also a third location when the nursery is not nearby. A 2014 study by the American Enterprise Institute found that, despite huge progress in women's labour participation and earnings since the 1950s, there are still many obstacles that prevent millions of women in the US from fully participating in the workforce at a level matching their skills and qualifications.[30] The study quoted research from the Brookings Institution showing that, across every income segment, women have a greater likelihood of being 'downwardly mobile'—and identifying high childcare costs as the main reason for this.[31]

More research from the US and Canada also substantiates the importance of funded childcare in women's ability to work. According to one study using data from the 1999 National Survey of America's Families, childcare subsidies in welfare programmes were associated with a 13% increase in the likelihood of women being employed.[32] A strong positive impact was also found in Quebec, which introduced highly subsidised universal childcare policies in the late 1990s,[33] as well as in the case of two Kentucky childcare subsidy programmes from the early 1990s. In the Kentucky case, it was estimated that introducing a subsidy of just $46 a week had increased maternal labour force participation by anywhere from 8.4% to 25.3%.[34]

So what support should women get with childcare, and should it be free? There is some interesting evidence of externalities from the UK's Sure Start programme. This support scheme for disadvantaged under-5s has been running since 1999 but reached its peak in 2009–10, when it was receiving £1.8 billion in funding (in 2018/19 money terms); Sure Start spending has now been cut to just £600 million a year. A 2019 report from the Institute for Fiscal Studies shows that, even at its reduced rate, the programme has a major positive impact on children's long-term health—a great benefit to society—and on reducing hospitalisations, again saving short-, medium- and longer-term costs. In fact, the IFS estimates that, through improved health alone, the programme can recoup some 6% of its annual costs. In terms of inequality, Sure Start has halved the gap in hospitalisations between poorer and richer areas in the community.[35] Beyond literal life chances of disadvantaged children, state support can help to fend off the vulnerabilities created by their families' socioeconomic status. Studies have shown that children growing up in poorer households are more exposed to the possibility of engaging in antisocial behaviour; it has been estimated that societal costs related to antisocial behaviour in the US are somewhere between $1 and $2 trillion per year.[36]

We know that the market struggles to measure the wider economic benefits of free childcare, but it is essential that we do so. We also know that many less-well-off children now live in households headed by a single parent, most often a woman—though even two-parent families are struggling. Danny Dorling, who has written a lot about inequality in the workplace, is adamant that the policies we need include universal childcare free for under-5s and flexible working across all businesses and sectors, to help with parenting without reducing parents' chances to earn a decent living or advance their careers. One might add that we should also be valuing properly the contribution a woman makes to our economy in looking after its children—again, not something the market can do by itself. I would say that this is all starting to look like the beginning of an argument for a universal basic income, geared towards women with children—but I will leave that argument for another day.

Capitalist production does not reward the bringing up of children or wider household production, but, as we saw in the Introduction, a man who works would have to pay a sum equal to the average yearly wage for someone other than a stay-at-home partner to look after his children. What is more, if a woman abstains from work for a while, the opportunity cost in terms of future earnings is greater, and the combined household income is less that it would otherwise have been. We have seen that, when childcare is difficult to find, or too expensive in relation to household income, women's labour force participation drops, which reduces an economy's ability to operate at maximum efficiency.

It is however a problem trying to find what the right demand will be when the price is zero or near zero— some may make Malthusian warnings that free childcare would lead to rising fertility, which would ultimately make free childcare unaffordable. But the evidence in fact suggests that fertility rates fall as a nation becomes richer. In countries that have instituted free or heavily subsidised preschool education, there has been no evidence of any significant rise in fertility rates. When you look across Europe, there is no connection between birth rates and labour force participation rates. For example, EU countries with a fertility rate of around 1.8 children per woman (the UK, the Netherlands, Sweden, Finland, Germany) also have the highest participation rates, while those with the lowest fertility rates (Greece, Italy, Poland, Malta), below 1.4 children per mother, also have the lowest labour participation rates.[37]

Instead what one finds is that, if childcare costs are high, it is only the richer section of the population that can afford to 'buy' more. In other words, children become a 'luxury item'. The well-known financier Dame Helena Morissey, head of the 30% Club which campaigns for more women on boards, has nine children. The multi-millionaire politician Jacob Rees-Mogg, Leader of the Commons at the time of writing, has six. Alright—I have five children myself, but I can tell you, I came to the UK with not a penny and have been the major breadwinner in my family for most of my working life. But why should a bigger family be a privilege of the few, while others have to restrict numbers because of the costs? That creates an immediate inequality that is then difficult to shift through the generations. As the American Enterprise Institute has demonstrated, average childcare costs represent some 7% of US family income, but for families in poverty—a good number of them headed by a single mother—it amounts to some 30%.[38]

So childcare is vital, not just for mothers but for the economy as a whole. The academic literature provides conclusive evidence that its costs impact on mothers' labour market decisions. Put simply, high childcare costs are associated with less paid work, and subsidised childcare costs are associated with more paid work. Research by Jean Kimmel found that the relevance of childcare costs to labour force participation is stronger for married mothers than for single mothers, who clearly also have other issues to deal with.[39] But it matters for both, even if it's at a slightly different rate. In any case, it is clear that employment of single mothers also goes up if the state pays more of the childcare costs.[40] Kimmel's overall findings suggested that a 10% increase in childcare costs results in a 7.5% decline in women's labour force participation.

Evidence from Germany comparing the former West and East German experiences after reunification found that, where there was greater availability of regional or local government provision, women earned higher salaries and maintained their career path more easily.[41] A study of mothers in Italy showed that those women who chose to shorten their maternity leave to take advantage of state-subsidised childcare were much less likely to leave the labour market and thus be lost to the economy.[42] Research by David Ribar in the US also looked at the juxtaposition of wages versus childcare costs, and found—unsurprisingly—that wages have a strong positive impact on married women's willingness to work, while childcare costs have a negative impact.[43] Policies that increase effective wages would therefore encourage more women to work, as would policies that reduce childcare costs, such as tax credits or subsidies.

Of course, the impact of childcare costs on labour supply varies from country to country. But even in places where women's workforce participation is already comparatively high, such as Sweden, Norway, France and the Netherlands, studies there still show a positive causal relationship between childcare cost subsidies and willingness to work. The impact is considerably bigger in places like Canada and the US.[44] Much, in the course of the analysis, depends from where you start and what policies were already in operation before the introduction of subsidised/free childcare. The UK's Institute for Fiscal Studies tried to anticipate the impact of the move from 15 free hours of nursery education for 3–4-year-olds (introduced in 2010) to 30 free hours per week for working parents (from September 2017).[45] It used, as a proxy measure, what happened when mothers moved their children from preschool, where they only had 15 hours free each week, to a free full-time school place at age 5. The IFS found that there were more women who joined the labour force each year when their child started proper school, but that the increase was not that significant. Thus, without drawing firm conclusions, the report suggested that a move to 30 hours' free nursery care for eligible parents might not substantially increase women's labour force participation.

But that isn't surprising. Firstly, as the IFS report itself acknowledges, there is already record work participation in the UK and this may not be a proper test case. Secondly, it is very likely that many women had joined the labour force already, precisely in order to qualify for those free 15 hours. Thirdly, the reduction in costs may not be very great if women were either looking after the children themselves at preschool age or relying on informal systems such as fellow parents or other relatives to do the caring. But the real factors preventing more women from returning to work, even with 30 hours of free childcare, are about our economy more broadly—what it values, and what it doesn't. For one thing, school hours do not normally translate well into normal working patterns, and still present difficulties for women who want to combine both work and principal childcare activities. For another, returning to work after a big period away means that the skills and experience of others in the workplace are greater and they will therefore tend to command a higher salary. So what we need is both better state provision of care, and adjustments to working culture in terms of how parenting-related absence is viewed and how much flexibility is offered—exactly as health workers in France have suggested.

The likelihood is that the direct costs to the state of providing free or subsidised preschool education will be higher than what may be paid back into the pot in terms of taxes. But does that matter? I argue that it doesn't, because of the significant externalities—the broader factors that determine the full, true cost or benefit of something. We know, of course, that substituting maternal for non-maternal care can be prohibitively expensive, but if we take the externalities into account, then state-subsidised childcare, properly structured, should in fact pay its way over the longer term. Women who work will earn more, require less in benefits, consume more, pay more in direct and indirect taxes and contribute more to GDP. The fact that this is not already the case leads to continuing 'parenting inequality', thus perpetuating wider inequality—as various studies in the developing world have shown, the intergenerational impact of losing out through motherhood can be significant.

A free or heavily subsidised childcare/early education system can help to reverse these losses to the economy, this market failure. As argued above, if properly applied, it should raise the average net income of a household, improve children's life chances, and, over time, reduce the likelihood of a mother or household moving into poverty. Indeed, over the past 50 years, many countries have moved to offer free or very highly subsidised education for all preschool children. The belief is that these policies should help to improve children's learning and educational achievements, but crucially should also allow more women to stay in or return to work, which will help the economy overall. The IFS has found only a small initial increase in numbers returning to work as a result of the UK's increase in free pre-school childcare, but the think tank also points out that the benefits of universal preschooling continue for several years, beyond the initial maternal return to employment, since the provision also enables mothers 'to gain more job skills and increase their attachment to the labour force'.[46]

We are not just talking about the higher paid, who perhaps can afford private childcare anyway. The IFS has shown that the most positive labour market impacts are felt by low-income single mothers, which substantiates findings from other research.[47] According to the Brookings Institution, for example, women make up 64% of all workers on the minimum wage in the States and, according to the analysis, this results in huge loss of opportunity, as some half of the population is not contributing at the right level. Again, the high cost of childcare was pointed to as a reason for this finding.[48] Its report also found evidence of the greater gains we've discussed among women with high levels of education and experience before motherhood. So the question of whether we can 'afford' to subsidise childcare is not the right question to be asking. The question is, can we afford not to?

In a cost/benefit analysis of improving conditions for working mothers through greater state spending, it's worth returning to the arguments that better maternity leave, better maternity pay, better childcare provision and so on will cause a crisis by encouraging rising fertility. In truth, Europe needs more people, not less. But, although there have been some signs of a small increase in births accompanying state support for parents (in Sweden for instance), the overall impact has been marginal. Germany is an interesting case. Like France, it encourages larger families, due to concerns about projections of a sharp population reduction, with all the fiscal problems this would entail. At a dinner in June 2019, I met Ursula von der Leyen, the German politician who would become the European Commission's first woman president a few months later. She was still Germany's Defence Minister at the time. I was astonished to learn that she had seven children—even more than me!—which always ends up being a sort of comparator in conversations with successful women. Do you have home help, how do you cope with all this travelling? That sort of thing.

Well, as the announcement came of von der Leyen's new EU role, and amidst the excitement that it generated, I found an article from 2011. It turns out that when von der Leyen was Germany's Family Minister (2005–9), she introduced a series of family-friendly policies, including 14 months' paid parental leave, with the father forced to take at least two of those months. Depending on income, the pay could be as high as 65% of salary throughout that period. What is more, the child allowance paid to the mother for each child goes up for every subsequent child—in total opposition to the UK's abolition of child benefit for third and subsequent children (soon to be reversed), which some felt was reminiscent of China's One Child Policy.[49]

Germany has another quirk that others can only look at and marvel: the payment per child almost doubles when you get to number seven, and the President officially becomes the godfather of the seventh child! This has been the case since 1949, an attempt to repopulate the country after the devastation of the Second World War. The 2007 von der Leyen reforms aimed to make Germany an even more family-friendly country. But, since that time, the fertility rate has fallen further, and is now only sustained by massive immigration—more recently, from the Middle East, with Chancellor Angela Merkel's consent. The country as a whole continues to have one of the lowest birth rates in Europe, and in 2010 there were just 603 seventh children. For a slightly less strange-sounding example, in Greece—a place I know well—nursery for 2-year-olds and above is free for working parents, though there are also many private-sector providers for even younger children. The public nurseries are run by the local authorities, from 8am to 4pm every day, and much use is made of them. Yet the fertility-mongers have nothing to fear: despite huge migration, Greek reproduction rates are still declining, and there are forecasts that the current population of some 11 million may be down to just 8.5 million by 2050.

In the US in particular, the cost of childcare is a heavy burden on families and the economy—exacerbated by the lack of statutory maternity pay. In parts of the country, high-quality childcare is not even available. You could worry that the lower starting-point of provision would make an increase in support for mothers and parents particularly damaging to the US economy. But pressure has grown, proposals have been made—and they have been costed.

In June 2019, the Democratic senator and presidential primary candidate Elizabeth Warren introduced her Universal Child Care and Early Learning Act to Congress. The bill proposed to create a network of federally funded, but locally run, childcare centres, to ensure that no family spends more than 7% of its annual income on childcare. Quality standards were to be matched to existing federal programmes like the successful 'Head Start', the inspiration behind the UK's Sure Start scheme, and would require care workers to be paid on par with public school teachers. Lower-income families would pay nothing, and overall the typical American family with young children would see their annual childcare costs decline by 17%. Senator Warren insists that 'Access to affordable and high-quality childcare and early education should be a right for all families rather than a privilege for only the rich.' A Moody's analysis of the economics of Warren's proposal says:

> The Universal Child Care and Early Learning Act would substantially increase the number of children able to receive formal child care. An estimated 6.8 million children, equal to about one-third of those younger

than age 5, receive formal care today. The proposal would ensure an estimated 12 million children, equal to 60% of those younger than 5, will ultimately receive formal care.

The estimated total direct fiscal costs were $1,720 billion over 10 years, but as the positive impacts would also lead to more growth over the 10 years (and so more tax), the dynamic cost is reduced to $707 billion across that period. On current estimates the scheme ultimately puts back into the economy about half of what it costs, but a fiscal expense of $707 billion is still a lot of money to find, and so the bill also proposes a wealth tax:

> The proposed universal childcare and early learning services could be paid for by revenues generated by Warren's proposed 2% tax on household net worth above $50 million and 3% tax on net worth above $1 billion. That is, $700 billion out of the total 10-year revenues generated by the proposed net worth tax could be used to pay for the child-care proposal. The Universal Child Care and Early Learning Act is thus deficit neutral over the 10-year budget horizon on a dynamic basis.[50]

But Moody's view seems to be that even these cost estimates—concluding that the Warren bill is deficit-neutral—are too high, and the benefit estimates too low. We need to look at the externalities. Not only would the scheme generate income after tax, but there would be other social and fiscal benefits. Moody's notes:

These results likely understate the economic benefits of the proposal. The model does not consider that ... According to the best-known study on the issue, the benefits, including greater lifetime earnings, the non-earnings benefits of reduced transfer payments and remedial education expenditures, and savings from less demand on the criminal justice system, are substantial. Studies conducted on a variety of other preschool programs find similarly large increases in earnings and societal benefits.

Overall, the Report concludes that the Warren bill is a fiscally responsible proposal that would significantly reduce the cost burdens of childcare for most American families, and would support increased labour force participation. It would also lead to stronger economic growth and may well prove fiscally neutral overall. Except, of course, that it would take time for those long-term benefits to materialise—and time is what politicians, like the markets, are usually short of.

Dependents and mobility: why we must change capitalism's work culture

On top of better support for parental and especially paternity leave, and better support when it comes to childcare, there is one more shift that needs to happen in our capitalist society to level the playing field for mothers. The EU Commission and Parliament noted in 2019 that work/life balance is particularly challenging nowadays, because of 'increasing prevalence of extended working hours and changing work schedules, which has a negative impact on women's employment ... The imbalance in the design of work-life balance policies between men and women reinforces gender stereotypes and differences between [paid] work and care'.[51] It should be obvious by this point in the book that women's different needs and abilities when it comes to flexibility and work/life balance is strongly connected to the fact that it is women who are depended upon for domestic and caring responsibilities, including of course childcare.

Many women still feel that the only choice they can make is to take time off after becoming mothers. Ann Bentley of the global construction and quantity surveying practice Rider Levett Buckland says that she actually turned down a promotion when she had children, and continued to turn down other opportunities for some 7–8 years, as she couldn't see how she could combine the required travel with bringing up children. She admits that 'Where I was probably very fortunate was that this didn't count as a black mark against me. For me it was a period of time [that came to an end]'. One wonders whether a father would have been so inhibited in taking that step up. The evidence suggests otherwise. But this market failure forcing women to choose between career and family works both ways. Not only should we be doing better by mothers who want to continue advancing their careers—we should also be doing better by women who would rather take more time off. They should not feel the pressure of knowing that they must get back to work quickly to avoid a permanent black mark against them and their future careers, and it shouldn't be a choice between working exactly as they did before or not working full-time at all.

The greatest kind of gap that Harvard economist Claudia Goldin has identified in the US is witnessed within organisations, suggesting a difference between women who are mothers and women who are not. But part of the widening pay gap for mothers is also found to be due to gender differences in the propensity to move between organisations. This suggests that mothers are less able or willing to seek opportunities elsewhere that could have resulted in promotion/higher salaries, no doubt partly because—as we saw with my ex-colleague in the Introduction—they fear they would face greater bias if applying to a new employer, as a result of having had children. But another reason why mothers avoid moving jobs is because they are more constrained than men in terms of the journey time between their home and their workplace.

A very revealing piece of research by the Institute for Fiscal Studies has similarly linked pay to difficulties for women accessing good jobs that may be further away from home in the UK.[52] The IFS tracked pay gaps against distance to work, and found that the two were closely correlated. In other words, the longer men's commute by comparison with women's, the bigger the pay gap; the two differentials aligned closely. According to ONS data, men account for the majority of UK commutes lasting more than an hour, and women account for the majority of short commutes lasting less than 15 minutes. This unwillingness or inability to travel further may well be linked to the need and expectation for women to be closer to home, because they are still perceived to be the main carers. They are the ones who must provide childcare themselves, be able to travel easily to a provider such as a nursery or school, and to be close to their children in case of emergency. What's more, the need to juggle both kinds of work naturally makes avoidable stresses, such as commuting, even more undesirable.[53] Compare the graph opposite with the one above—there is a striking resemblance between the evolution of the gender pay gap and the gender commute gap.

So motherhood creates a reluctance to go for good jobs that are further away, and this lessened mobility is a constraint on earning power, choice in the labour market and ability to work full-time. This may be a major part of the reason why, apart from the lowest-skilled 'elementary and process plant and machine operative' occupations, men are more concentrated in the higher-paid occupations, while women are more concentrated in lower-paid occupations. The ONS reported that in

Men's and women's average commute time in the years before and after arrival of their first child

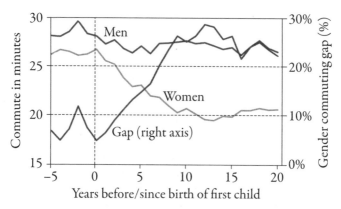

Source: IFS, 2018.[54]

2017, men and women working full-time in the UK's highest-paid occupation group (chief executives and senior officials) earned a median hourly pay of £48.53 and £36.54 respectively, and that men had 72.8% of the full-time employment share in this occupation. Similarly, men had 70.2% of the full-time employment in the second-highest-paid occupation group (managers and directors), and a median hourly pay of £23.69, which was £2.62 higher than for full-time women.[55]

Employers generally seem reluctant to help redress the unequal mobility of mothers. This effectively gives local employers what economists call 'monopsony power' over employment of women (they employ such a large proportion of the labour in one area of employment that they can effectively dictate wages for that job). To induce more women to travel a greater distance, an employer further away would have to raise wages—but this means raising the wages of all employees, even the ones who live very close by and who would be quite prepared to have traded off wages for proximity. The employer may notice that there is a high marginal cost of raising all women's wages in order to attract a few more, and therefore refrain from doing so.

Of course, women are more able today to switch to more remote working after having a child. Advances in IT are changing patterns of work, and there has been increased flexibility from many employers. This is important, but we should keep things in perspective: John Maynard Keynes had anticipated that by now we would probably only work half the week, with the rest of our time spent on leisure, education, retraining and so on. In fact, if anything, people now work longer hours than they have done for some time. And, frankly, technology is not particularly the friend of the working mother here: if employees are expected to answer emails at all hours of the evening, this will continue to put mothers at a disadvantage compared with men, due to their disproportionate burden of household labour. This reinforces the need for changes to work culture, to allow for greater flexibility and stop over-valuing presenteeism, if we really want to level the playing field for women with children.

We have a long way to go yet. The site Working Mums carries out an annual survey; its 2016 results suggested that some 18% of working mothers had had to quit their jobs after being refused flexible working.[56] The number not taking up positions, or discouraged from even applying for a job better matched to their skills levels, must be even larger if a CBI survey from the same year is to be believed: it found that only one in ten job listings specified that the role could be done flexibly.[57] Equally if not more worrying is a Europe-wide survey from 2014, which tested the hypothesis that women willingly accept low pay for greater flexibility. It found that, in fact, women—and workers generally in women-dominated sectors—had no better access to schedule control than in other areas of the economy.[58] In other words, they may be simply opting for lower pay in the hope of more flexibility, but not necessarily receiving it.

This is going to have to change. A report by the UK's Equality and Human Rights Commission on Pay, with particular reference to the situation of women, concludes with a quote from Charles Cotton, Senior Performance and Reward Adviser for the CIPD, the UK's professional body for HR and people development:

> Many employers will need to review their recruitment practices so they are able to attract women into roles or professions where they are under-represented as well as creating more flexible jobs and working practices that enable both men and women to achieve more fulfilling working and family lives. Another area of focus for

organisations is providing mentoring support for women to help them prepare for senior roles and ensuring that more women are short-listed for interview for senior positions. The key is to develop robust action plans to reduce pay gaps and improve gender equality that are backed by senior level commitment.[59]

There has been much anxiety about how workers' rights will fare once the UK leaves the EU, but, perversely, Brexit may actually force firms' hands in relation to women's employment. The worry of losing EU workers in many of our sectors—especially hospitality—is encouraging change in terms of the type of workers being sought. As with the sudden shortage of traditional (men's) labour sources during the Second World War, employers are turning wherever they can to find extra hands. In some cases, this has involved attempts at greater flexibility, with the hope of encouraging more women and mothers to work.

Travelodge, for instance, announced in mid-March 2019 its intention to open another 100 hotels over the next 5 years, but the fact that 27% of its workers were from the EU has been causing some headaches. As net immigration from the EU is falling in anticipation of Brexit, Travelodge has had to rethink its hiring and employment policies, including introducing much more flexible working and abolishing zero-hours contracts. The aim was to give more guarantees and show a clear path of career progression into management posts. CEO

Peter Gowers told the BBC's *Today* programme that, as a result of these changes, the company has had tons of new applications, and a large rise in the number of 'working parents' applying—a shorthand for women.[60] The question of how much they will be paid remains, but the Travelodge example shows that adjustments to working culture and workplace practices can help mothers to participate more fully and more equally in the labour market.

The state to which we must aspire and for which we must strive is one where women contemplating taking time out of the workplace in favour of domestic activity are able to make their decision in a system that values both choices to their real worth. This must come through government action to improve both maternity and paternity leave and pay, to support childcare, and to foster greater flexibility at work—employees should not just have the right to ask for it, but should be entitled to it automatically. For those who do take leave, the path of return to work and career must be made as easy as possible. There is no excuse for inaction here, given the strides made with technology, the ever-louder calls for a 4-day week, and the mounting evidence that greater flexibility can substantially improve productivity and profitability. But these measures are only part of the necessary steps to gender equality because of continued bias and flawed assumptions about women's work, which remain very much embedded in the system. It is to these that we turn in the next part of the book.

PART THREE

BIAS

3

BIAS

Lots of social factors impact your pay. For example, there is no doubt that the quality and level of your education has a strong bearing on your later earnings and class, while your original class plays a clear role in determining your educational attainment. This is particularly so for the UK, given its fragmented schooling system: the OECD has found that the UK has a much stronger correlation than most developed countries between the social class of one's birth and one's educational performance (and hence life opportunities).[1] But these aren't, ostensibly, 'gendered factors'. In most richer countries, men and women are fairly equally represented in each category of social status, education, genetic inheritance and so on—what economists would call a 'similar distribution of variables'. Yet a gender pay gap exists in all economies to varying degrees, even ones where the genders have equal educational opportunities, for example. This seems to be the case even when women work full-time or have no children. So there are clearly other forces at play beyond education and beyond motherhood.[2] A study of the lifetime earnings of women in the US who had worked full-time all their lives still reveals a pay gap at every educational level.

So what we see is income inequality existing between otherwise 'equal' individuals. We know that education levels have an impact on earnings—on balance, the more educated you are, the more you earn in your lifetime, and the more you contribute to the economy as both a consumer and a taxpayer. Thus textbook economics would predict that income discrepancies narrow with the narrowing of education discrepancies. In other words, in theory, twenty-first-century women, especially in developed nations, should be at least as well paid as men, given the largely improved access to education for girls in the last century and more. Yet it is still apparently harder for women than for men to get their due recompense for their education levels. As the Institute of New Economic Thinking argues:

> It is clear that the economy treats men and women differently. This is much more true in some countries than in others, but it is true for all countries. Income disparities between men and women among otherwise similar individuals are one measure of this inequality ... any differences in the figure are not due to women having more time out of the labour force (on average) because of child rearing ... Yet for every level of schooling, women can expect to earn much less than men.[3]

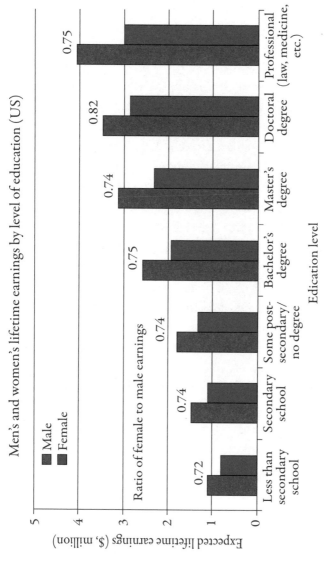

Men's and women's lifetime earnings by level of education (US)

Source: Institute of New Economic Thinking.

This is not just the case in the US, of course. The experience is repeated across most developed countries. As we've already seen, in France the pay gap between men and women increases as the women's education level rises, reaching an astonishing 31% for those at the highest level. This is a mix of bias and the (related) fact that women end up doing jobs below their skill levels, or have skills that simply aren't recognised or valued appropriately by the capitalist system in which they operate. Women earn more as their skills levels go up—but not as much more as for men with the same qualifications. At a time of increased economic uncertainty, the fact that women cannot utilise all their talents represents a huge loss to society. A better educated workforce that can apply its skills to meeting the needs of the economy and society is good for productivity and growth. This means that we are facing a market failure, given the continued existence and acceptance of both overt and hidden barriers preventing even highly educated and skilled women from participating equally with men in the economy. Economists, both men and women, should be focusing on this—and governments and employers should be thinking about the reason for it. What else can it be, but bias?

* * *

While I was writing this book, a friend and former colleague told me about an incident that neatly illustrates some of the problems I'll look at in this part of the book. He described how he was once on a plane for a business trip with his colleagues—two women and the boss, a man—when a female voice introduced herself over the Tannoy as the pilot. My friend's boss found this too unusual to ignore, and felt he had to say something: 'Oh dear, we might be late. She'll probably stop to ask the way!' When the flight actually landed twenty minutes ahead of schedule, the boss then cracked, 'Well, she probably had to get back early to pick up the kids.' The two 'girls' in the work party were expected to laugh along too, and everyone knew that to say anything would have soured the atmosphere with a boss they had to work with; and after all, he was merely engaging in friendly teasing, rather than trying to offend. So the women let it go, as women so often do, and my friend likewise didn't want to rock the boat, or rather plane, by championing the women, who may well have resented his intervention anyway.

What is or isn't acceptable humour is not the point here. This anecdote is a succinct example of something deeper than a 'boys-will-be-boys' excuse or the passivity of both men and women towards sexism. When we look at this phenomenon repeated across society, it amounts to a more serious problem: the (neo)liberal 'free market' is allowed to operate unchallenged on the basis of conscious and unconscious biases, which in the end fail the economy—and the people who live in it—by perpetuating inequalities. This is the reason that so many 'plane stories' exist. Take my own version of it: in early 2018 I took part in a Union debate at Durham University, arguing against the motion 'This House Believes That Feminism Has Lost Its Way'. A male member asked, with all sincerity, 'But surely, if we had more women pilots, wouldn't we need to lower standards to accommodate them?' I was surprised that there was no hissing, general outcry, or any serious disagreement from the floor—and there were many young, sophisticated-looking women there. I lost that debate.

This is the deeper issue I want to explore in this book: how capitalism interacts with gender roles and expectations, and with life chances, for both the main genders. All of this bias is part and parcel of how capitalism fails women.

Women's employment has gone up significantly since the 1970s, with women making an increasing contribution to, and considerable inroads into, many occupations and professions. But we have seen that the pay gap is still alive and kicking, across the world. The public sector is better on this, but data from UK government departments, for instance, indicates that women's pay in the civil service still lags behind men's. Some organisations that are private in constitution but in fact rely heavily on government funding, such as universities, have often been revealed to have some of the largest pay gaps, not only in salaries but also in bonuses. Multi-academy trusts reported huge pay gaps in the UK's first round of statutory pay reviews (2018), often in excess of 50%.[4] We've already looked several times in this book at the example of the BBC, but it's a particularly interesting one, as a publicly funded corporation that has to compete in the marketplace. The pay reviews showed that it cannot escape from contemporary capitalism's in-built bias against women: the BBC pays its female on-screen talent far less than their male counterparts, and has far fewer women than men in top positions.

A 2018 report for the UK government by Professor Wendy Olsen et al. suggested that the persistence and scale of the gender pay gap reflects the negative impact of traditionally gendered ideologies, held by both employers and employees. The chart below represents their summary of the observable characteristics that increase or decrease the pay gap. Perhaps more importantly, it also shows their estimation that 'Unobserved Factors' associated with gender accounted for 35% of the pay gap. That is, even allowing for differences we can easily measure (and these are themselves related to gender), there is still an unexplained pay gap of over a third.[5]

Main drivers and protective factors of the UK gender pay gap, including 35% 'unobserved' contributing factors

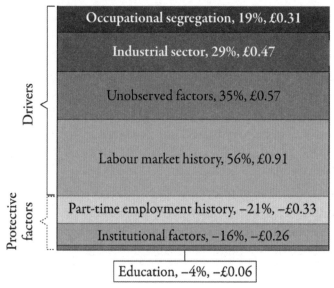

Source: UK Government Equalities Office, 2018.

Using a similar method but different data, the ONS found the unexplained (or 'unobserved') gap to be even greater, as large as two thirds. This leaves a lot of room for explanations that relate to direct discrimination against women, but it is not correct to assume that this would account for all of the 'unexplained' pay gap. As the ONS fairly points out:

> The analysis would benefit from information on family structures, education and career breaks; without these

the unexplained element is over-stated. Factors such as the number of children, the age of children, whether parents have any caring responsibilities, the number of years spent in school and the highest level of qualification achieved are likely to improve the estimation of men's and women's pay structures and consequently decrease the unexplained element of the pay gap. As a result, the unexplained element should not be interpreted as a measure of discriminatory behaviour, though it is possible that this plays a part.[6]

Nevertheless, what this chart shows is that, even allowing for impacts heavily related to gender roles, there is a gap of one to two thirds in which direct biased discrimination can be expected to play a part. And there is strong evidence of direct discrimination against women in the jobs market, where perceptions persist that women either don't want to move up or wouldn't be up to the job if they did.

One of the quotes related to this issue that I have always found the most striking is from Dame Fiona Woolf. I first met her when I was Head of International Privatisations at the major accounting multinational KPMG and she was fronting her law firm's various joint attempts to restructure energy sectors around the world. In an interview after she became the third ever female Lord Mayor of the City of London, she talked of the time she had had to actively ask for partnership to become her law firm's first female partner: 'The senior partner was actually quite surprised I might want a partnership, he told me,' she said.[7] It was clearly assumed at that time (the early 1980s!) that women had no ambitions. They do—it is just that they get put off. But if they overcome the discouraging environment around them, and do ask for a promotion or pay rise, they may get it—provided they work in a more women-friendly environment. Otherwise they might be considered too pushy.

When I became the first female client-focused consultancy partner at KPMG in 1990, I was told that I could become a member of a club paid for by the firm—not a sports club, of course, but a 'gentlemen's club'. I immediately replied with my choice: the Reform, where my previous boss used to take me all the time for lunches and meetings with other senior bank economists and Treasury officials, and which had been among the first clubs to open membership to women a few years earlier. Despite that change, the shock of the senior partner at my suggestion was palpable. He was speechless for a while, and I worried about whether I had said the wrong thing and if my partnership was going to be taken away from me. But he then recovered and said, 'Great—I will sign the book for you.' He meant the members' book, which is left open for all to see who is applying to join, and for them to add their signature in approval of you as a new member. He kept his word, approved my application and I became a member of the Reform Club pretty soon after. KPMG stopped paying for all our club subscriptions a few years later as a matter of policy, but of course I carried on my membership, and am still a proud member to this day.

So if you don't ask, you don't get. But, while this might work for some, it doesn't for many, as sometimes-insurmountable unconscious bias remains. Ann Bentley of construction group Rider Levett Bucknall has this to say about her first years working as one of an organisation's very few female engineers: 'What I could definitely see in myself and my female colleagues at this stage was that we waited to be asked to do things. And I definitely changed my behaviour in my late 20s/early 30s in this respect. If I didn't put myself forward, we would be deemed not to be committed, whereas I thought [early on that] if I was good enough I would be appointed. I definitely adopted the "stop me if you dare" methodology, otherwise I felt I would be passed over for opportunities.'

Bentley went on to become a very successful business owner, in what is still perceived as a man's world. So clearly there is no lack of ambition among women, even those who refrain or once refrained from making demands. But women know they are being viewed differently and therefore treated differently. And the frustration is palpable, as the watch entrepreneur Rebecca Struthers made clear in conversation with fellow entrepreneur Beverley Nielsen: 'There is certainly a bias against women in my industry, which is still incredibly male-dominated both within the sector and within the client base. There is no research in my industry, to my knowledge, examining the challenges women face in the workplace and in starting their own workshops; likely because too few of us exist to put together a significant case study group. I have personally witnessed men with less experience, fewer qualifications, and a limited track record being given opportunities that I have been refused. I've met with industry organisations who claim to be doing all they can to support women in industry, [but which] however, have treated me with blatant bias when it came to the application of that support.'

Of course, legislation in the UK and a great many other countries prohibits any difference in direct treatment of men and women, in terms of pay and conditions of employment. But establishing equivalence of jobs can be difficult, and we know that occupations are often segregated, making direct comparisons difficult. Men who have a particular preference for jobs in sectors dominated by women will tolerate the lower pay that is generally the norm in those sectors, but obviously they will be in a minority. As the ONS notes, 'When employment within an occupation is heavily skewed towards either men or women, it is likely to introduce occupational segregation—where some occupations become more attractive than others to either men or women.'[8]

This in itself can lead to a pay gap. If most of an employer's workforce can be filled with women workers, then costs may be reduced by only using men to make up the residual. This might help explain, for example, why in 2016 some 84.6% of nursery and primary school teachers, 91.4% of teaching assistants and 82.2% of school support staff were female.[9] (The latest figures have little changed from these.)[10] If women are crowded into certain occupations, they may earn less than their other personal characteristics, such as education and work ethic, would be worth in other occupations. The ONS again: 'The gender pay gap for full-time workers is entirely in favour of men for all occupations; however, occupational crowding has an effect since those occupations with the smallest gender pay gap have almost equal employment shares between men and women.' So job segregation lies behind some of the gap—19% of it, according to Olsen's chart above. But there is something else happening too: under-representation of women at senior levels of organisations, due to bias.

Bias in hiring decisions

The UK's Hampton-Alexander Review, mentioned in Part 1, published its interim report in mid-2018, which incorporated the results of surveys of company chairmen. Among others, these surveys produced the quote 'We have one woman already on the board, so we are done—it is someone else's turn'.[11] Of course, having a single woman on your board changes very little in terms of the organisation's overall gender bias; you hear very often from women on boards that the impact they can make increases hugely if there are at least two of them, and not just one token woman to show 'compliance'. Yet this belief that having just one woman does the trick persists in hiring decisions. A study in the *Harvard Business Review* showed that, if you had one woman on the final shortlist of four, the chances of them being hired were not one in four. They were practically zero. That is because being the lone woman candidate highlights your 'difference' from the perceived 'norm', which makes it harder for hiring personnel to view you as suitable for the job. The chances of a woman being hired increased dramatically, to 50%, if there was just one more woman on the shortlist—and to 67% if the majority of candidates (three out of four) were women.[12]

This finding rings true for, and reflects the frustrations of, many senior women I know, who are put on longlists to ensure enough women are on them, and then on shortlists where they are the only woman. This tends to satisfy a company's requirement to be seen as open to women, but this 'minimal' system ensures that women are rarely the ones selected for the non-executive director positions, which usually go to (white, middle-aged) men. The same study found a similar bias in hiring patterns in relation to ethnic minorities. Whether it's women, people of colour, or women of colour, such bias in recruitment and promotion clearly results in resource misallocation. We know by now what that means: it amounts to a market failure, as it reduces competition.

Lack of women in a particular workforce has the same effect as lack of women on a particular shortlist, making 'others' or 'alternatives' of the type of person that makes up more than half the world's population. The antique-dealing sisters Emily and Victoria Ceraudo told the *Sunday Times* style magazine that 'It is unusual to see a female antique seller or auctioneer ... we are normally the youngest there and the only women. The smallholders in the antiques business often look at us as though we're homeowners and just dabbling. They are even more confused when we know what we're talking about or outbid them on something'.[13]

According to Sukhi Clark, former Head of Engineering Operations at Jaguar Land Rover, 'As an observation, people tend to like people like themselves. It takes a braver manager to employ someone who's different. So choosing a female engineer as the boss is harder because of this unconscious bias.' Construction suffers from this issue, too. It is a particularly tough sector to recruit into—there are constant skills shortages—and recruiting more women is therefore a must. Yet not enough of them are currently coming into the industry, and so there are not enough women designing our future buildings and cities. Just waiting around for things to change in this regard will be like waiting for Godot.

Ann Bentley, who is on the board of Rider Levett Bucknall, believes in targets and has been known to defend them publicly on panels; without them, she says, the industry is just paying lip service to gender equality. She quotes Thames Tideway as a good example: the CEO has set a very challenging target of 50% women employees, arguing that this may be incredibly hard to achieve. However, just setting the target will encourage more women to want to join. It is a good plan, as in Bentley's experience, women are far more loyal: 'Our evidence is that women don't move much at all.' This makes them particularly worth recruiting from a business perspective, to improve retention, and firm policies should encourage women to want to stay. But it won't be easy to improve recruitment. As Bentley says:

> I definitely believe in quotas in terms of shortlists. I accept we do need to recruit a person who is likely to fulfil the role. However, I don't know how good people will be until they are around a year into their roles. I'd like to see at least 30% of our shortlists containing women. But even coming up with diverse shortlists is harder work for recruitment companies.

Women in top management positions are far more likely to be viewed as individuals rather than as the 'token woman' if the group is more gender-balanced overall, regardless of the skills or qualifications that may have led them to be appointed.[14] When there is only one woman in the picture, women are just as likely as men to suspect 'tokenism'—appointing the odd woman to a top position for the sake of form, while doing very little to change the biased way an organisation functions.

Indeed, tokenism can even make gender bias worse, since it fosters the resentful view among some men that all women who've risen to the top are only in their senior roles as an undeserving sacrifice on the altar of political correctness. Far from 'solving' the gender inequality issue or making a concession to women, tokenism makes the place look uninviting to women, since it suggests a failure to consider ways to alter the overall gender balance in a sustainable, long-term way.

On the other side of the gender ratio scale, one of the professions seemingly dominated by women is interior design. The experience of a young man I know well, a friend of the family, is telling. Having just graduated from the Courtauld Institute of Art, and looking for his first job, he walked into a fabric shop in Chelsea looking for employment. He managed to get an interview, but was then quizzed about how he could cope working in a predominantly female environment, and in particular how he would interact socially. He was told, 'We don't talk about football here, you know'. He is the last person I know who would ever talk about football, as he has zero interest in it, and he did tell them this—but obviously the fact that he was a man acted against him. He didn't get the job.

Obviously women still have a lot to learn, particularly on how to use the power they have once they get to senior roles and the importance of helping other women into those top roles, avoiding stereotypes and prejudices themselves. We have all been conditioned under the same system. But men have kept these top positions for themselves for much longer, and a further push is needed for this to change. Until we see a change in the make-up of those making recruitment and promotion decisions, we will not see a change in hiring bias. A culture that deems some jobs to be 'men's work', and others 'women's work', together with the gendered bunching in occupations that we have noted, results in active job segregation. Unfortunately, the 'women's' jobs are also often the worse-paid and lower-ranked ones, with adverse impacts on women's long-term earning power and overall empowerment. Once these patterns become ingrained, they are difficult to shift, from either side.

As we saw extensively in Part 2, much of this job segregation is due to women's lower mobility and greater domestic commitments, and their over-representation in part-time work to accommodate this, particularly among mothers. Yet there is ample evidence of organisations discouraging women—either consciously or unconsciously—from staying on in higher-ranking jobs, irrespective of whether they are mothers.[15] This is because, beyond specific concerns about retention of mothers, we tend to favour people who are more like ourselves: male managers hiring for a senior position are more likely to hire another man, and the more men there are running the show, the greater the chance that another man will be hired the next time. That leads to a serious lack of women role models in most sectors.

Some women will rise to the top, of course, and analysts will always try to understand why. Some make it through inherited wealth—or family business connections—and others for more unclear reasons. Tracy McVeigh, writing in the *Observer* in 2014, linked the success of Angela Merkel, Hillary Rodham Clinton, Christine Lagarde, Oprah Winfrey, Sheryl Sandberg, J.K. Rowling and Beyoncé to the fact that they were all first-born children in their family. I was sadly the second born, but still the first daughter—does that count? In seriousness, what is clear is that women who have succeeded in a man's world have done so by being (at least) twice as good as the men. Why it is acceptable that a woman, possibly with children, is often expected to work so much harder than a man to make it? This is a question that society needs to ask itself. And the question that a free-market capitalist society needs to ask itself is: why aren't we fixing the obvious market failure that this represents?

Sukhi Clark, reflecting on her own career to the top of engineering, says: 'It was not easy simply because it was not that easy, and in part [also] because I was doing it as a woman'. It is not easy or comfortable when there aren't many of you at the top to act as a challenger or disruptor—a highly essential role in any organisation. As Beverley Nielsen puts it: 'As a woman, it is likely that if you are in this role, you are a mould-breaker, and this in turn will mean there are few others to compare notes with, or to gain moral support from. But, more than that, [there is no one] to learn useful lessons from. You will be left to make it up as you go along. And that is a hard way to learn.' So being a woman at the top is lonely. It's also very hard work. Sukhi Clark adds:

> You almost need to be twice as good as a woman, as if you make a mistake, you stand out. Female engineers are fantastic. They go out of their way to really understand what engineering is and how to get it done. I am not saying they don't make mistakes, but they have a way of working to make sure of things.

This tells us not only that women are likely to be more diligent in their work, but also that there is an insecurity more common among women. To succeed, then, a woman also needs to develop a thick skin, which many self-confident men seem to have in abundance. A very respectable, politically centrist newspaper ran a long article in 2018 on the women at the top of UK firms who had had to resign, bringing companies down while at the helm and so on—this has happened with countless men who don't, on balance, get that negative coverage. What is more, the implication of such stories is: well, we have tried having women at the top, and look where it has led us!

So there is clearly an attitude problem, and it seems that only a 'tipping point' number of women breaking through can change this. Women making a difference is what we want to see become the norm—that is how we can deal with all the issues of gender discrimination that are increasing inequality and hardship for women and their families, and keeping the economy from performing sustainably and at its best. The Overseas Development Institute think tank reviewed the global evidence on the factors that enable women to gain a substantive voice—a role in leadership and decision-making. Its 2015 report concluded:

> The combination of economic capital (e.g. women's ownership of productive assets and control over income) with other types of resources associated with social and cultural capital (e.g. education, skills training, awareness raising with men, and logistical support to engage in collective action) increases the likelihood of women gaining more power at the household level, and the potential for change at the community and national level.[16]

The report found that, across the world, women still 'overwhelmingly' had limited access to positions of leadership. Yes, there were some improvements in the percentage being elected to central or local government—more so in some parts of the world than others—but they were less likely to be in key cabinet positions or in executive branch posts. The ODI did find women in leadership roles in social movements, and in organisations that focus on women's and gender issues, but they are under-represented elsewhere, and certainly hugely absent from senior roles, as the report points out. In the private sector, this is particularly so in business management and business associations, meaning that women are largely excluded from corporate decision-making.

India makes for an interesting example, being one of the most populated and fastest-growing countries in the world, and also one that is undergoing a rapid technological revolution in the twenty-first century. Yet a 2016 report by the Indian sociologist K. Bhavani Shankar showed that the percentage of women represented in parliamentary seats was just 8%; for cabinet posts it was 6%, and less than 4% in the high courts and the Indian Supreme Court. Women were almost non-existent in senior private-sector posts. This is despite the fact that Indian girls often outperform boys in education.[17]

The problem is an urgent one. Beyond active measures taken by senior women to close the pay and promotion gap, having more women at the top also organically helps this, because—as various studies have shown—the presence of women role models raises the aspirations of others.[18] Having more women among the world's business leaders could be instrumental in better supporting women's retention and progress, while also ensuring better decision making and outcomes—most research studies link presence of women in executive positions with greater profitability (see below).

As we saw in the Introduction, with women in the EU becoming better represented in politics, the 'power' index has improved slightly. But the overall European gender balance index hardly moved at all in the 10 years to 2015, because the economic power—in other words, the money—has hardly changed hands. Yes, having a few successful and self-confident women at the top provides a few role models for others to emulate. But the problem with the short-termist way capitalism works, as critics of the 'lean in' philosophy would point out (see Part 4), is that individual women's 'assertive action' and self-belief would only help the 1% who rise to the top, leaving some 99% of women unaffected, their lot unimproved.[19] Any progress on the number of senior women has come about not through a 'can-do' attitude among leading women, but mainly through the imposition of quotas or strong voluntary targets. It takes time for the culture to change fundamentally: for work practices to change appreciably and for any consistent effect to come through.

As long as the pressure keeps up, one can and should remain hopeful. But we should also get more women involved in the process of change. As Ann Bentley of Rider Levett Bucknall put it, there is still 'a lack of women in senior management roles, and consequently, too many decisions about what support women need to advance their careers and businesses are being decided by men'.

Bias in hiring: bad for business

Of course, hiring after your own image does not guarantee that the best person will be hired, or that they have any idea how to lead a team. The (female) head of the UK's Serious Fraud Office, for instance, has warned that due to recruitment bias 'we are not getting the best decision-making we could'.[20] Professor Tomas Chamorro Premuzic, an organisational psychologist at Columbia University, argues that men tend to interview better, and that narcissistic men are good at getting jobs in interviews but make lousy leaders—presumably doing more harm than good to a business. Women tend to lose out in interviews because they come over as more hesitant, but in fact, Chamorro Premuzic says, would have made good leaders. Those 'feminine' qualities of cautiousness and consideration are a good thing for business, whether in men or in women, and 'women lead in a more transformational way, are less likely to be absentee leaders and have more emotional intelligence'. So instead of wanting to see women behave more assertively in interviews, Chamorro Premuzic sees the solution in women staying as they are, but with their qualities recognised through promotion. But unless the dominant hiring ethos shifts, men will hire men in perpetuity, and the potential benefits for individual employers and the economy as a whole will be lost.[21]

Not all men are narcissistic, of course—nor is this the main argument here, and there are narcissistic women out there too. But there is a general rule of thumb about gendered behaviours, because society as a whole and our labour market in particular perpetuates them. Men who are not naturally narcissistic are far more likely than women to act that way anyway, because this is what is expected of them if they wish to succeed in the workplace. At the leaving reception for an outgoing permanent secretary (a high-ranking UK civil servant), their coach—who works with some very senior people—told me that all the women come to her saying they lack confidence and want it boosted. The men, even if they feel the same way, don't ever admit to it, and cover it up in the way they behave. Instead their interest in coaching is to get help in sorting out their career path, so that they can move to a better paid job—simple! But the damage is done if the practice of hiring people like oneself does not lead to getting the best person for the job.

The homeware entrepreneur Emma Bridgewater says: 'An equally weighted group in terms of sexes would deliver a more sustainable answer in business and politics, in pretty much any situation; I really believe this.' She worries about whether men care equally about some of the issues that bother women who have had children:

> The fact we bear and care for the babies when they're small, perhaps that makes us more concerned with what we leave behind, our legacy. Just look at the reception [teenage climate activist] Greta Thunberg has had from

a lot of men as a young girl. One of my daughters is studying in Rome at present. She commented to me, 'It's so lovely here. Do you think it will still be here so I can visit with my daughter one day?' She was asking if there will still be a world when she herself has grown up children. I'm ashamed that my generation can laugh off that question.

Not everyone would agree that mothers will make better decisions because they have more at stake, but it's hard to argue with the fact that women work differently and in ways that can bring huge benefit to an organisation. Angela Burman of Burman Bears also believes that, if women were more involved in business, business models would be more sustainable. And they can be an inspiration to many others coming up: 'I've been around a lot of strong women and I feed off it and I have learnt a lot from them, which has helped me to grow'.

The academic evidence on this is strong. The tendency for organisations to select people similar to the leaders they are replacing has been described as a form of cloning—one that perpetuates unequal representation, risks 'group think' and discourages appropriate challenge. One analysis of the lack of women leaders in higher education looked at these phenomena, bringing together previous research on the subject and pointing out that none of them are beneficial to good governance of a university.[22] Ann Francke, CEO of the UK's Chartered Management Institute, despaired and fumed in a *Sunday*

Times interview about the 'groupthink' of all-male boards: 'Typically, it is a bunch of almost exclusively white men sitting around a table, reinforcing each other's beliefs'. She believes this to be at the heart of almost every corporate disaster in history.

On the contrary, there is a strong business case for a heterogeneous executive management team reflecting a diversity of backgrounds and talents. A 2018 report by the major consultancy McKinsey, which calculated the business benefits of including more women in the executive team, found that those companies with the greatest gender diversity were also likely to be some 21% more profitable, and 27% more likely to create superior value for shareholders.[23] This is clearly due to the different skills that women can add to leadership of an organisation. A study in 2007 by Professor Øyvind L. Martinsen of the BI Norwegian Business School found that, of the 3,000 subjects analysed, women scored higher in most areas of competence, including communication, openness, innovation, sociability and offering support, as well as in methodical management and goal-setting. Although men were more able to cope with work-related stress—maybe because they didn't also have the stress of domestic work to deal with!

But here is the perennial problem I have been outlining throughout this book: free-market capitalism is not inclined to take the long view like this. It demands quick and easy results, and the men who largely make the world's hiring decisions can see a safe and lazy option in 'more of the same'. Unless the state intervenes to force their hand, they will continue to take that option. To understand the full scale of this market failure, we should look at a few different sectors of our economy that are suffering from bias against women.

Bias in the legal professions

To start with, there has been a lot in the papers since about 2018 on the way in which women barristers and solicitors are belittled in courts and by male colleagues. Baroness Hale, the most senior female judge in the UK, was the first woman to be appointed to the UK's Supreme Court, of which she is now the President. In 2013 she was voted the most influential woman in the UK by the BBC. In a 2014 interview in the *Evening Standard*, she spoke of the misogyny in some parts of the profession and said that progress in boosting the number of women in senior judicial roles remains 'painfully slow'.[24] In earlier interviews she has also referred to the culture of 'unconscious sexism':

> There are women of my generation who've had to face the fact that some people may judge women's behaviours differently from how they've judged men. They accuse women of being ambitious, as if that was a bad thing, or of being strident, or opinionated. No thing that a man is ever criticised for.[25]

The latest data on female progression in the law makes for grim reading. There was a bit of confusion in 2018 when six of the UK's ten largest law firms did not include partners in their first annual pay gap figures. As with accountancy firms, the law does not require inclusion of partners in the pay review, as they are technically self-employed and do not fall into the category of workers whose salaries need to be reported. The following year, 2019, all ten of the largest legal firms did include partners, revealing a median gender pay gap of 43%—as opposed to the 28.3% shown if partners are not taken into account. Both figures were higher than for the previous year (42.6% with partners, 27.6% without).

There are now three women among the 12 Supreme Court judges, Baroness Hale, Lady Black and Lady Arden. In an interview in 2018, Hale once again decried the lack of women represented in the senior UK judiciary. She acknowledged that entry levels had changed—when she was studying law she was one of six women in her class of 100 students, whereas now women are there in larger numbers than men. But she expressed concern at the high rates of attrition later on and higher up, with talented women choosing to take on legal jobs in the government that allow more flexibility and fewer work hours. She was clear about the reasons for this: 'It is not easy to combine practice at the Bar or in a big city solicitor's firm with family and other responsibilities.'[26] But this means that fewer women remain in the private-sector pool from which the senior judiciary is traditionally recruited.

Dana Denis-Smith is the founder of the First 100 Years project, which charts the history of women in the law in the UK. She agrees with the President of the Supreme Court, arguing in *City AM* in 2019 that, for women, 'the rigid and inflexible structures in many firms are still preventing their progress to senior positions'. Her concern is that women are still not represented in sufficient numbers in senior positions across all segments of the legal profession—whether as equity partners in law firms, as QCs or in the judiciary more generally. She is also worried that they are paid less than their male counterparts. In her view, quotas are necessary, since self-regulation only takes you so far.[27]

Bias in the public sector

In general, the UK civil service has been way ahead of both the private sector and the professions more generally when it comes to promoting women into leadership roles, and there is a lot to learn from best practice. In 2014 women made up some 37% of the senior civil service.[28] But this is not necessarily the case across the public sector as a whole, where senior women are considerably less evident. The percentage of local council chief executives who are women, for example, was just 24% in 2018, improving only fractionally in recent years.

Although women account for 75% of local government jobs, women councillors are only 30% of the total. There are concerns elsewhere that parts of the public sector are going backwards on diversity and inclusivity. A 2019 report by the NHS Confederation found that the percentage of ethnic-minority chairs and chief executives of NHS trusts in England had fallen from 15% in 2010 to 8% in 2018. As for women, their representation had dropped from a rather high 47% in 2002 to just 38% in 2018. Yet the workforce is 77% female.[29]

The figures are even more extreme for public finance. The gender balance index produced annually by OMFIF, a think tank and financial sector consultancy on whose advisory board I sit, tracks the rate at which women are rising up public financial institutions such as central banks, sovereign funds and public pensions institutions. In 2019 it found that things have improved, but at a disappointing rate.[30] Globally only 14 out of 173 central banks were headed by a woman, and some 20% of them had no women at all on their boards. The figure rose to 63 central banks with women in top positions if you took into account deputy governors. Only eight sovereign funds were run by women. The countries with the best gender balances were spread across the world and the wealth scale, from Iceland to Albania to Rwanda, but some trends could be seen. On the whole, Europe did best on senior women, Asia worst, and the US somewhere in between, though improving.

As I write, none of the Bank of England's four Deputy Governors are women, but it is trying hard to increase the gender balance on its policy-making committee. The Prudential Regulation Authority, which supervises and regulates UK financial institutions, now has two women—both Dames of the British Empire, for some reason. Maybe that is the nearest to a man one can get! But there is still only one woman on the Monetary Policy Committee, which fixes interest rates in the UK. The furore has been so strong that the then-Chancellor of the Exchequer Philip Hammond, under whom the Bank's Governor is appointed, hired an all-women recruitment firm to find the next Governor—it specialises in finding women board candidates. Does that tell us something about change to come? Let's hope so.

The obvious beacon of women's leadership in public finance is Christine Lagarde. She says that she hasn't faced sexism, because she is 'too old and too tall, it is hard to be sexist towards someone who is older and taller than you.'[31] Well, many of us are old, though maybe not as tall, but we are not all head of the IMF. Not all women are born equal, and we need gender equality for the many, not the few. Also, without wanting to detract from Lagarde's achievements, she was the first woman ever to get the top job, and we could have been waiting even longer if the stars hadn't aligned: she was lucky that her male predecessor had to resign, mired in a sex scandal, and that another French person had to be found in a hurry to replace him. But Lagarde has set a trend—it looks, at the time of writing, as if her successor at the IMF may well be another woman, if the EU candidate (a Bulgarian) is accepted as her replacement.

Bias in the financial sector

It is true that the IMF has championed gender equality strenuously and is prepared to call out bad practice where it sees it. Lagarde herself has been part of that leadership. In the same interview where she quipped about being too tall for sexism to hold her back, she expressed concern that some firms may have become more reluctant since 2017 to hire women, due to fear of issues that the #MeToo movement might expose. If this is the case, and the response to revelations of harassment and assault is to avoid women rather than confront men, then it seems clear that the world of finance still has a way to go in committing to righting the wrongs done to women in the sector. The research Lagarde has been doing to construct a gender equality index for the financial sector suggests that there may indeed be something of a 'backlash' against diversity. Many institutions or firms she and her organisation spoke to thought that they were perhaps focusing too much on diversity, at the cost of other things they should be doing. In other words, short-term profits and savings still come first.

Even when steps are taken towards better gender equality, this too may well be out of worries of a negative reputational or regulatory backlash, rather than being motivated by principle. Kat Usita is an economist in the City of London. Now in her early 30s, she started her working life in the Philippines, where who you know is crucially important—her family knew someone in the Ministry of Finance who knew someone in a bank, and so on. She describes the culture of that world as very male-dominated; women were few and far between, and sexist comments were common. There were no senior women in the bank where she worked. She says it was only when she came to the UK that she realised that those comments would be considered harassment in Britain, and she finds her working atmosphere in the UK much improved as a result. But, she wonders, how much of this is because firms and individuals in UK finance believe in gender equality and understand the benefits of diversity? And how much is because they have suddenly started 'talking the talk' to avoid litigation and scandals negatively affecting their reputation? Most large firms these days have diversity officers who do and say all the right things, but she doubts that the underlying unconscious bias has shifted at all. As Usita puts it, 'meritocracy only works when the level playing field is even'.

So it is not surprising to see the analysis of 20-first, a gender balance consultancy, which finds that the make-up of executive top teams, rather than of boards, is the best measure of progress. It looked at the top 20 financial sector companies in the Fortune Global 500, and detected only some very slow progress in recent years. The percentage of women in top teams rose from 14% in 2014 to 18% in 2018. In the technology sector, which has been another laggard, the percentage for the 20 leading companies has inched up from 11% to 14%—though this is entirely due to the shrinking of the size of executive committees in the sector, which has increased the share of female representation. In fact, the rise over that period in the number rather than the percentage of women on executive committees was just one.

20-first goes one step further than most researchers of women's progress, awarding extra 'good' points to the companies with women on the executive committees who have line roles—in other words, women who are CEOs or CFOs with subordinates reporting to them. The consultancy makes clear that support roles such as HR, legal or communications, though important in an organisation, 'rarely lead to the very top'. Indeed, its research suggests that, although the UK saw a 2% rise in the top 20 companies from 2014 to 2018 (16% to 18%), most women are stuck in staff roles, and there was actually a sharp reduction of women in line roles, from 41% to 25%. As Kat Usita wrote in a bulletin on her research for OMFIF's Global Equality Index, we have a long way to go still.

Even a cursory look at the UK proves her right. The private finance entities seem to be ahead of the public institutions, but are not great performers either. As the IMF has reported, women do not feature prominently in leadership roles in finance. In 2018, less than 20% of bank board seats were held by women and women made up a minimal 2% of bank CEOs. The statutory pay review data for 2019 shows that the gender pay gap in finance firms is now some 26.3%, up from 25.7% the year before and way above the average of 14.2% across all sectors. The differences in bonuses, according to Bloomberg analysis, was even worse, at 48.1%. These figures are an indicator of how little impact women make in senior positions across the sector. At HSBC UK the bonus paid to women was just a quarter of that paid to men. And Reuters reported that one third of the financial-sector firms had gone backwards in the year.[32] Private equity firms and hedge funds have generally escaped having to report, but Blackstone was one of few to publish its pay gap—and it has announced that an active recruitment drive for senior women had allowed it to reduce its bonus gap from 75.4% to 'only' 67.7%.

Overall, the picture in the financial sector seems to be one of too little, too late. Virgin Money, now owned by Clydesdale Bank and Yorkshire Bank, achieved a small fall in its gender pay gap from 32.5% to 29.7%, but its own former chief, Dame Jayne-Anne Gadhia, has been critical of the financial sector's performance, arguing that 'businesses need to realize that they will not succeed unless they embrace diversity as a key driver of results and growth.'[33] Now running the government-backed Women in Finance charter, Gadhia has challenged finance firms to take gender equality seriously, measure how they are doing, take action in terms of targets, and make senior executives accountable for failure to meet them. My experience in the civil service was that permanent secretaries' bonuses were linked to achieving diversity targets, and that was certainly helpful. But nothing like this seems to be happening in the private sector, at least not in a transparent way that may send signals further down the organisation. The UK government also recommended that, alongside their statutory pay reviews, firms should publish action plans on how they intend to tackle gender imbalance—but this has not happened, and it is now left to individual firms to decide whether they want to do so. Many, of course, don't.

It can't be said that there's nothing more to be done by the state here. Other countries have gone much more firmly down that route. In Sweden, for example, every company with more than 25 employees needs to produce such an 'equality plan'. Nicky Morgan was the UK's Equalities and Women Minister and Secretary of State for Education from 2014 to 2016. She then took on the role of Chair of the Commons Treasury Select Committee, and in that capacity ran an inquiry in 2018 on women in finance. The inquiry highlighted the usual failings of the sector as a whole, urging City institutions to sign up for the Women in Finance Charter, reduce unconscious bias and increase female representation particularly in senior roles. However, it concluded that much needed to be done not only by private banks, but also by the Bank of England, the Treasury and the regulators in ensuring more women in senior positions.[34] Morgan called for women on the shortlist for the next Bank of England Governor, castigating the Bank—and by association the Treasury, which approves of candidates—for choosing the only man out of the five candidates for the latest appointment to the Monetary Policy Committee. Interestingly, after Morgan's criticism the two dames mentioned earlier were appointed to the Prudential Regulation Authority.

The Government response to the inquiry was lukewarm.[35] In an interview framing Bloomberg News' equality summit in May 2019, Morgan said that her committee was 'very disappointed' with the 2018 Pay Review figures, which showed that Goldman Sachs Group Inc, HSBC Holdings Plc and Barclays Bank Plc were all paying men at least 49% more than women. But given that there are no plans to punish the banks for their pay gap, or even the organisations that fail to report at all, all she could promise was the intention to summon these banks, and others with appalling records such as Lloyds Banking Group and Clydesdale Bank, and grill them publicly about their future intentions. The proceedings of the Select Committee are televised on BBC's Parliament channel. Mentioning me as an advocate of quotas, Morgan told Bloomberg's David Hillier, 'What we need to do is change the culture and quotas don't do that ... My target is to no longer need to speak about this issue because it's gone away.'[36]

All I can say to this is, well, hardly! After all this time and with so little progress at the top, it seems a forlorn hope to think that a telling off by a cross-party select committee will indeed achieve what she wants, namely 'changing the culture that underlies the discriminatory practices' of banks and other financial institutions. It requires a little bit more than that! And Morgan is simply wrong to summarily dismiss quotas and say they 'don't change culture.' They have not failed in the UK, for they have never been systematically applied or enforced, and where they have been in place (anywhere in the world), they have generally focused on the wrong target—board representation, rather than senior management as a whole.

Morgan, back in the Cabinet as I am writing, wasn't wrong that we've seen disappointing results so far from the financial sector's few attempts to implement quotas. Investors like BlackRock, JP Morgan and Standard Life Aberdeen have all declared their intention to push FTSE 350 boards to achieve 30% female board representation, and to ensure that FTSE 100 companies achieve that same percentage of female senior managers. And yet those investors are themselves lagging behind. Tortoise, the news organisation run by former *Times* editor James

Harding, has compiled statistics for 2019 showing that BlackRock has just 3 women on its global executive committee, out of 21 members, despite declared intentions to change things; JP Morgan has only 2 women on its 11-member board, and only 3.6% of its environmental, sustainability and corporate governance funds have more than 30% female representation among their directors. At least Standard Life Aberdeen can boast 40% female representation on its board.[37]

Gordon Stoker is a doyen of the consulting profession, chair of a mentoring organisation and 'father' of the Worshipful Company of Management Consultants of which I was Master in 2010/11. He told me of a nurse of Indian origin who had looked after him at Lewisham Hospital in London after a bad fall. He was taken by her intelligence and the innovative way in which she handled his accident. She told him that her family were keen she should work in finance and she had duly joined a bank. But when she'd gone for a promotion, she had simply been told that her face didn't fit! Was it her face, or was it her gender? Or both? In any case, she had decided to leave and retrain, despite her parents' disapproval, and had become a nurse. Stoker was shocked that this kind of overt discrimination still happens, and that no one stops it from happening. This conversation spurred him to refocus his mentoring service on people in higher executive positions, as they are the ones who can bring change. But unless the system is forced to change faster from above, the individual piecemeal progress that can be made with such endeavours will not be enough.

Bias in higher education

The same goes for higher education; complacency seems to rule here too. A 2015 survey of UK university governors, commissioned by the Leadership Foundation for Higher Education, found that equality and diversity 'barely registered as a concern'. Only some 3% of governors identified the issue as a key institutional challenge and only 17% believed that it was harder for women than for men to succeed in their organisation. Staff views differed considerably from this viewpoint, with some 42% believing that it was harder for women to succeed.[38]

In 2017, Sue Shepherd of the University of Kent looked at why there are so few women leaders in higher education, focusing particularly on the more traditional pre-1992 universities (before many polytechnics were converted into universities). She chose this focus because the older universities have increasingly been moving from the more traditional internal methods of promotion to also considering external candidates for the top posts, something that the newer universities have long been practising. Her findings questioned the notion of women's 'missing agency'—in other words, she rejected the argument that the lack of senior women is due to a lack of female confidence that deters them from applying. Instead she attributes women's continued underrepresentation to other factors, such as difficulty of labour market mobility due to women's disproportionate domestic and caring commitments. Shepherd highlighted the importance of three structural factors associated with the selection process: mobility and external career capital, conservatism, and homosociability.[39]

In actual fact, women are as ambitious as men, with more or less the same percentage applying for higher posts within their institution such as Pro-Vice-Chancellor. But that rate falls to about half if you look at whether women apply across any other institution, suggesting that they are more constrained in terms of job mobility, for reasons we explored in Part 2. They also seem to be less successful in getting the top jobs: Sue Shepherd's research found that women academics were twice as likely as men to be unsuccessful, which itself suggests that unconscious bias is at play—a tendency to hire people after one's own (predominantly male) image. This leads to another disadvantage for women: jobs at the top of higher education have become more managerial, and there is quite a lot at stake these days, with universities being multimillion, if not multibillion, institutions. As a result, there is often a requirement of experience in a similar role elsewhere—which women generally lack, having failed to get promoted as often or as fast as men.

So the chance of greater gender diversity in higher education leadership is killed from the word go. An earlier study by Sue Shepherd (2015) found that the increase in the UK's percentage of female Pro-Vice-Chancellors between 2005 and 2013 was just 0.4%.[40] At this rate, certainly in the UK, it will take 100 years to achieve equality in the number of professors, and even longer for those in executive positions such as Pro-Vice-Chancellors.[41]

This situation of despair is not only the case in the UK. In 2012 the European Commission estimated that, across the whole of the EU, just 15.5% of higher educational establishments and 10% of universities that awarded PhDs had a female head.[42] Incidentally, we can see the same pattern in school education, even though it is a female-dominated occupation. As we know, the clear majority of teachers in UK schools are women, and the World Bank reports that this is the case in most countries.[43] But even so, they only comprise 62% of UK secondary school headteachers—significantly lower than their representation in the workforce. In primary schools, men make up 15% of the workforce, but have 28% of the headteacher roles.[44] The under-representation is simply repeated at higher education level.[45] We know that the 'women lack ambition' argument is a fallacy, so what else is left to explain this but bias?

Do women-only colleges help the number of senior women in academia? It's difficult to draw too many conclusions, as there are very few. In March 2019, *The Economist* carried the news that one of Cambridge's three women's colleges, the mature students' college Lucy Cavendish, was moving to accept students under 21 for the first time. The fall-off in UK mature students reflects the increase in fees and greater difficulty in getting funding, which is particularly bad news for women, who are more likely either to have missed out on education early on or to want to retrain after time off due to motherhood or other domestic/caring duties. So perhaps it is logical that Lucy Cavendish has also decided to open up its doors to men, leaving just two women-only colleges, both in Cambridge—Oxford opened up its last one in 2007.[46] But what was interesting in the latter case was the reason given. The then college principal, Lady English, said that it made sense, given that the men's colleges had been opening up to women, but also argued that 'The ability to consider men as well as women for fellowship appointments will have immediate benefit by allowing us to strengthen our science teaching. However, our commitment to supporting women's careers remains a priority.'[47]

The lack of women academics specialising in science subjects was clearly proving a problem, as we know it is in society more widely: to this day, the gender gap in take-up of STEM subjects (science, technology, engineering and mathematics) is still only closing slowly. The lack of women role models forging careers in STEM then limits what girls consider achievable aspirations for themselves, and limits the examples available to counter men's bias about women's suitability for STEM—and the vicious cycle continues. At least the world now has a new heroine, who has managed to get the recognition she deserves in an area usually the preserve of men: Katie Bouman, the 29-year-old scientist who led a team developing an algorithm that has been instrumental in photographing a black hole for the first time, in April 2019. The image featured on the front pages of most UK and many foreign newspapers.[48] Dr Bouman, an MIT graduate, became an instant sensation. This is clearly brilliant and should be helpful for many young women whose scientific and other contributions are often obscured, if not lost, amongst their many male co-workers—who tend to shout loudest.

Bias in media and entertainment

Progress on the elimination of bias in the media remains decidedly patchy. A *Guardian* weekend magazine cover story in spring 2019 had the headline 'Rage On— Glenda Jackson on power, politics and her second take on Lear'. The celebrated international actress and ex-Labour MP, now in her early 80s and still working on stage, was asked about #MeToo and its impact. According to the piece, 'she pulls an extraordinary face of disgust. "It's everywhere, it's everywhere. We have raised [awareness levels], no question, but it's by no means universal and we still ain't got equal pay, have we?"'[49] Well, this sums it up. Campaigns here and there bring down some people and raise awareness, but they only tackle one aspect of the issue, and the overall power imbalance remains. This is no surprise given that women are still being treated economically as inferior. Rose McGowan, one of the women who accused Hollywood producer Harvey Weinstein of rape in 2017, said in a *New Statesman* interview, 'I will always look up to a woman in a man's world'.[50] But there aren't many of those. Despite the huge increase in debate and conversation since 2017 around the lack of women headlining music festivals, many of 2019's festival line-ups looked much the same as ever, with rarely more than a token woman to placate critics.[51]

Why is that? Why has it not been sorted out after so many years of campaigns and raising awareness? It seems that perceptions of men and women—gender expectations—are deeply ingrained and hard to shift. A report in 2012 by the training and campaigning network Women in Journalism showed that sexist stereotypes dominated British newspapers' front pages, with some 78% of front-page articles being written by men, and 84% of those quoted or mentioned in these articles being men.[52] Similarly, in the United States, men were found even to be dominating stories that covered 'women's issues' such as abortion and birth control; men were in a big majority—in the 80s, percentage-wise—in anything to do with political election issues.[53] That research is from 2012 for both countries, but an event led in late 2018 by Professor Suzanne Franks, an ex-BBC journalist and then Head of Journalism at City University in London, showed that nothing much has changed in the UK, despite pledges to the contrary following various public inquiries. Similarly, the US Women's Media Center reported in 2019 that, despite some gains, men still dominate in every part of news, entertainment and digital media.[54]

A comment from the veteran broadcaster Joan Bakewell says it all. In a March 2019 piece written for the *Sunday Times* magazine column 'A Life in the Day', she took readers through her day, starting with listening to the news at 7am on BBC Radio 4: 'I never listen to the Today programme after the news because that is too much testosterone for me at that time of the morning.'[55] The lack of women interviewees on politics and current affairs shows may partly be because the culture and exposure that comes with such interviews is a negative experience for women, who choose to avoid it. Homeware entrepreneur Emma Bridgewater points out that 'There are real reasons why women don't want to put themselves in full view; social media and the media in general are gruesome. There is a sense that women get a pretty tough critique when they air their views.' But, as with the 'women aren't applying' defence, this isn't the full story.

What we need, if we want women to be given more airtime and column space, is more senior women journalists. Media staff deciding what to cover and who to give a platform to operate under the same unconscious bias as hiring managers who recruit in their own image. This is the reason why a survey of Women in Journalism members found that women's issues were given a low priority and that journalistic work culture, for decades male-dominated, looked unfavourably on those with family responsibilities. The women surveyed felt that more women in decision-making roles would be helpful in achieving a more women-friendly news agenda and a more women-friendly work environment.[56] But until that happens, it is not surprising that women don't stay for long and don't rise up the career ladder as well as they should. Again, that is a market failure. And it is a shame, since women are naturally drawn to journalism— Suzanne Franks reckons that on average in the Journalism MA at City, they outnumber men by two to one. Even financial journalism attracts a good number of women, despite the vast gender inequality issues in the finance sector itself.

It is only later in their career that women discover this path is not as straightforward as it is for men; as Suzanne Franks puts it, the women are shocked when they realise that being good and working hard is not a guarantee of success or recognition if you are a woman. There are obstacles along the way, of a different type and harder to overcome than for the men. But maybe things will start moving in the media now that the BBC's editor of the

Today programme and Political Editor are both women, as well as the senior interviewer on *Newsnight* (Emily Maitlis) and the host of *Question Time* (Fiona Bruce). In her diary in the *New Statesman*, the *Newsnight* presenter Kirsty Wark has joked that the three women presenters (herself, Maitlis and Emma Barnett) should form a Newsnight Presenters Social Club. Even if it won't have as many members as a gentlemen's club, and even if it won't be based in Havana, it would at least allow the new 'sisterhood' of three to develop and influence the way in which the flagship BBC programme is produced and presented in the future.[57] We'll all wait with bated breath for the change to come.

Bias in the creative sector

An interesting set of data also centres around women in the arts, such as movies and games. It should be no surprise that culture is particularly susceptible to being influenced by societal culture more broadly, and little seems to have changed in terms of harmful gender perceptions despite the #MeToo movement, as we are hearing from younger women in the creative industries. Ella Road, a British playwright in her late 20s, gave an interview in 2019 to promote the second airing of her debut play *The Phlebotomist*, at the Hampstead Theatre. She spoke about the difficulties still faced by actresses, a profession she had previously pursued herself: 'It's still really hard for women, not just in terms of the roles you are offered but the ways you are treated and talked about.'[58]

During 2019, news came that the next 007 will be a woman—but Daniel Craig is still to appear as James Bond, with the black British actress Lashana Lynch inheriting no more than a codename. Phoebe Waller-Bridge, brought in to liven up the new film's script, has sparked controversy in her seeming defence of James Bond's misogynistic behaviour as run of the mill stuff, saying:

> There's been a lot of talk about whether or not [the Bond franchise] is relevant now because of who he is and the way he treats women ... I think that's absolute bollocks. I think he's absolutely relevant now. It has just got to grow. It has just got to evolve, and the important thing is that the film treats the women properly. He doesn't have to. He needs to be true to this character.

Well, there might be an argument post-#MeToo that James Bond's misogyny is not remotely outdated, and perfectly in keeping with our times—but does this mean we need to keep making room for such characters? And how will a Bond film manage to 'treat the women properly' while continuing to shine a heroic, glamorous light on a protagonist who doesn't? Maybe it's about time to have heroes who treat all people with respect.

Lynch also had a role in the Disney movie *Captain Marvel*, released earlier in 2019 to coincide with International Women's Day on 8 March. It was marketed as the first Disney action film with a woman protagonist, and the first time a woman had been seen in the role of Captain Marvel—great stuff, loved it. But the *Telegraph* quote my local cinema used to advertise the film said it all: '[Brie] Larson's terrific lead performance can be understated and self-questioning, yet also big on girl-boss attitude when it counts.' Do I take it that women should now think that they have made it because of admiring comments about 'girl-boss attitude'? Had there been a man in the lead, as with all Marvel movies until this one, would there have been an equivalent reference to 'boy-boss attitude'? Or would that remark have been redundant, since it would have been automatically assumed that leadership qualities would exist in a man? We know the answer to these questions, but women in proper leadership roles, as opposed to stereotypical roles, will continue attracting that kind of comment until there is greater economic equality for women in the film industry. Only then will there be sufficient numbers for a culture shift to occur.

Also in 2019, the British Film Institute, run by its first female CEO, Amanda Nevill, came under attack for an exhibition entitled 'Playing the Bitch'.[59] Use of the term sparked protest, but underlined the view of women given by the film industry, mainly falling into male viewers' or creators' stereotypes of women 'as the femme fatale, scheming social climber, or untrustworthy double-crosser'—basically as 'nasty bitches'. The predominant phenomenon that this exhibition sought to expose was a culture in which male characters can misbehave without this reflecting on their morality or likeability, but misbehaving female characters are an unfavourable caricature of distressed/wronged/angry women. Of course, most of the films shown in the exhibition were directed by men.

These differing standards of behaviour for men and women do not only apply to fictional characters: they also dominate 'in real life'. Veteran actress Kathleen Turner has commented: 'There is an allowance for bad boy behaviour. Not just with our stars but with men in general … But the other side of male entitlement is fear. Fear of losing it…'[60] In this context, the tolerance and even rewarding of men's sexual misconduct in the film industry makes sense. This has been highlighted by the controversial and outspoken American actress Roseanne Barr, who says she is not in favour of the #MeToo movement herself. Whatever your views of Barr, her comment to *The Sunday Times* in March 2019 was a hard-hitting critique of the film industry's systemic power imbalance and its manifestations: 'I'm one of the few women who's made it on talent in Hollywood. I tried to sleep my way to the top but there were no takers.'[61]

Sexual harassment, exploitation and assault is certainly one half of the gender inequality that is being increasingly discussed by actors. But there is a second key issue of gender inequality facing actresses: the question of who gets paid more. (It's usually the men.)

However violent and unacceptable the sexual politics of the film industry, this should not trivialise or distract from the industry's economic inequality. It is this economic imbalance that allows a broader cultural power imbalance to fester. How can we expect women to be equally valued morally so long as they are not equally valued literally? If women can't earn as much or control the processes of production and creative decision-making, then their role in the industry remains subservient. And if women will have a harder time making a living as actors, then they, like Ella Road, will leave the profession, in greater numbers than men—perpetuating the cycle. This will shape the aspirations of younger generations of girls, who won't see many options or examples, and will also shape the gender attitudes of all people who view culture produced through a male-skewed lens.

Beyond acting itself, in numbers women tend to dominate the cultural sector as a whole, but this doesn't seem to help them. Research published by the Sociological Review Foundation in 2015 found that large numbers of them were involved in what are seen as more 'traditionally female' professions such as marketing, PR and production coordination, with men dominating in the creative roles and technical jobs that are generally more prestigious and better paid.[62] The study, based on many interviews with people in the industry, concluded that there was a legacy in the arts of associating masculinity with creativity. To be creative, the logic goes, you have to be able to disregard the rules and think outside the box. This doesn't sit easily with the continued overwhelming association of women with domestic and caring work. Men are perceived to be less bound by rules, while women are seen as 'more caring, supportive and nurturing ... better communicators ... and better organised'. In other words, they are there to enable and promote the work of men. Although some of those perceptions are changing, this is not happening fast enough, and job segregation continues.

A 2016 report on the cultural sector looked at this problem in greater detail.[63] It was prepared by the Culture Action Europe network and co-funded by the European Union's Creative Europe programme. It looked at broad heritage and social issues of gender equality that are still troubling, but when it came to the situation on the ground in the cultural sector itself, it also used analysis incorporated in a UNESCO 2014 report.[64] Between the two analyses, we end up with an absolute challenge to the conventional belief that the creative sector, employing a high percentage of women, is a haven for gender equality. There is indeed a larger number of women than men enrolling in university courses related to culture and the arts. However, when you look at what actually goes on in the professional arts world, this is not reflected in women's career progression or representation. They tend to dominate the administrative areas of public cultural institutions, are overrepresented in the informal sector, and are underrepresented in decision-making roles.

In the context of this glass ceiling and limited choice of career paths within the sector, we see job segregation manifesting itself again in what becomes a vicious cycle. There still seems, to this day, to be an underrepresentation of women artists, film and theatre directors and composers, and works by women that do exist rarely seem to get the prominence they probably deserve. In the decade from 2009 to 2019, only 18 of 180 films in competition at the Cannes film festival were made by women.[65] There are, of course, exceptions, like my friend and godmother to my daughter, Norma Percy of Brook Lapping Productions. She has been celebrated for her innovative, hard-hitting documentaries, which have won her a series of awards. But my goodness she has worked hard—I have witnessed the masterly bringing together of her interviews for a recent programme on Europe in which I had some small involvement. And, as with Christine Lagarde heading the IMF, a few women who break through is not enough to spark change. The UNESCO report in particular also referred to the number of women making it to senior positions being too small to create a 'domino effect' in hiring patterns. Instead we have a catch-22 situation, where women remain underrepresented and so fail to 'gain credibility with their (male) peers'.[66]

Let's take yet another example: video games. Apparently, an equal number of men and women play them, which I had not realised—I thought that maybe women had better things to do! I have only once played a video game, with one of my grandsons on his little iPad. We were trying to get a man to jump over a cliff edge and on to safety across, without him falling into the abyss below, which signified the end of the game and no points earned at all. Disaster, in other words, and screams of disappointment from my grandson. We did it again and again, and finally we pressed buttons fast enough for the escaping hero to make it through! Of course, it was a male character trying to escape from something horrid. Maybe a woman would not have found herself in such a difficult situation?

But, in all seriousness, it is a disturbing fact that just as many women as men play video games, yet only 3.3% of top video games feature female protagonists.[67] Just one reason for concern about this is that it helps to perpetuate the stereotype of men as the people who are expected to be strong and assertive—and aggressive, in many video games involving violence. It's not hard to guess the reason why video games are hardly ever about women: the vast majority of the people making video games that get released are men. Women account for just 5% of people working in interactive content sectors, and only 6% in the game industries as a whole. In the UK, it is believed that 19% of those working in game development are women.[68] This gender imbalance of the video game industry reflects that of the tech sector more broadly.

As in film, the lack of senior women in 'real life' and the lack of strong, complex female characters in games of course perpetuates the myth that decision-making in tough environments doesn't come naturally to women. Senior roles—and senior role models—remain few and far between. According to the comedian Sandi Toksvig, co-founder of the UK's Women's Equality Party, 'invisible women syndrome' is not just the result of the biases and barriers preventing women from succeeding, but can also be a deliberate erasure that hides from view those women who have succeeded. In an interview with Julia Gillard, ex-Prime Minister of Australia, Toksvig accused the predominantly male volunteers who man the free online encyclopaedia Wikipedia of 'actively editing women out'. Only one in five biographies on the site are of women, and there was a furore when it was revealed that in May 2018 an editor had apparently rejected a page created for Donna Strickland, on the grounds that she didn't meet their 'notability guidelines'. Strickland went on to win a joint Nobel Prize for Physics a few months later![69] What more evidence do we need that unconscious bias is holding back women?

There is no reason why quotas for women in senior leadership can't be applied to the creative industries. The Oscar-winning Julianne Moore, who has been nominated for an Academy Award five times, spoke for many in an interview from Cannes in May 2019 when she said that more needed to be done so that more women filmmakers could compete for the Palme d'Or. She said, 'I do believe in quotas, I really do. I believe in trying to level the playing field ... You have to open doors, we've been in a culture that's been one way for a very long time.'[70] We know that private organisations like film studios or production companies are unlikely to move too far on this without being forced to by legislation or state policy, but that doesn't mean that public bodies can't apply financial pressure and make the short-term business incentives clear. British Arts Council funding for films, for example, now requires a certain number of individuals on the project to be from ethnic-minority backgrounds, both behind and in front of camera. The cycle can be broken for women too, using the same type of methods.

Bias in sport

We know that differential treatment of women's sport has existed for ages. Put simply, sport has been a laggard when it comes to women's emancipation. At the Rio Olympics in 2016, the number of women athletes finally rose to represent some 45% of all competitors. In fact some countries sent more women than men, including Bahrain, China, New Zealand, Puerto Rico and Australia. Yet, if you look at the leadership of the international sport associations and federations, 33 out of 35 were run by men in 2017, and a number had no women at all on their executive committees. That included federations representing sports that mainly attract women, such as the International Handball Federation! Others with no women on their executive boards were the International Basketball Federation and the International Golf Federation.[71]

The biased attitudes around motherhood seem particularly problematic in this profession which depends on the physical body. The US track and field sprinter and Olympic gold medallist Allyson Felix has revealed that her sponsor, Nike, wanted to reduce her pay by 70% after she gave birth to a daughter in 2018. Others have also come forward telling of suspended or cut payments during their pregnancies, even if they then went on to win more titles soon after their child was born. There is clearly lack of insurance in the sports sector for women athletes, who often choose abortion to carry on performing and being paid. Recently the outcry has forced the likes of Nike to offer women athletes improved maternity rights.[72]

In the UK, the excitement over the progress of England's football team (the 'Lionesses') in the 2019 Women's World Cup appears to have helped, with record television audiences, but much still needs to be done internationally and nationally. It must have come as a surprise to the younger generation caught up in the excitement to learn that the UK's Football Association banned the use of its clubs' grounds by women footballers for five decades until 1971, considering the sport 'quite unsuitable for females'.[73] The Women's FA was only formed in 1969. In some countries, women weren't allowed until very recently to go and watch live football. At a Bloomberg Equality Summit in May 2019, I had the chance to listen to a panel on women's football, which looked at the way the game and its attraction to the public is changing. The women's game is now finally classified as professional in the UK, meaning that women footballers are to be paid proper wages.

But of course the pay gap will remain enormous so long as viewing figures for women's football, though rising fast, remain below men's. In 2017, footballers in the English Women's Super League were being paid on average £26,752 a year; by contrast, the men in the Premier League were earning an average of £2.64 million. That means that the elite of men's football were being paid £99 for each £1 paid to an elite woman player.[74] If anything, it looks like the pay gap is widening. Perversely, as UK clubs' purchasing power is rising, they are still focusing mainly on their core competition—vying for star male players and raising their salaries even further, instead of helping to correct the imbalance by putting more money into the women's game.

The picture in the US is more worrying still. Despite the fact that women's football is much more popular there than men's football, and although the US boasts the best-paid women footballers in the world, their wages remain below those of men in the sport.[75] Women athletes have revolted, suing for fairer pay, but about the only sport that now pays the same to men and women is tennis. This is mainly due to the efforts of the likes of Billie Jean King, the former World No. 1 US tennis player, who famously won a match in three sets against Bobby Riggs in 1973, becoming an icon for women's prowess in the game. That match is now immortalised in the 2017 film *Battle of the Sexes*. It is only now that the huge unexploited commercial value of women's sport is beginning to dawn on sponsors and others in the sector, with sell-out crowds at the Women's Cricket World Cup, and the football Women's World Cup in 2019. I myself didn't hesitate for a second before ordering my tickets for the first Chelsea Ladies' Premiership game in early September 2019, taking some very excited grandchildren along! But proper recognition and equal pay across most sports is yet to come. The result is that fewer girls and women than boys and men are choosing to become athletes, an obvious market failure that is preventing the best talent from reaching the top—which, of course, reinforces the biased expectations that women are a less natural fit for sport, or can't really be as good at it as men.

The truth is that, wherever we see cultural or social inequality, there is sure to be economic inequality behind it. Lots of voices in different countries are now asking for a rethink in the way sport is taught and managed in schools, to encourage greater diversity in the sports available to boys and girls. It stands to reason that we need some top-down intervention, rather than simply relying on grassroots campaigns, because the change we are asking for here is a fundamental one: a change in perceptions. If measures aren't imposed to allow for women to be properly paid for their training, and if that training isn't properly funded, then women's sport will never be able to overcome the decades of neglect it has suffered. If performance can't go beyond a certain level, then the sport's attraction for fans will also be limited—which will in turn limit what the big business of global sport is willing to do for women's equality. It is worth reminding ourselves that the lifting of the UK ban on women's football in the early 1970s coincided with the passing of landmark equality acts. The Norwegian Football Federation has introduced a system of redistributing wages between men and women players at international level, and some clubs in Europe do try to achieve parity. We can only hope for more of the same.

Bias: conscious or unconscious?

Thankfully we have made some progress on overt prejudice and explicit sexism. It is less acceptable than it was decades ago, and the worst offenders are likely to get a public rebuke. Legislation on sexual harassment and discrimination has been tightened, as the shamed Nobel laureate physiologist Tim Hunt learned the hard way.

Trump's 'locker-room talk' was widely condemned even by most, though not all, of his own supporters. You might argue that Trump's victory and installation in the White House shows that such advances have been for nothing, but there is no denying that women stand a better chance than they once did. British entrepreneur Beverley Nielsen told me a story from her early career in the 1980s. She started talking to the CEO of a well-known UK textiles business, and asked him why she had not been interviewed for a role she had applied for as a graduate a few years earlier.

> After much prevarication, he admitted that it was 'simple in my case, they did not interview any women'. I was staggered. 'Why was that?' I asked. Again a lot of prevarication. However, after further probing, it turned out that 'as a lot of manufacturing plants are in far off places, we worried that a young woman might have an affair with their manager'. Another stunning answer. 'Well, did you not think that a young man might have an affair with the bored manager's wife?' I asked in return. He had no response. Except to say that if I were to apply now I would be given an interview!

Even if individual attitudes for their own sake have proven resistant to change, firms across all sectors are now at least becoming increasingly aware that the image they project is crucial both in ensuring customer loyalties and in attracting and retaining talent. It's hard to imagine a UK business getting away with such an overtly negative attitude to hiring women in 2019. Nowadays, at least in the West, the discrimination that exists is more unconscious, more hidden, and so more worrying, as it is trickier to detect or counter.

The Confederation of British Industry (CBI) has reported that its diversity conferences are often oversub-scribed.[76] It published employment trends surveys in early 2019 showing that some 93% of respondents had been taking steps to deal with the gender pay gap, and putting in place measures to increase diversity in their organisations—some 30% more than the year before. It was also reported that the headhunting firm Egon Zehnder, hired by Waitrose and John Lewis to find them a new chairman, had been called in to run 'a workshop on unconscious bias' for the top team. It seems to have worked—the John Lewis Partnership recruited a bril-liant woman to succeed the outgoing male chair of the group, from an ethnic-minority background, and an economist to boot! At least we now have proof that the 'naming and shaming' publicity since 2018 over the pay gap is having some small effect—but, again, only because large firms were forced by regulation to publish their results, when previous voluntary agreements to do so had met with very little enthusiasm. And the steps being taken, while better than no effort, don't seem to be achieving much.

It seems that most current efforts in business are focused on increasing overall gender balance throughout the organisation, with still only a minority reported to be actively working to enhance the representation of women in leadership roles. As the CBI noted, only a third of the 250 respondents to the survey, employing between them some 1 million people, were prioritising better gender diversity at the senior levels of their organisation. Let's look once again at the financial services industry, since it's one I'm familiar with. At the time of writing, my 'alma mater' KPMG has never had a woman chair or senior partner, though the Deputy Chair is now a woman, Melanie Richards, whom I interviewed for this book. At PricewaterhouseCoopers, the Chairman and Senior Partner, the Head of Tax, Head of Markets, Head of Regions, Head of Consulting, Managing Partner and Chief Operational Officer are all men, with the women relegated to roles such as Head of Risk Assurance, Head of People and General Counsel. Only one woman executive board member has a proper business role, as Head of Deals.[77] Deloitte and Ernst & Young are much better, with more women in leading business roles, but the Senior Partner and Chief Executive are again men in both firms.[78]

An *LSE Business Review* blogpost highlighted another reason for the ineffectiveness of many company gender initiatives so far: they are failing because women are penalised for displaying non-stereotypical behaviours in the leadership context. In other words, organisations' voluntary responses to gender inequality have not been enough to counteract the depth of unconscious bias against women. Ann Bentley started work as a British rail engineer in her 20s, one of only three women in the division at the time. She says that the plus side was that she was noticed a lot and was given opportunities—the downside was that she was often looked at with incredulity and asked what she was doing there. It was even commonplace not to have any women's toilets on building sites. Bentley was fortunate in getting a lot of help and support to step up, but says that with age she is now much more sensitive to unacceptable behaviour by men, which includes the condescending habit of addressing women as 'darling' even in a work situation. She says:

> I'm quite militant about the way women are represented in business externally. Keen to see that it is not about glamorisation, or tokenism. For example, I got a sales brochure recently and every picture was of a man, and I asked the sales and marketing consultancy why they thought I would buy their product. What it shows to me is that, although the law has changed and there is a gloss of compliance, you don't have to go far to see [that] things are [in practice] different [from the spirit of policy], and that the world [still] changes when you have childcare responsibilities.

Bentley recounted to my colleague how, during a lunch break at a diversity and inclusivity workshop, the woman catering assistant brought in the lunch and a director said, 'Thanks, darling.' She picked him up on it at once and he joked about how she was not the first to have issued such a challenge. Beverley Nielsen told me of a meeting she had helped set up between the NHS and a new healthcare company, at which one of the male directors suddenly stated, 'Oh no darling, that is not how it works at all.' Even when she objected to the term after the meeting, he later called her 'dear', explaining that this was just a habit he was unable to break and that it was meant well. As Nielsen said, 'The idea was that I should just get on and accept it!' Presumably such men feel confident they can get away with this kind of language since the then-UK Prime Minister David Cameron refused to apologise for telling opposition MP Angela Eagle to 'Calm down, dear' during a 2011 parliamentary debate about NHS reform.[79]

How are we going to change this, without regulation? The *LSE Business Review* piece mentioned earlier quotes a detailed study of some 800 medium to large companies in the US, which found that diversity and bias training—apparently costing some $8 billion a year in the US alone—is the least effective way of increasing diversity in management positions.[80] Another study in the US concluded that, in fact, the most effective way to reduce gender imbalance in business is to have externally imposed and monitored programmes and measures that engage managers.[81] A review of practices in Norway looked at how that finding applied in the Scandinavian country after decades of quotas and regulation. It found that the 'forced' introduction of substantially more women into senior and managerial positions had led to greater inclusion of women by that business more broadly. In other words, state intervention in the market is needed if we are to improve women's economic equality. In the next part of the book, we'll explore in more detail why this is so, and what kinds of intervention would be useful.

PART FOUR

SOLUTIONS

4

SOLUTIONS

Why don't women just employ themselves?

All of this raises what may seem an obvious question. If it's tougher for women to be recruited at senior level or to rise through the ranks in so many existing organisations, why don't they just start their own businesses? Well, for a start, they would typically need a business loan to do this. There are many countries where women face unequal treatment in relation to running a business, for example in access to credit, signing a contract, registering a business, or even opening a bank account. Raising funds or investment is also more difficult for women. Globally the European Bank for Reconstruction and Development calculates that over 70% of small and medium-sized enterprises led by women are either receiving no credit from financial institutions or are receiving too little for their needs. It estimates a gender funding gap in the order of some £285 billion. By any reckoning, this is a huge unmet financing gap that urgently needs to be plugged.[1]

Research has shown that amending legislation to take away this discrimination has a positive correlation with female labour force participation. This type of discrimination is more pronounced in developing countries, but it exists in many developed ones too. There is ample evidence of gender-based discrimination among lenders in the UK and US, for example, and in many countries on the European continent. A study across 94 economies found globally that laws prohibiting that type of discrimination have a positive association with female business ownership.[2] But there is still a long way to go. According to OECD calculations, in Israel—the home of tech start-ups—only 1.5% of women run their own companies, versus 6.2% of men. Even in Sweden, often held up as a bastion of equality, only some 1.4% of women run their own businesses, as against 5.3% of men.

The UK once set a good example, with the advisory Women's National Commission set up in 1969, which did serious work ensuring action against all aspects of gender discrimination. Its erstwhile Chair, Baroness Prosser, chaired a study in the mid-2000s led by the then Secretary of State, Patricia Hewitt, to calculate the impact on the UK economy of its lack of women entrepreneurs. This was when I worked for the Department for Trade and Industry, later the Department for Business; I seconded someone from my economics team to work with that commission, which was the first time the economic value of women entrepreneurs had ever been investigated using proper economic techniques. We estimated then that if we had a similar percentage of women entrepreneurs as the US, then GDP would be a good few billion higher.

Yet the UK closed its Women's Commission in 2010 when the coalition government came to power.[3] The justification, as the government put it, was that this was 'part of its cost-cutting drive to reduce and streamline quangos'. The Commission's core functions were moved into the Equality Office in the Cabinet Office, but the focus was lost. The then Chair, Baroness Joyce Gould, denounced the closure as 'yet another blow for women across the UK, at a time when the Comprehensive Spending Review [in other words the coming period of austerity] is likely to hit women and families dispropor-tionately'. In the field of entrepreneurship, women in the UK fare very little better than they did in the mid-2000s when we made that estimate. A 2019 report by the state-owned British Business Bank found that only 1% of venture capital funds go to women-only enterprises, even though 20% of single-person businesses and 18% of smaller firms are majority-led by women.[4] A prominent female entrepreneur was quoted recently saying, 'We all know we don't get money, we all know it takes time to build a business, we all know women invest less and we all know there is no gender equality.'[5]

Women entrepreneurs make up only one third of the total in the UK, and only a fifth of small or medium-sized businesses with at least one employee (19%) are owned by a woman.[6] This imbalance was acknowledged in 2019 in a briefing paper on women in the economy: 'Men are more likely than women to be involved in "total early stage entrepreneurial activity", which includes owning or running a business less than 3.5 years old'.[7] A review of women's entrepreneurship by Alison Rose, then head of commercial and private banking and now CEO at the Royal Bank of Scotland (where I started my career), has found that extraordinary discrimination and barriers still exist.[8] The review, commissioned by the Treasury and published in March 2019, found that only 6% of women in the UK run their own business, compared with 15% in Canada, 11% in the US and 9% in Australia. It is important to make these comparisons with other Anglo-Saxon countries because, like the UK, they have very advanced capital markets, allowing a high degree of fundraising and investment to take place—an area in which the UK usually excels.

The EU country closest to the UK in terms of capital markets is the Netherlands, but even there the UK lags behind: the Dutch ratio of entrepreneurs is 0.9 women for every man—in other words, almost at parity, whereas the Rose Review calculated that the UK is stuck at 0.46. This means that more than twice as many men are entrepreneurs in the UK, considerably worse than almost everywhere else in the OECD. The ratio is 0.8 in Spain, and around 0.6 in Sweden, Israel, the US, Australia, Canada and Greece. In this context, it's unsurprising that the *Sunday Times* 2019 list of the 1,000 wealthiest people in the UK features virtually no women other than sport and pop stars and heirs to family businesses. Even once they get started, women are less likely to be able to scale their businesses beyond a certain point, with only 13% of women running established businesses in the UK ultimately achieving a turnover between £1 million and £50 million, whereas the figure for men is 29%.

Given the size, sophistication and supremacy of the UK capital-raising model, and the fact that the UK is, as the Rose Review points out, 'the start-up capital of Europe', it is odd that things have not been better for women entrepreneurs. Rose identifies a major market failure behind this: a 'perceived bias within the UK venture finance community'. What she means by this is that the UK investment teams that make decisions on funding tend to be dominated by men, and nearly half have no women at all. Women make up just 13% of senior members of investment teams. The review's astounding content got the headlines it deserved when it was published, particularly the finding that only 1% of venture funding goes to all-women start-ups. As a result men are five times more likely than women to build a business with a turnover of £1 million plus.

Why did Rose identify this bias as a market failure, and not simply an injustice? The answer is in the economics. The Rose Review calculated that if women entrepreneurs in the UK started new businesses and scaled them up at the same rate as men, that would add some £250 billion to the economy. Even just getting to the same rate of women's entrepreneurship as the best-performing countries studied would add £200 billion. The Women's Enterprise Taskforce's final report in 2012 came to a similar conclusion, suggesting that 900,000 more businesses would be created if the UK could match the level of women's entrepreneurship in the US—England alone would see 150,000 extra businesses created per year.[9]

There is also some evidence coming through now that women have better success than men in sustaining and growing the businesses they start, once they become an established entrepreneur. A KPMG review of 91 new fintech companies, published in May 2019, found that the median internal rate of return for the women-owned or -co-owned companies was more than twice as high as in the companies started by men.[10] However, this better performance may just have reflected investors, perhaps unconsciously, requiring more stringent due diligence tests for the women-run firms. So the correlation doesn't necessarily prove that women are better at running a business—just that the businesses women start end up having more solid foundations than the average male-founded business. But regardless of the reason for better performance from women's startups, the ones that get going are a better bet for investors in terms of future growth. In other words, both in theory and practice, the evidence is there that more firms started or owned by businesswomen should be supported. Beyond these specifics, we know that—by free-market capitalism's own logic—the more firms enter and compete in the market, the more innovation should take place and the higher productivity should be. Entrepreneurship is a must in a free-market economy, but if the support for women entrepreneurs just isn't there, the system will not allow it to happen at its optimal level. Bias is restricting competition, and this is a clear market failure.

In response to the country's dismal record on financing women's enterprises, the UK government has announced a series of measures it intends to take, including sponsoring a new industry-led taskforce aimed at securing change in this area. The Treasury, working with the UK Finance trade association, is establishing a new 'Investing in Women' code of conduct. The idea is that financial institutions will sign up to this code, which should raise awareness of the issue and improve decision-making in allocation of funds, to achieve a target of 50% more female-run businesses by 2030, and 600,000 more women entrepreneurs.[11] This is better than nothing, and at least knowledge about the problems facing women entrepreneurs slowly increases with every new report.

But gentle measures or assistance may not do the trick given the scale of the problem, as the Rose Review argued.[12] The government response to the review referred to the above target figures in terms of 'ambition', and we all know what happens to ambitions, particularly when other issues like Brexit remain on the horizon, as do changes in government and therefore priorities.

One thing that we know could help is an expansion of enterprise teaching in schools, and targeting it towards girls in particular. This UK curriculum innovation, originally introduced by Labour, involves contact with businesses, and girls who benefit from it become four times more likely to want to start their own business. Boys, interestingly, only grow twice as likely. This is no doubt because girls are in more need of awareness, exposure and 'leading by example' to find their way to entrepreneurship, due to the unconscious bias encountered by potential women entrepreneurs, those starting out, and those trying to grow their business—both in their business dealings with men, and within their own social conditioning. The Rose Review was partly guided by evidence from interviews and survey work, which influenced its proposals on solutions—we have undertaken some small amount of extra interviewing during the research for this book, to add to those findings.

My Birmingham City University colleague Beverley Nielsen has been encouraging entrepreneurship and innovation in that city, keeping close to entrepreneurs of both main genders and from various ethnic backgrounds. A number of women have spoken to her about their experiences, and it is interesting to see some of the sentiments expressed. Rebecca Struthers of Struthers Watchmakers talked about the difficulties in raising capital to set up a business during the recession, and her disproportionate reliance on women investors. For her and her associates, 'Private investment was our only means to secure significant capital to generate growth, and that came from a female investor and very success-ful entrepreneur.'

The surface pattern designer Sara Page, who started her business in her mid-40s some 10 years ago, has encountered both misogyny and ageism:

> When I first went overseas on business, I was treated well. More recently, I've found the businesses more complacent. Often, when my husband came, I found this made a difference to the way I was treated, and it was apparent sometimes that they spoke to him, not me, until he explained, 'Sara is the designer, it is her business.' It may also be to do with not just being a woman but being older. I am seen as another 'middle-aged woman with a hobby'.

Page is not alone in experiencing this unconscious bias causing men to be more respectful towards fellow men, with women struggling to be taken equally seriously as businesspeople. Nicola Milne, who started a successful business in 2004, says that overall she didn't at first find it very difficult starting a business, with £10,000 she borrowed from her then boyfriend and a £10,000 over-draft facility from HSBC. But she did encounter unconscious bias: 'This one's interesting because the accountants "assumed" that my [then] boyfriend was a partner in the business (his money was actually a pure loan), and they gave him 50% ownership. Now that was difficult to undo!'

Dame Barbara Stocking, President of the all-women Cambridge college Murray Edwards, has been quoted saying, 'The college's job is to prepare young women for a working world dominated by men by encouraging them to take risks, and that [this job] will only be finished when there is true gender equality.'[13] This emphasis on risk-taking is interesting. We've seen throughout this book that evidence suggests women tend to be more cautious. Angela Burman of Burman Bears says that, in her experience,

> the women artists and designers I have taken on in the shop have thought carefully about their businesses and what they are taking on in terms of risk. I do not see this as being risk-averse, but being sensible in assessing what they are getting into. I think some women have more 'common sense' and avoid silly risks. They are used to running their homes and run their businesses in the same way. They tend to think of the whole thing rather than one 'glory bit'.

When it comes to entrepreneurship, greater adventur-ousness among women might be a good idea, in moderation. But there is ample evidence that, in our male-dominated society, women are not encouraged or rewarded for being willing to take risk, hence their conservatism. As specialist watch manufacturer Rebecca Smythes points out:

> In my own career I have faced a constant battle of being accused of holding myself back by being too quiet and not speaking up, but then, as soon as I've spoken up and demonstrated my authority within my field, I am accused of being bossy/aggressive/domineering/pushy and told to pipe down again. All of those terms have been used to describe me in the past.

Unfortunately, I don't think that's an uncommon experience for women in business, and it often leaves them feeling less secure. That, in turn, makes women less likely to have enough belief in their abilities to take risks. As with the 'queen bee phenomenon' of senior women supposedly pulling up the ladder for other women (see below), there is a debate about whether this is a fundamental difference in women, or whether it is born out of the gender inequality that permeates our society and culture. Emma Bridgewater expressed the feeling that 'I definitely think that women are less adventurous. They tend to be more cautious ...This is probably due to our lack of self-belief in our ambition. I think this is inherent in women.' Well, that is more of a perception, and it must be broken. There is no evidence that women are less bold if they find themselves in a gender-neutral environment. But it is possible that they simply recognise that their ambitions won't be met, given the rarity of such environments, and so they let them lie dormant, playing safe within the limits of what society will let them achieve. The Rose Review hasn't exactly proven them wrong.

What can women do to counter unconscious bias?

Sheryl Sandberg, Chief Operating Officer of Facebook, is one of the world's most powerful women. In her book *Lean In*, she famously suggested that women facing inequality in the workplace should be staying put, working to change the culture in their firms, and pushing for change.[14] But that is likely to be hard, and certainly will only work for a handful of elite, relatively well-paid women. It will probably do little for the many down the pecking order. Instead the best solution may in fact be to cut your losses and run—to an organisation that is perhaps more open to change. In *Lean Out*, the columnist Dawn Foster criticises the 'lean in' brigade's focus on a relatively small collection of professional, highly educated women with good family and partner support, who do nothing to shake the capitalist system in its current, male-dominated free-market form, except for enabling their firms to get some good PR. In Foster's view, there is very little trickle-down effect, and therefore the answer is to exit not just the particular organisation, but the entire patriarchal corporate world, and to fight for change from the outside: 'Few women will sit in boardrooms in their lifetime, and adding a few "golden skirts" in places of high responsibility doesn't translate straight to a hastening improvement in women's rights and quality of life'.[15]

Well, I have sympathy with both viewpoints. The research suggests that the trickle-down does happen, but very slowly, and mostly not as a result of having women in boardroom positions. In other words, the evidence backs my argument throughout this book: left to itself, the system will not correct in a hurry. And, as Dawn Foster points out in her book, even in Norway, hailed as the doyen of women's empowerment, most women in boardrooms are non-executive directors who would be hard pushed to really understand an organisation's culture or make the time to ensure that their appointment to the board is reflected in a greater number of women coming up from within. It is only if quotas are applied to executive directors, involved in the leadership culture and promotion practices of the company, that the trickle-down can really begin to happen.

One of the most obvious demonstrations that there's only so much women can do to overcome systemic economic sexism is the phenomenon of the 'glass cliff'. This is a term used by women leaders to describe a fate that befalls women who seem active, interested and ambitious: their (usually male) managers give them pretty difficult, sometimes hopeless jobs that men are wary of taking on, expecting that they would fail. There is simply too much discussion and experience of the phenomenon to deny its reality, particularly since it is often brought up by women who have managed to overcome it.

The *Financial Times* has attributed the term to none other than Christine Lagarde, Chair of the IMF (2011–19) and the next President of the European Central Bank, but as far as I am aware it was in fact first used by the psychologists Michelle Ryan and Alex Haslam, following a UK study of FTSE 100 companies that found evidence of women being appointed to leadership positions at times of crisis. A typical 'glass cliff' job is sitting or chairing remuneration committees for big public limited companies, only to find that you have to support the committee's recommendations despite knowing they are outrageous and will get you into trouble with shareholders and the press. You may even receive a summons to explain yourself in front of the House of Commons Treasury Select Committee, as happened to a friend of mine who was involved in a 2018 payoff to a well-known departing chief exec, unusually a woman.

Belinda Phipps, former Chair of the Fawcett Society, described the phenomenon to me as follows:

> My first glass cliff job ... Marketing Manager for [pharmaceutical giant] GSK. At the time the lead product Zantac was the main profit earner for the company and was due off patent within a couple of years. New competitors were coming out and it was believed, with

good reason, that the ulcer market in the UK was saturated, i.e. all ulcers were being treated with an H2 antagonist, so growth could only be achieved by displacing competitors. No one wanted the job and, although I had not applied, I was actually offered it, and became the third most senior female in the UK. The challenge I had taken on quickly became evident, and it also became evident I was to be the fall guy. However, I found a new indication for Zantac, created a new market of patients for it, and sales rocketed. The strategy was repeated round the world. This, along with the major and 'mission impossible' coup of getting a patent extension for the product—achieved by another woman—supported GSK's fortunes till its next blockbuster came along. I was later told I was paid less than my male predecessor by some considerable margin. I left shortly afterwards to do an MBA, having been refused the opportunity to run a factory within the company. This not being seen as an acceptable job for a 29-year-old woman.

Perhaps even British Prime Minister Theresa May (2016–19) unwittingly took on a 'glass cliff' job: implementing Brexit. All of her rival leadership hopefuls, including the one other woman, peeled off from the 2016 contest to replace David Cameron as Prime Minister after the EU referendum that year, and May entered Downing Street by virtue of being the only person left standing. As we have seen in the years since, she could only slide downwards from there! At the time of writing, alpha male 'Boris' Johnson who ducked out of the contest that brought May to victory has replaced her amidst chaos and political stalemate over Brexit, concluding his debut speech as Prime Minister with a thinly veiled swipe: 'after three years of unfounded self-doubt it is time to change the record.' The message being, of course, that he is the strong, confident man needed to clean up a weak woman's mess. We shall see!

I am now also wondering whether the very same thing might have happened on the other side of the Brexit saga, when two major jobs in the EU ended up going to the second-tier candidates, both women, after EU leaders failed to agree on their respective first-choice candidates, who were men. The press—and I, in a way—rejoiced that the appointees were women, and strong, very successful and prominent women at that: Christine Lagarde and Ursula von der Leyen. But they are certainly set for a hard time, given that neither is perfectly suited to the very difficult job they have been asked to do, at a critical time for Europe when reforms must be carried out to keep the EU together. Might this undesirability of a potentially thankless task have had something to do with their appointments?

From a personal perspective, if you can't get anywhere in your own firm—despite reassuring words from HR and a well-put-together corporate and social responsibility policy—or if you can only get promoted to a doomed job that you're expected to fail in, then there's no point 'leaning in' and hanging on, in the hope that the organisation's culture will change. Best for an individual to move to a more open and flexible environment that allows her to be appreciated, do well and move up. But for all to benefit, the answer is a more interventionist state that shakes firms out of the inherent short-termism and bias pervading our current capitalist system. Instead we will need more active intervention to tackle the market failures and reduce the inequalities that this system creates. The change must come from employers, and though they will move a certain way under peer pressure, they are unlikely to implement the full changes needed unless they're also pushed by the authorities.

What should organisations do to counter unconscious bias?

The UK government has helpfully produced and disseminated evidence-based guidance to employers on how to close their gender pay gap. The Behavioural Insights Team, working with the Government Equalities Office, has looked at the evidence on what works in organisations, and again emphasises the effectiveness of processes that circumvent bias, conscious or unconscious. To summarise, the guidance recommends the following actions for employers as having a strong evidence base to support them:

1. Include multiple women in shortlists for recruitment and promotions: shortlists with only one woman do not increase the chance of a woman being selected.

2. Use skill-based assessment tasks in recruitment: ask candidates to perform tasks they would be expected to perform in the role they are applying for.

3. Use structured interviews for recruitment and promotions: unstructured interviews are more likely to allow unfair bias to creep in and influence decisions.

4. Encourage salary negotiation by showing salary ranges: women are less likely to negotiate their pay. This is partly because women are put off if they are not sure about what a reasonable offer is.

5. Introduce transparency to promotion, pay and reward processes.

6. Appoint diversity managers and/or diversity task forces.

7. Improve workplace flexibility for men and women.

8. Encourage the uptake of Shared Parental Leave.

9. Recruit returners: many of them, as the evidence suggests, have taken an extended career break for caring or other reasons, and are either not currently employed or are working in roles for which they are over-qualified—in other words, the evidence suggests that they are working below their skills level, a huge loss to society.

10. Offer mentoring and sponsorship.

11. Offer networking programmes.

12. Set specific, time-bound internal targets so that progress towards them can be tracked.[16]

This list is quite an ask. Implementing it would be costly, and require firms to think long-term, which is certainly not what our current short-term profit structure encourages. And often, as we know, translating HR principles into action is no small thing. So I'd go further and add quotas to this list. Most HR heads I speak to, usually women, are sympathetic to this. It's just that saying it openly would mean that they are supporting extra regulation, which could be a career-limiting move for them—unless they are already part of the top team and aren't worried about being sacked. But we have to assume that organisations prepared to engage sincerely with the government's guidance on closing the pay gap can see that regulation may be necessary to change practices across the economy, improving the pipeline of senior women who will serve as disruptors and role models.

At this point we need to look in more detail at the supposed 'queen bee phenomenon'. Its supporters argue that if only a limited number of women are breaking through the glass ceiling, it is not men stopping them, but the women already up there. On becoming successful, it is implied, women assimilate into the masculine culture they have joined, and behave 'like men', thus legitimising the gender inequality that is widespread in big organisations. Those who believe in it would argue that quotas for senior leadership will change nothing, since having more women at the top will not lead to better gender equality throughout the organisation.

To this I would say that the reasons for the 'queen bee phenomenon' in Western societies are often misunderstood as something biological and inherent—in other words, unavoidable in an organisation—when it is in fact a social phenomenon dependent on the environment in which women are operating. Yes, we often hear that women coming up the ranks have, at some stage, experienced lack of empathy from women higher up their organisations, but that seems to be changing, and there is a clear social reason for this. I wrote about it myself, observing that when I was growing up women at the top seemed to be either unmarried or without children.[17] It's understandable that this situation could lead to judgement or lack of sympathy on both sides. But it's also perfectly understandable why this divide emerged: forgoing a family was almost a must for the older generation of women managers, given that the surest way to get fired or never be promoted again was to announce that you were either about to get married or about to have a child—hence the colleague I mentioned at the start of this book who simply hid her pregnancy and family life from the employer. Where this issue once created friction or lack of understanding between more junior and more senior women, the problem is thankfully much smaller than it once was.

More broadly, even if senior women do behave unhelpfully towards women lower down, the chances are that it isn't because women are naturally 'jealous' or 'catty'—as the 'queen bee' argument often implies—but because the system makes them feel a desperate need to assimilate and belong, in other words to adopt 'masculine' characteristics and suppress 'emotion' to prove that they can be strong and effective leaders despite being women. You can easily see why this might prevent them from behaving in a naturally generous or open way towards any colleagues, whether men or women, and especially their juniors.[18] Some findings have suggested that women at the top may try and dissociate themselves from less successful women further down the ladder.[19] But this says more about the masculine, outcome-focused environment in which women work, particularly in the private sector, than it does about the nature of women. If we're imagining a scenario where the organisation as a whole does not reward such behaviour or attitudes—which is far more likely if it has adopted the government's proposals for eliminating bias and pay gaps—then the 'queen bee phenomenon' should melt away.

We can see that this is true when we look at businesses that are run or started by women. When they are at or near the top, women—like men—tend to hire and promote more of their own kind, or at least what they perceive to be their own kind, which is welcome until we have redressed the imbalances of the male-run system.[20] Take the incredible story of Conna Walker, the retail entrepreneur who started a clothing label at the age of 17 with a £3,000 loan from her father. In 2019, at the age of 26, she is making a yearly profit of £12 million, and employs a woman-heavy team, arguing that 'women understand our customer, so they know what we want to achieve'.[21] It makes sense, and clearly no inherent sense of resentment or hostility towards other women interfered with that logic. This example is supported by research. The Norway study mentioned in Part Three found very little evidence of any widespread 'queen bee' behaviour.[22] Another study by Credit Suisse concurred: looking at microfinance institutions, the bank found that female-led companies are much more likely to have a woman chair, a greater percentage of women clients, and more women on the board.[23]

In my interviews with women in top industrial positions, it is invariably the case that they are actively employing women in their teams, often as a conscious effort to bring women up, even in traditionally male-dominated industries such as engineering and aerospace.

In March 2019 I attended the launch party of *Commentland*, a new compendium on how the media has covered various political, social and economic crises in the decade since 2009. The volume was put together by the knowledge networking company Editorial Intelligence, and I had been invited to the launch by Editorial Intelligence's founder, the writer and networking professor Julia Hobsbawm, as I had contributed a piece on the financial crisis. The event was at the Mayfair Hotel, which had associations for me—I had started my working life there at the age of 17 as a fresh arrival from Greece, working as a room service telephonist in the kitchens in the afternoons and evenings, while studying for my A-levels in the mornings. I walked into the launch at the same time as a self-confident-looking lady called Benita Walia, who then proceeded to tell me that she had been an architect and had now become quite a successful artist. Benita insisted that she had suffered no discrimination as a woman, but on questioning attributed this entirely to the fact that many of the senior people she'd dealt with in her earlier career had been women—the leadership of local councils' architectural departments, which had been her main clients. Now, in her new incarnation as an artist, she again sells mostly to women in galleries and museums. How nice, I thought! And it supports the argument above that having a woman making the buying/hiring decisions is helpful to other women—in other words, that the 'queen bees' are few and far between.

Beyond my anecdotal encounters with women, research has also shown this. An extensive questionnaire on senior men and women in Norway found that the women in the survey, having themselves made it to top management, remained keener on gender equality measures than their male counterparts. It's true that, when one focuses on sectoral differences, the report found that senior businesswomen in private companies were less inclined to be sympathetic to gender equality measures than those in sectors outside business, such as the public sector or academia.[24] But the research suggests that any 'queen bee' behaviour that may exist is relatively limited in its impact—women in top positions had not pulled up the ladder for other women. Surely there have to be more than a couple of senior women for them to be held responsible for the lack of gender equality in an organisation! One assumes that in the case of business, there were still too few women, so that those who had made it were enjoying—or fearful for—their privileged positions too much to want to change things. This evidence from Norway, which is an overall example of good practice and early board quotas, suggests once again that the number to watch is how many women are on senior executive boards, and in senior positions more generally.

Are quotas part of the answer?

As you'll have guessed by now, my view is a resounding yes. The suspicion is that capitalist economies, despite already being subject to considerable government intervention, need a further strong dose of extra measures to deliver gender equality, for the reasons we explored in Part 1. The legislation of the last fifty years has helped in establishing basic principles and measures of equality, but the problem is still far from being solved in practice. Of course, women who want to opt out of the labour market for any reason, even temporarily, should be able to do so—but this should be out of free choice, not because they think they have no other choice. Does this matter? It certainly does! Not only is there an unquestionable issue of fairness and equal opportunity, but it is also through financial empowerment that the rest will follow, allowing women to be more involved in making policy and in shaping our culture. What's more, the economy will be more prosperous and society more equal. Resetting the gender power imbalance is a 'win-win', and if we need quotas for senior women to do it, then one can legitimately ask: What is there to object to?

Yet there is still resistance to the idea of quotas in many quarters. Occasionally, of course, one finds enlightened people at the top—and it helps if they are women. So quotas should gain acceptance as a reasonable and necessary policy as more women make it to the top. I did a panel discussion for the news outlet Tortoise with Ana Botín, head of Santander, on what needs to be done regarding gender equality. She said that, if you'd asked her ten years ago whether she was a feminist, she would have said no, but now she declares herself as one. She was against quotas then, but no longer opposes them, as things are moving too slowly. Botín told the panel how, when she first took control of the bank, she had a talk with her team in Spain, who were choosing new regional managers. On top in terms of capability was a woman, Carmen, but the head of HR told her that she wouldn't be appointed because she was away on maternity leave. Botín was shocked, and countered the decision. The woman was appointed and was still with the bank when we did the panel, one of Santander's star performers.

To those who argue that quotas have been 'done'— that they've been tried and they've failed—I would argue (as I have argued before)[25] that they have not yet been visited properly, at the right level. Ed Sibley, Deputy Governor of the Central Bank of Ireland and chair of the bank's diversity and inclusion steering group, has spoken of the need for 'targets', though in fact what he was describing sounded very much like 'quotas'. Of course, he wanted the 'targets' to be realistic and to 'target' the right variables. He referred to the Scandinavian board 'targets' (in fact, as we know, they are 'quotas'), worrying that they don't really change the culture of an organisation, as the women are just 'parachuted in'. The real 'targets', he says, need to be further down, at levels where women are involved in the running of affairs, so that they affect the pipeline to the top.[26] A very good point and one I agree with entirely.

I am not advocating tougher quotas on boardroom representation, which are irrelevant and just provide 'jobs for the girls'. Such quotas already exist, and are being tightened in many European countries, but their impact on senior representation in the private sector in particular has been very small. My suggestion is for a series of quotas for senior executive positions, adjusted by sector, with a time frame, penalties for non-compliance, and a sunset clause once cultures change. This is the only thing that will force firms to think and act long-term, in a consistent way that marks a real culture shift and takes investors and shareholders with them on that journey. Of course, they will ultimately benefit too, with better-balanced decision-making, a culture that attracts and retains the best men and women, greater productivity and, eventually, larger profits. And for the economy, greater presence of women decision-makers will allow for a more compassionate and flexible approach to working life, for mothers, fathers and all others. It should end long working hours, stop the rewarding of overtime and 'boys' club' networking, and maybe even herald the move to a formal 4-day week—rather than the informal one that exists today among many high-ups. (Who works on Fridays? Anyone? The Tube in London is empty on that day of the week, and the cafés full!)

Women's quotas for senior management, adjustable by sector and to be achieved over a period of years, would force companies to change their culture, work hard to keep the women's pipeline going to the top, and reduce any bias. This would also appeal to men, who could take advantage of the more flexible operation that would hopefully develop. No one likes regulation, but if it is done cleverly and flexibly then there's no reason why it can't work. In her research in this area, Beverley Nielsen has had feedback from young women in the legal profession, who point out that in Scandinavian countries where there are statutory quotas, women can leave their jobs to have children, knowing that there is a good chance they'll still make partner after they return. For Nielsen, this cultural impact is the biggest reason to implement legally binding quotas that force the effort required to drive the system, from school onwards, to produce equality.

Anything approaching gender equality is still a long way off, and the environment won't improve any faster until we have more women rising to be decision-makers. Only then will a culture develop in which fellow women can get the skills and experience they need to rise to such positions. Is there a chicken and egg situation here? It sounds like it, and if that's the case then we need considerable intervention to break the cycle and force a shift. As we saw in the Introduction, the Commonwealth Secretariat—which encompasses both developing and developed economies—argued that economic empowerment, through quotas, was a prerequisite for advancing women's participation in politics— and hence decision-making at all levels of government. It makes sense, therefore, for quotas to be continued where they exist and introduced where they do not.[27]

We can only hope that more governments and international organisations will soon start to agree.

Pay transparency

In the Introduction I talked about the problems created for women by information asymmetries. The market clears at suboptimal levels, because it doesn't allow them to know—or get paid—what they are really worth. A recent survey in the UK showed that most workers would welcome pay transparency if it meant an improvement in their relative position. This is what the UK Pay Reviews were meant to achieve. Predictably, this exercise in transparency revealed substantial pay gaps. At the BBC, large differences in salaries were revealed between men and women—and between different men, to be fair—doing effectively the same jobs. The gap was addressed by forcing men to accept pay cuts, rather than giving the women the difference in salary over a number of years. As a result, the BBC's percentage gap has now been reduced, not so much because of 'affirmative action'—though there was some—but also because many of the top-paid men have left rather than face salary cuts. And this was also the case in an example studied by academics in Denmark, who found that, once there was transparency, the result was eventually more equality—not because women got a pay rise, but because men's wage projections slowed. The company's profits improved! What an outcome!

Some progress has been made. But all the meaningful changes that have happened so far in Britain, for example, have required top-down intervention: the Equal Pay Act (1970), the Sex Discrimination Act (1975) and the Equality Act (2010), which made it illegal to pay people different rates for 'work of equivalent value'. It was under the Equality Act that the women cleaners of Birmingham triumphed in claiming pay equal to that of the men who collected refuse. Meanwhile, the practice of paying men more continues, as we saw in a UK case involving the majority-state-owned Royal Bank of Scotland. This centred around a female worker in the bank who was being paid some £30,000 a year less than men in a comparable role; she was sacked in 2017, but agreed a £150,000 settlement, as she was about to take her case to an industrial tribunal. The Unite union had said that this worker had been underpaid for seven years, and that there are still many other women in her position who will also be asking the Bank to make up for years of underpayment. It is extraordinary that this is still possible nearly 50 years after the Equal Pay Act was passed.[28] Again, we clearly need more than equal pay rights to achieve actual equal treatment.

In April 2017, the UK government implemented regulations compelling firms with more than 250 employees to disclose any gender pay gaps, after too few firms took part in a voluntary disclosure scheme.[29] This amounted to just over 10,000 Pay Reviews, including

200 small and medium enterprises that reported voluntarily. Put together, these reviews suggested a median pay gap in the UK as a whole of 9.7%.[30] The worst offenders were the construction industry, with a gap of some 25%; finance and insurance, at around 20%; and education close behind. Practices of course differed hugely within sectors. In higher education, for example, things may have seemed fairly uniform on the surface, with over nine out of ten British universities paying men more than women on average—but the 2018 Pay Reviews disclosed a mean pay gap ranging from 1% to 45%, and a median pay gap between 1.9% and 37.4%. For women in the top quartile of pay, the gap ranged from 22.4% to 64.4%.

As Bloomberg's David Hellier has written, the City is one of the worst offenders in the pay gap stakes. Women often represent the bulk of the workforce, and yet are mostly absent from senior leadership in many financial institutions.[31] The men at Goldman Sachs in the UK earn on average twice as much as the women, and those at HSBC more than twice as much. How long will it take for that gap to disappear if insufficient numbers of new women are promoted to senior positions? What is required is investment in the long term, which won't happen of its own accord given the instinctive short-termism of the City. In the financial sector in particular, there are also differences in bonuses, with women getting some 35% less on average. HSBC Holdings Plc, UK has a policy of increasing numbers of senior women, yet reports that only 23% of senior positions have gone to women, and the mean (average) pay gap has gone up to 61%, the highest among UK banks.

Professor Susan Vinnicombe of Cranfield University suggests that making organisations produce data about their gender pay gaps nudges them into action.[32] It's early days, perhaps, but the results to 2019 have been disappointing so far. The average hourly pay gap at the British operations of Goldman Sachs has gone down slightly (from 55% in 2018 to 51% in 2019) but remains very high.[33] According to the bank, the gap is not due to men being paid more for the same job, which is illegal—so the gap is mainly blamed on the lack of women in senior positions. The problem is that we can't be sure if this is true—not only do more women than men work in generally lower-paid part-time jobs, which complicates the picture, but there is often little transparency about individual wages. At the BBC, women are getting organised to sue for back pay, which will cost the Corporation a huge amount of money. But, of course, one can't do that until one knows what others get paid—not just between men and women, but also those going up and down the hierarchy. A recent survey suggested that, in fact, most British workers would like full pay transparency, as is already the case in places like Finland, Sweden and in particular Norway, where tax records, for example, are available for all to see online, for every worker in the economy.[34]

Pay transparency is important. But there are no financial incentives for good behaviour, nor fines for underperforming in this area. 'Shaming' does not appear to have a substantial impact. It seems to me that, until we introduce quotas to force financial institutions to increase appreciably the number of women in executive positions, nothing will change—a pay gap will remain so long as senior women continue to be severely outnumbered by men. But at least what pay transparency there is in various countries has exposed the gap in women's economic empowerment in a pretty stark way. And for women, despite the shock, there is something positive to be taken from it. Emma Bridgewater, MD and founder of a design group that now employs some 200 people, says:

> The gender pay gap law is one of best pieces of legislation to have been introduced in recent years. It has led us to be more searching in our conversations and it has revealed much to us. I wish government would make reporting more and more detailed as I think everyone should have to report these figures, they are crucial. Across the board we need equal representation. ... Now there are big women on the move and some fiefdoms are being defended. Unless there is equal representation in politics and in the boardroom we will not have reached our goal.

She went on to tell me: 'I used to think "tokenism" was not good. Now I don't. 50/50 is a reasonable goal. That will drive a lot of changes. We need to get power, and when we do, not behave like men'.

Would having more women economists help?

So we need policy-makers to be far more bold, and willing to commit openly to improving women's representation at senior levels of all kinds of organisation and work. But how can we achieve this? Well, one thing that might help with improving women's position in our economies would be having more women among economists themselves. As a result of the 'great recession' that followed the financial crisis in 2008, and the long time it has taken for countries to recover, particularly in the West, concerns about inequality are back at the top of the agenda amongst economists. The idea that 'the free market can't be wrong' and that it is always efficient no longer convinces anyone, other than a few die-hard free-marketeers. In many countries, real wages still have not returned to the levels they were at before 2008, and many women in lower-paid occupations have been particularly hard hit. To finally redress this gendered economic inequality, which existed before 2008 but has worsened since, is the only way to empower women in society more broadly. And it will need good economists who care about the issue, men and women.

In the UK the Royal Economic Society (RES), listening to its members, decided to make diversity its core area of focus in 2019/20. Its strategy document outlines the Society's intention to promote diversity in all its manifestations, including gender. People differ in the type of economics they are interested in studying, and gender plays a role in this. In a session on women economists at the 2019 RES annual conference, it was made very clear that we still have a long way to go to ensure that economics is taught in a way that encourages more women to take it up as a subject, both early on at school and later on as a degree or a career. There have been some improvements: 20 years ago, 25% of university economics departments in the UK had no women in them at all, and 75% had no female chairs. RES research suggests that all departments now include women academics, and it is rare to find one with no women holding a chair. But even so, only 26% of economics undergraduates in the UK today are women.

It's been clear throughout this book that we need government policy, leadership and regulation to tackle women's economic inequality, so of course the number of women economists in the public sector should be of particular importance. Thanks to more active government policy, the UK Civil Service generally has more women in senior policy positions than it once did. Yet even here we find that it is harder for women to rise to the very top. There are only a handful of female Permanent Secretaries, and there has yet to be a female Cabinet Secretary or Head of the Civil Service. The

Governor of the Bank of England has been a man since the Bank was established in 1694, though this may change with incumbent Mark Carney's replacement— at the time of writing, the search is on, and is being led by the all-women headhunters Sapphire. I was lucky to receive a couple of landmark appointments myself, becoming the first woman Chief Economist of the Trade and Industry Department in 2003, and the first female (joint) head of the Government Economics Service in 2007. I'm glad to report that after my male co-head David Ramsden went to the Bank of England as Deputy Governor, the GES is now headed by two women, again one from the Treasury and one from my old department, Business.

Other encouraging news is coming out of regulated services. At the time of writing, the head of Ofcom, the UK's media regulator, is Sharon White, an economist who was the first black person and the second woman to become a Permanent Second Secretary at the Treasury, and who has now been appointed as the first female chair of the John Lewis Partnership. So the influence of women economists is spreading. The Director of the Serious Fraud Office is also a woman, Lisa Osofsky, who in April 2019 attacked the lack of diversity at the top of society, arguing that this reduces the quality of decision-making. Following her policy announcement to this effect, the executive team of the SFO itself is now bucking the trend with a 50/50 gender balance.[35] But the truth is that we are still missing women from the economics profession around the world, and their absence in decision-making across all fields in the economy is being felt, particularly as the economic costs of homogeneity are increasingly evidenced.

The positive side of this is that there is now increasing focus on tackling the lack of diversity in the profession, as the above examples perhaps show. We can see this in both the public and the private sector and in academia. In April 2019 the Centre for Economic Policy Research (CEPR) launched a new Women in Economics initiative with the Swiss bank UBS. The CEPR President, Beatrice Weder di Mauro, said at the inauguration, 'The missing women in economics have become an issue, essentially because their share in academic positions is not progressing. It's a good time to showcase exceptional female economists and their research to encourage others.'[36] The initiative is led by CEPR's Vice President, London Business School Professor Hélène Rey, and its aim is to work with its member organisations to reverse the lack of information about women economists' achievements and redress the gender imbalance in the profession, in the hope of inspiring future generations. As Rey put it:

There are a number of exceptional women who do extremely interesting work in economics, from development to labour, to macroeconomics to finance. So the first thing is that we would like to showcase this exceptional work, because it is interesting and deserves more visibility. Second, we would like to use this CEPR Women in Economics project to create some role models for younger generations of girls and boys because we think that seeing that these women have achieved so much can inspire a lot of people.

All admirable thoughts. It is a shame, though, that the work of women economists has been obscured for so long, not helped by the absence of women economists in senior positions. We've seen throughout Part 3 that even where women are equally or over-represented in a profession, they are still under-represented in its leadership—so when there are far fewer women than men even entering the industry, what chance do they stand? Academic economists across the globe remain overwhelmingly male. *The Economist* calculates that only about a fifth of Europe's senior economists are women. A look at the US also reveals that, among full professors of economics, women make up only 15% of the total. According to a study published in early 2019 by the University of Warwick's Centre for Competitive Advantage in a Global Economy, the share of women academic economists was some 48% for lecturer positions, but 38% for senior lecturers and just 18% for professors. On a related note, women were also bunched at the lower end of the pay scale. Around 50% were in the bottom two salary brackets, and only 28% of those on a salary above £56,000 were women.[37]

It seems harder for women than for men to reach the higher career levels in economics, or any other subject, whether as a practitioner or as a professor. But it is not for want of trying, or lack of the necessary qualifications. Even Stephen Pinker—who believes that it is differences in preferences that lead women to go for particular professions rather than others—has been quoted referring to a study by Cornell University showing that, in almost all academic disciplines, women are more likely to land an interview for a post than a man. Aside from the fact that this doesn't make them more likely to get the job, the one subject area where women were less likely than men to land the interview is economics.[38]

Why is that? *The Economist* ran a long article in March 2019 outlining the relative lack of women economists, particularly in senior positions. But the one germ of an idea contained in the article struck me as genius. It is very likely that economists really believe that the free market works—especially economists in the States who believe that Friedman was right, the market can do no wrong, and market forces will eventually, inevitably, right the gender imbalance. Unfortunately, they don't. To my mind, there is no stronger proof of the need for intervention in the market than the poor outlook for women academic economists. The *Economist* piece quoted a study by the American Economic Association, which found that the academic environment for women economists is particularly intimidating.[39] According to the survey it conducted, some 46% of women respondents have apparently decided not to ask a question at a conference or present any ideas, worried that they may be treated unfairly, interrupted or attacked for lack of deep knowledge or understanding, as is often the case in academic seminars. The percentage for men was only 18%.

In the same survey, some 48% of women said they had faced discrimination at work.[40] For those who think that the balance has now in fact switched too much, against the men, the equivalent figure for men economists in academia was just 3%. A US study has shown that men are more likely to end up getting jobs in top-ranking departments offering economics PhDs, and more likely to publish in top journals, even if they graduated with similar types of qualifications to the women. There is also data suggesting that it generally takes longer for a woman economist to acquire tenure in an academic institution. Women seem to be as productive as men in terms of their output if it is judged by research papers, yet they are treated more harshly in peer reviews, and if they produce joint papers with a male economist, the man is more likely to be promoted first and to rise faster. There have been a number of studies focusing on the US which show that, in comparison with other academic subjects, women's career progression in economics seems to be slower.[41]

This may explain why, all through the system, few women become academic economists. It is not therefore surprising that, while the third woman has just won the Nobel Prize for Physics, a profession also dominated by men, only one woman has managed it for the Nobel Memorial Prize in Economic Sciences: the late Elinor Ostrom. Of course, the economics prize was a bit of a latecomer, having only been established in 1968, and Ostrom had been recognised for her work in all sorts of ways before winning the Nobel. But, for the moment at any rate—and I would love to be proven wrong—there doesn't seem to be anyone near joining her as number two. I said as much in my *Prospect* piece of October 2018, wondering where the next female Nobel winner would come from.[42]

The Nobel is an international prize, and the problem is clearly a global one. But research in the UK and the US may give us some clues as to the reasons behind it. According to one recent study, whether or not women university students enrolled in higher-level economics classes was majorly influenced by whether or not they knew women who were successful in the field. If not, they chose to do something else instead.[43] The article in *The Economist* also demonstrated this, quoting a recent issue of the *Journal of Economic Perspectives*, which showed that the number of female graduate economic students goes up if a woman is department chair, without any reduction in quality of candidates.[44]

* * *

So one thing is very clear: not enough women are entering economics, and the culture of the profession does not encourage them to. What can we do about this?

Part of the problem may well be the perceived requirement to be good at mathematics. A study by the Institute of Education at University College London suggested that maths is too masculine in the way it is taught at school, and that the types of careers perceived to be associated with the study of maths seem less appealing to girls.[45] Further up, the way economics is taught may also be reinforcing the notion that maths and economics are for boys and men. Something urgently needs to change if we are to close the pay gap, in economics and across the economy. Dame Frances Cairncross used to be Management Editor of *The Economist*. She has suggested a strong correlation in the UK between high lifetime earnings and an A-level in Maths.[46] Yet figures for 2015 show that, in England and Wales, only 18% of girls taking A-levels were doing Maths, compared to 37% of boys, among whom Maths was the most popular subject of all. For the subject Further Maths, often required to study STEM subjects at undergraduate level, the figures were 7% for boys and 2% for girls.

Sadly, economics is not taught as an A-level subject in all schools in the UK—many state schools don't offer it at all, so it is privileged students in independent (private) schools who have more exposure. Often, state-school students have no opportunity for the familiarisation required to encourage interest in a subject and its pursuit at university level. Surveys of 15–17-year-olds suggest that young people's image of economics is all about making money: of white men in suits! This may have something to do with the fact that only 30% of girls study the subject at A-level. There is a perception problem not only with economics but also with the core STEM subjects, where again only 24% of UK undergraduates are women—their numbers have gone up over time, but so have the men's, so the proportions have remained more or less the same. Girls making their choices at school will be affected by the lack of examples and role models. Dame Sue Ion, a leading UK nuclear engineer and Honorary President of the National Skills Academy for Nuclear, has pointed to the loneliness of women in science and engineering in a *Sunday Times* interview. She talked about what would happen when she and colleagues came out of a difficult meeting:

> all the men go to the gents' and I am left wondering what they are talking about in there. It was only later in my career that I was lucky enough to work with some extremely talented women and I'd be in the ladies' thinking: 'Well, this is a unique situation, we can have a discussion about what we are going to go back into this meeting with, just like the guys do in the gents'.[47]

The lack of confidence among girls in their ability to pursue STEM subjects is wider than in relation to maths and economics alone. A study by the Institute of Fiscal Studies, with which I have had a long association, in partnership with the STEM Skills Fund, examined the barriers to girls taking A-level Physics and Maths.[48] It found that girls get discouraged from continuing these subjects even if they did really well in them at GCSE, the qualification before A-level. Among high-achieving pupils who received the top grades (A* or A) in their Maths GCSE in 2010, only 36.5% of girls went on to do the subject at A-level, whereas the take-up by boys was 51.1%. For Physics, it was even worse: only 13.2 % of girls continued, against 39.3% of boys. This was not the case for Chemistry and certainly not for Biology, where more high-achieving girls than boys take the subject at A-level. A plausible explanation for this is that, while STEM careers overall are seen as 'for boys and men', the caring professions that require Biology and Chemistry, like medicine, have more women role models and are more appealing to women. The IFS report noted that:

> Teachers also perceive that the gender gap in STEM A-level is partly driven by girls not aspiring to work in STEM, and that this is strongly driven by male dominance: 75% agree or strongly agree that 'these girls don't aspire to work in STEM occupations and so don't need to take A-levels in STEM subjects'; and 80% of those agreeing or strongly agreeing say this is because 'STEM occupations tend to be male dominated'.[49]

How can we explain all this, other than by unconscious bias? It is confirmed, for teachers and students, boys and girls alike, that these are 'boys' subjects', because that is who does them—and so the cycle continues.

There is clearly a job to be done by economic institutes, such as the Royal Economic Society in the UK, going round and explaining what economics can offer, particularly to girls. An economics degree from, say, the LSE is one of the qualifications most valued by prospective employers, after computer science. The subject is changing, and that should be better conveyed to prospective students. This will hopefully erase the perception that economics is all about maths and modelling, and increase girls' confidence to tackle the subject. Behavioural economics is becoming more prevalent, combining economic decision-making and psychology, while a renewed focus by various universities on the need to equip economics graduates with the analytical thinking skills to support policy-making is attracting new entrants. There needs to be better understanding and publicising of the contribution that economics can make in addressing social problems, climate change, inequality and barriers to wellbeing. This is particularly important as research suggests that, overall, women care for the environment a bit more than men, and worry more about the future impact of things such as climate change.[50]

If we don't speak to our young people—especially our young women—about why different subjects might suit them, and about the financial benefits of certain subject and career choices, then we are perpetuating a market failure, because women are not ending up where they should. I spoke with a woman called Laura, a part-Asian and part-European charity worker in her late 20s. She loves her work, travels a lot to developing countries, and is enthused about the contribution she is making. The charity sector has a considerable number of senior women to act as role models. But now she feels that her career choices may be limited from here on in by the typical low pay in the sector, and that gender expectations played a part in leading her down this path. At school, she was just as good at sciences as at liberal arts subjects, yet no one steered her in the direction of STEM studies, which she now realises would have put her on a much higher wage trajectory than the voluntary sector. She studied English and languages instead, but is regretting not opting for science subjects, now that she knows how much better-paid she might have been.

The consequences of how we are educated, and of how schools present subjects to us, are felt by all, up and down the pay scale. These consequences are more dramatic for some than for others. Alex Marcham, my lovely 30-year-old hairdresser and single mother of a mixed-heritage baby, has been cutting my hair for a good ten years or longer—while an apprentice. She says that, at her school, a good girls' comprehensive (state school) in South London, there was very little career guidance, and she was left to choose for herself—there was no push to do well even in English or Maths. It was only when she decided she wanted to retrain in mental health counselling that she realised it was a major problem that she doesn't have even those minimal qualifications. Like many others in her position, Alex has been a victim of severe cutbacks to further education provision in the UK, leaving her unable to gain those qualifications in adulthood in order to pursue her dream. Instead she had to pay £600 to train as a barber, which she could ill afford. Even the teacher on that course informed the class that this was the last course they were running at all, as funding had been cut.

There is a desperate need for clear support and guidance for girls and young women that will open up career paths, while preparing them for what it will take to succeed. This is not only about encouraging them into certain subjects or professions, but also about making sure that they are as well-armed as possible against the gender inequality they will face. Suzanne Franks, an independent television news producer, published a book in 2000 called *Having None of It: Women, Men and the Future of Work*. In it she quoted a study of 900 previously high-flying female Harvard students, which concluded that those students had not been warned by anyone of how desperately difficult some individual personal choices would become for them as women in pursuit of a career.[51] Of course, we're hoping for a day when this is no longer the case, but until then, we at least need to equip our young generation as best we can.

Women vs robots

Before we end this reflection on ways to tackle economic inequality, we need to think especially about those future generations, and about the future in general. One thing that has surprised me is the gender imbalance among those bringing us the new AI age, which has not yet been well documented. The underrepresentation of women in the tech industries is a particular worry if this encourages data bias against women, which can be detrimental to women's interests. Certainly the feminist Caroline Criado-Perez, herself a behavioural economist, argues that it does in her book *Invisible Women*: just as poor, groupthink-based decisions can be made in board-rooms that aren't diverse, algorithms and interpreta-tions of data can be limited and skewed by a lack of consideration for women's particular and differing needs or circumstances, due to lack of women in the room.[52] Given their absence, and especially the lack of senior women working on the development of new technologies, we should be especially worried about what those changes will bring for women.

Elsewhere in this book we've discussed job segrega-tion: the effect of some sectors being more populated by women, and others by men. This by itself wouldn't mat-ter much, if it reflected an optimal allocation of workers throughout the production chain—if it were a sort of 'natural selection' that somehow ended up this way. But it is obvious that job segregation results from cultural and social norms that perceive some things as men's work and others as women's—doctors are men, women are nurses, for example. We know this is harmful to the economy, because it is not putting talent where it can best serve production and productivity—but even this might not be economically harmful to the individual, if the men's jobs and women's jobs were equally respected, valued and remunerated. The problem is that women are not just segregating into particular types of work, they are segregating into less well-paid types of work.

Figures for the UK in 2018 show that the vast majority of women work in relatively low-paid sectors: 21% of all women's jobs are in health and social work, 14% in wholesale and retail, and 12% in education, where the slashing of funding has had many deleterious effects. In fact, out of all healthcare and social-sector jobs in the UK, 79% are held by women. The figure in education is 70%.[53] The free market is clearly unable to deal with the driving bias behind this segregation, and as long as it is allowed to carry on unimpeded, progress towards women's empowerment—both economic and overall—will stall. This is a long-term problem, and urgent intervention is needed. As with climate change, we must address the iniquities of gendered job segregation, and broader gendered economic inequality, before the costs of reversing the trend become too large to handle. And that point of no return may be approaching much faster than we think.

The technological revolution taking place in the twenty-first century is likely to affect jobs across many sectors. But the IMF has calculated that the risks are higher for women. It argues that 50% of women educated no further than high-school level, in other words with no further specialism, are most at risk.[54] That compares with 40% of men. (The risk drops to just 1% for those with a bachelor's degree or higher.) The reason for this is obvious. In the current configuration of the global economy, women are found mostly in caring occupations, working as nurses, carers and teachers, and in service-sector jobs, such as hospitality and retail. These are precisely the areas that will be most touched by emerging technology around automation and artificial intelligence. Indeed, the IMF calculates that, even if you take into account differences in skills, experience and choice of occupation, some 5% of the global gender pay gap is due to working women's over-concentration in more routine functions.[55] So with many routine, middle-skilled jobs particularly threatened by technological change, addressing the iniquities of women's work and ensuring that they break the glass ceiling becomes an even more urgent task. Not only do women take home less pay than men through their lifetimes, but now they are also facing a greater risk of their job being taken by a machine.

There is a precedent for vast socioeconomic change disproportionately impacting women, and it is both recent and ongoing: the sobering experience of women during the era of austerity that followed the 2008 financial crisis in many countries. As we saw during that period of recession, women are often most affected when costs are cut, whether in private-sector firms needing to make redundancies or the public sector needing to make savings. The UK serves as a good example of this. Even in sectors where women are meant to be better represented, such as media, looking back at data and reports from the height of the recession makes for extraordinary reading, in terms of where the job cuts have fallen. *The Guardian* reported figures for 2009 suggesting that, since 2005, some 5,000 women in the UK had left television. The number of men was just 750.[56]

The 'belt-tightening' of state spending and public services has also dealt a disproportionate blow to women. A review found that by the end of 2014—when the bulk of the cuts had been implemented—85% of the burden from changes in the UK's tax and benefits system had fallen on women.[57] Danny Dorling's *A Better Politics* attributes much of the rise in women's mortality since 2008—faster than men's—to the Conservative/Liberal Democrat coalition government's cuts to social services in 2010–15.[58] Women tend to live longer and, unlike men, don't usually marry younger partners. As a result, elderly women often live on their own. They are also generally poorer, because they have generally done lower-paid jobs and therefore receive a smaller pension.

Thus they are more reliant than retired men on state provisions of social care. Worryingly, evidence from Scotland shows that women from a disadvantaged area have more years in bad health at the end of their lives than men, for example—the difference between advantaged and disadvantaged areas being 9.2 years for men, but 13.3 years for women.

Austerity in the UK also involved very substantial job cuts in the civil service and the wider public sector. Women have traditionally been over-represented in public-sector jobs, and some half a million of those jobs were lost. An extra 2 million jobs have been created in the private sector since the crash, many of them taken up by women, but these have often been lower-skilled and lower-paid service jobs, or self-employment, often on zero-hours contracts. The so-called 'gig economy' has brought about a more uncertain wage packet for all who work in it.

This is not replacing like for like, as many of these new jobs are far less secure and worse-paid. Public-sector jobs tend on average to be higher-paid, because the average level of qualifications is higher, and the pensions benefits are considerably higher. For women—and for many men—one of the advantages of the public sector is that it tends to have a more flexible attitude to working practices, which particularly suits the domestic and caring responsibilities that largely fall to women. The civil service, for example, operates a system of diversity targeting—even if it doesn't call it that—which allows greater flexibility, job-sharing at all levels, and fairer promotion processes. With the loss of public-sector opportunities, women have been forced to take flexibility at work where they can get it—often below their skills level, and without proper guarantees of holiday, pensions, income or even hours. Where will that leave them when even these lower-level routine jobs disappear?

And they are disappearing. The unstoppable rise of tech companies and online shopping, especially Amazon, is causing a huge decline in high-street viability and so in retail jobs, which has historically been a sector overwhelmingly occupied by women, and to which many new women migrated in the 2010s as public-sector cuts began to bite. Unfortunately, the timing for this move was not good, with savage cost-cutting among even large retail chains and the substitution of self-checkout machines for people on counters. More generally, any role that involves performing the same task repeatedly, whether it's taking blood pressure or cleaning a floor, is obviously vulnerable to automation.

We cannot afford to be complacent. Now, more than ever, is the time to start taking seriously the solutions proposed here, because without them there will be no change. Already the impact of current trends on inequality is shocking, despite the fact that, across the world, both absolute and relative poverty levels are declining. Our capitalist system tends to move women to inferior positions within the economy, and the inequality this creates has been worsened by the post-2008 financial crisis and austerity regimes implemented to deal with it. If anything, we can expect women's inequality to be exacerbated even further in this century, by continuing globalisation, continuing growth of precarious work, and continuing technological change. As Douglas McWilliams argues in *The Inequality Paradox*, the coming wave of technological development known as the fourth industrial revolution presents even more challenges, particularly for the lower-skilled jobs that many women find themselves working today.[59] This is a crisis waiting to happen.

CONCLUSIONS

The only conclusion one can reach after looking at the place of women in our economies is that economic disempowerment remains the name of the game. Contemporary feminism may demand equality of status in all aspects of life, but it must focus on economic empowerment. Until that is achieved, it will be impossible for decision-makers—and a good proportion of them will need to be women—to change the 'capitalist' norms that currently prevent the market from working efficiently. Only then, when women are men's economic equals, will we have social justice.

What's more, the evidence clearly shows that only then will we have optimal economic efficiency and growth. Women's empowerment is critical to our ability to use our resources in the best possible manner. But, as with other historic injustices, overcoming women's economic inequality needs government intervention, for a simple reason. The current state of women at work—their lower pay and status in the labour market, the barriers to them participating in that market at all—represents a profound and quantifiable market failure, resulting from a capitalist system that cannot correct it when left to its own devices. And the emerging wave of new technology and artificial intelligence is likely to make things worse.

There are lots of scholarly books on capitalism, but as I was researching the vast array of articles on the subject, I came across one written not by an academic, but by a practitioner—someone who invests his money globally and has done well out of the system. He is the American billionaire Ray Dalio, founder of Bridgewater Associates, one of the world's biggest hedge funds. It may be that Dalio's very success encouraged him to look more closely at how capitalism works, and specifically to look at the statistics on how capitalism plays out in the US. Though the data is well documented, like many observers before him he was horrified by the poverty trap of single parents and their children, and also by the longer-term impact and costs of poor educational attainment, for both individuals and society as a whole. He could have been talking about women—in fact, he probably was, but hadn't quite realised it. Anyway, his paper, posted on LinkedIn, was about 'Why and how capitalism needs to be reformed'. We probably all agree, post-2008, that reform is needed. But I loved the simplicity and straightforwardness of his conclusion: 'The problem is that capitalists typically don't know how to divide the pie well, and socialists typically don't know how to grow it well.'[1] The answer is going to have to be a better version of the current, inadequate compromise between a centrally dictated economy and completely unregulated free markets.

Of course, attitudes change only slowly, and in many cases the transition requires long-term thinking which may not be forthcoming from businesses in a liberal-market economy driven by short-term profit. But changing attitudes doesn't seem to be the problem. Young women appear much more confident than my generation was at the same age—they are more aware of gender inequality and more empowered to speak up about it. Some organisations, stung by their public shaming and workforce anger following revelations about pay gaps, have been quick to announce measures to rectify the situation.[2] They have also been pushed to act by the way the younger generation is beginning to examine more closely firms' corporate social responsibility commitments.[3] According to the UK's Equality and Human Rights Commission, as of 2018 many prospective employees, and as many as two thirds of women applicants, are investigating an organisation's pay gap before applying for a job.[4] I have spoken with many young professionals who are not shy in coming up with their stories of frustration.

Yet they still have those stories to share—as soon as young women enter the labour market, the obstacles start to pile on. The evidence across the world remains bleak. For all that the cultural and social feminist move-ment has done to change what is or isn't considered acceptable treatment of women, they are still given an inferior place in our economies. And no wonder, when this is the case, that unconscious bias perpetuates the cycle of disempowerment.

Even if organisations feel spurred to instigate real change through improvements to promotion practices, and even if they are able to reduce or overcome their unconscious bias, this will take a very long time on the current trajectory, given that much of the pay gap is in fact a seniority gap between men and women. It will be difficult simply to find enough senior and trained women to fill the top posts instantly. This is why, as we saw in Part 1, results of greater transparency through published pay gaps haven't, in the first couple of years, been encouraging. If anything, it looks in 2019 as if the gap may have widened in the UK, with a median gap across 10,428 reporting employers of 11.9%, compared with 11.8% in 2018. There were still no sectors that reported paying women and men equally.[5] For the change to happen 'naturally' will simply be too slow to make any discernible difference for the younger genera-tions entering work. We need a way to speed up progress, or the girls among them will see their aspirations dashed.

There is no evidence that women are any less produc-tive than men doing similar jobs, or less effective in navigating politics; nor that they have fewer leadership qualities, or are less ambitious. They are not left poorer, in less senior positions and unable to fully utilise their skills—even when they are equally or better educated—because it makes long-term economic or business sense. We have seen throughout this book that the entrenched cycles of women's inequality are painful for individual women and their households, a block on national efficiency, and a threat to social harmony. None of this is good for GDP or for the externalities that GDP can't measure. We've also seen that women are unnaturally concentrated in certain sectors, and kept out of decision-making and creative roles, even in higher-skilled areas where they dominate the overall workforce, such as teaching or the arts. If women aren't given equal access to all sectors and to leadership, they will be most vulnerable to the coming AI and automation revolutions, as their jobs will be threatened with extinction.

But there is something standing in the way of society responding to these problems: the short-termism of free-market capitalism, which simply can't prioritise these concerns without intervention. It's worth us recapping just how this vicious cycle works against women.

* * *

There is lack of sufficient flexibility in the workplace to accommodate women's needs. Serious effort has gone into understanding the impact of flexible working on the economy in general, and research from the UK's HR professional body, the Chartered Institute of Personnel Development, has shown clear benefits to productivity, through better staff engagement and performance. New technology has helped, facilitating remote working, but it has also led to new business structures and models facilitated by digital platforms and apps. This has given rise to what is known as the 'gig economy', characterised by low pay, lack of rights and support, and high insecurity. Similarly, while UK law now allows any worker of 26 weeks' employment to request flexible working, such requests are often refused—many firms cite 'business reasons'. This inflexible work culture, seen across the globalised and permanently connected world, is a gendered problem, because the burden of domestic and caring work falls overwhelmingly on women. This is a market failure, because it results in suboptimal allocation of resources (not all women would best serve the economy at home).

This lack of flexibility leads to a large percentage of women doing part-time work. This trend is particularly pronounced in the UK, where 41% of women work part-time, versus 13% of men. This is clearly linked to childcare considerations: the academic literature, evaluating policy impacts worldwide, has found overwhelming evidence that lack of free or heavily subsidised preschool education or childcare has a strong negative impact on women's ability to work, with extensively documented negative effects on the individual, the household and the national economy. Of course, this is a market failure, because children are the future work-force—well-cared-for and well-educated children are a clear economic asset, and so childcare should be highly valued, whether that means compensating mothers for this work 'outside the labour force' or the state paying for somebody else to do it. Men's average hourly wage doing part-time work is actually lower than women's, because of the higher calibre of women who go part-time due to childcare considerations, but the pensions gap is exacerbated by women working fewer hours over-all, increasing the likelihood that women will end their lives in poverty.

Women being forced into part-time work also contrib-utes to the pay gap. Going part-time will harm your chance of promotion and career progression. This is partly a real loss of experience, skills, training, network-ing and time to move up, but it is also due to perceptions among management, because our inflexible work culture values presenteeism. The domestic and caring burden of women makes it difficult for them to overcome the information asymmetries that this culture perpetuates: the high importance of networking in a cut-throat capi-talist economy, if you want to gain knowledge about job opportunities and insider culture. The lack of senior women adds to the information asymmetry between men and women, as we end up with fewer role models and senior advisors, and this problem starts in school. Girls are not told clearly what it is in their best interest to study, let alone properly prepared for the gendered obstacles they will face, or encouraged to network. Again this is a market failure, because it leads to 'imperfect market competition'; if some are held back from competing, then the best will not win.

All of the above difficulties result in a concentration of women in low-paid sectors, and lower down in the internal hierarchy. These lower-status jobs are often easier to fit around domestic work, and when women are having trouble getting into more highly skilled or higher-paid jobs, they will have no choice but to take the work they can get. Not only does this affect the growth of the economy overall, but also has serious consequences for women's lifetime earnings. Segregation into low-paid or low-valued sectors reduces women's ability to achieve economic equality with men, and makes women more economically vulnerable. Women end up with no effective voice in society, and are unable to explain the public value of these services, for which they should be properly remunerated. This is a double market failure: it reduces the competitive forces that men would otherwise face across the economy (and market capitalism dictates that competition is needed to bring out the best), and the market does not allow for proper valuation of certain assets that women often bring to the market.

Lack of women in senior positions, and in certain sectors, creates 'bounded rationality'. Economists define bounded rationality as the idea that individuals are limited in their ability to make rational decisions by the information available to them, and the cognitive limitations of their minds. In other words, another source of market failure. One excellent example is the lack of awareness and understanding of the benefits that women would bring to the workforce in general, and to leadership of an organisation in particular. The IMF has argued that what is often missing is an understanding that women bring complementary skills—particular skills rather than simply equivalent skills—that would disproportionately raise productivity and economic welfare if put to proper use. These include greater consideration for the big, long-term picture and a more cautious approach to decision-making. We've also seen plenty of evidence in this book that diversity is good for innovation, productivity and growth, but this evidence is insufficiently disseminated and recognised. The US-born and -educated Ann Francke, Chief Executive of the UK's Chartered Management Institute and champion of diversity, declared in an interview with *The Sunday Times*: 'Look at the business case for gender balance. If you miss that, you will miss talent.'

Bounded rationality also creates the phenomenon of bias. If people can only make rational decisions within the limits of their knowledge, then it is harder for them to conclude a woman should be the chief executive of an engineering firm, if they don't know any women who are. The patterns of domestic responsibilities, part-time work, job segregation and difficulty of progression reinforce gender stereotypes, which leads in turn to both overt and unconscious bias, perpetuating those patterns. More men in senior roles means more men and fewer women being hired, even though the literature strongly suggests that hiring after your own image leads to suboptimal outcomes for your own organisation and for the economy as a whole. We can see pay gaps and seniority gaps even with all other things—such as social class or education levels—being equal, and often there is simply nothing to explain this but unconscious bias. Bounded rationality is evident here, in spades, and the market is failing to allocate its resources efficiently.

The same bias even disadvantages women who try to start businesses of their own. A global mix of covert and overt discrimination means that there isn't enough funding for women entrepreneurs, despite the fact that entrepreneurship is a major driver of productivity and innovation, and hence competitiveness in the economy. Women are less likely to get funding for their ideas, and gender expectations worsen the situation by inhibiting them from demanding what they deserve. Interviews with successful women throughout this book have shown widespread experience of 'impostor syndrome'— a fear that they don't really deserve or belong in the senior role they have reached. That suggests a continued lack of confidence and fear of failure to which they may have been conditioned, and it affects women trying to raise capital just as it affects women who deserve, but perhaps won't ask for, a pay rise.

Free-market capitalism is inherently short-termist, which prevents these issues from being measured, understood and confronted. Ironically, women might have the most to contribute in business, politics and economics or finance, since they're known to be more long-termist in their thinking, but their under-representation in decision-making roles makes this unlikely. The market is simply unable to sort out market failures by itself, as this requires a long-term commitment in capital and social policy, amounting in this case to a re-evaluation of the value of work and of women's contributions. In short, capitalism does not and cannot empower women.

So what next?

Women do not face a level playing field when it comes to paid work, and their work outside the market is not rewarded. Capitalism may be considered to be better than socialism at growing the pie, but in not knowing how to divide the pie more equably, it is also constraining the growth that can be achieved. The result is that we all, men and women, end up with a smaller pie than we could have had. So what can be done about this?

Firstly, across the world, there are countless statutory and societal or cultural restrictions on women's labour market participation, limiting their employment in certain sectors, their hours, their ability to complete education and receive qualifications, or their financial independence. In countries—most obviously, but not exclusively, developing economies—where there are legal or social restrictions on women's work, these barriers must be removed. Research signposted by the World Bank shows a negative correlation between inaccessibility of certain jobs and women's labour participation.[6] Even at the simplest level, removing small but common inhibitions, such as night-time restrictions on women's hours, increases their chances of moving to a top management position.[7] Delaying early marriage adds hugely to the human-capital and growth potential of an economy, as we can see in the history of the West. So does the presence of statutory women's rights, including property rights, the right to be the head of a household, and equal access to education. The research finds that, not only does this add to the availability of human capital, but it closes the wage gap, creates intergenerational educational advantages, and leads to a dynamic improvement in household incomes and GDP.

Secondly, Western governments that have already passed plenty of such legislation still need to intervene, to increase women's representation in leading roles across all sectors, and not just those where male numbers dominate.

The state is needed to fight the short-termism that the markets instinctively reach for by combatting unconscious bias. If the market won't acknowledge the long-term necessity of women's equality, then we need to make the issue an urgent problem for profits and growth. We need not just monitoring of the inequalities that exist, but penalties for not improving on them; organisations should be forced to publish plans on how they intend to deal with the issue, and over what period, so that failure to achieve these aims can be held to account. Voluntary targets are much less effective than quotas that bind.

On top of this regulation, what is also required is a better structure of support for women to succeed. The state should do its best to counter the information asymmetries getting in their way, starting with early careers advice making clear the possibility and advantages of study and career options. Women should be kept from falling behind due to motherhood or other caring responsibilities: governments should enforce non-transferable paternity leave, provide heavily subsidised childcare support, and oversee greater flexibility in the workplace. Both men and women would be helped to remain in an organisation by practices such as continuing to offer training during leave, granting properly remunerated flexible working after the leave is over, and enabling and encouraging job shares at senior levels. And, for those doing unpaid work, there should be a minimum pay per hour, above the minimum wage, to compensate women for this contribution to the economy.

It's true that governments have noted women's limited access to leadership, and have tended to intervene in the labour market mainly to legislate against discrimination. But, on the whole, these interventions have been rather meek, and insufficiently implemented and enforced. As a result, improvements in women's empowerment have happened too slowly in most countries. Conscious and unconscious bias against women in the workplace is too deeply engrained across most societies—Western, Eastern, Asian, African. We need radical, decisive and fully committed action for a long-term change, for the benefit of all.

* * *

The theoretical market economics case for tackling women's inequality in the labour market is clear. So is the business case for having more women in senior decision-making positions, as research has shown again and again.[8] The public sector is ahead, but most of the private sector is still lagging behind. Financial-sector firms, the worst culprits, are making an effort but are mostly just talking the talk. Although much has been said about the positive impact of diversity, there is still a lack of understanding of gender inequality's implications for an organisation's long-term sustainability, and the economy's. This is because the market's pricing mechanisms simply can't account for this unaided.

This book has explored all sorts of different ways in which governments and businesses have tried to address women's economic inequality. Some have been voluntary, others more prescriptive, and an insufficient number have been truly effective and enforceable. Overall, it has been legal interventions with real consequences for non-compliance that have had the greatest result. But even those have only moved things slightly forwards. Overall, there has been no system change: a man will still get hired to replace another one, as it is the easy, lazy, seemingly least risky solution. Money will be lent to a man's start up, as he will more easily tick the various boxes. And half the population is still suffering from lower incomes, poorer prospects and a greater vulnerability to leading a life of poverty, while the nations in which they live also suffer as a result.

Without a serious, big-picture intervention from governments, the market failures we've spoken about will continue to exist—in fact, they may get bigger, if the challenges of the twenty-first century play out as we suspect. It is time to take on the assumption that capitalism will clear all, and the 'invisible hand' of markets will solve our problems for us at anything more than a suboptimal level. It is time for us to call this gender inequality what it is—a market failure—and to redress it. It is time for governments and the private sector to partner in such a way as to turn this into a 'win-win' for all. The question is no longer: 'Can we afford to fix this?' It is: 'Can we afford not to fix this?' There is no way to justify failure to act here—capitalism simply won't save us.

APPENDIX

This Appendix contains a few more 'big picture' illustrations that can help us understand the nature and scale of the problem we are facing with women's economic inequality, and why all countries have an interest in fixing it. I am of course an economist, and we have a particular weakness for charts.

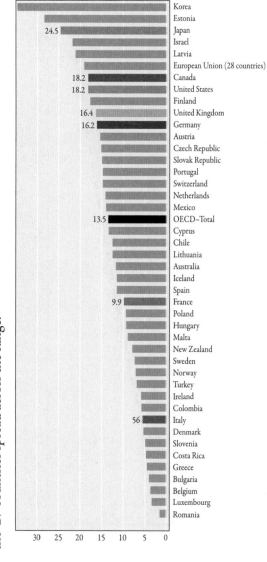

Fig. 1: The percentage median gender pay gap of different developed nations as of 2018, showing the G7 countries spread across the range.

Source: OECD (2019), Gender wage gap (indicator). doi: 10.1787/7cee77aa-en (Accessed on 26 July 2019).

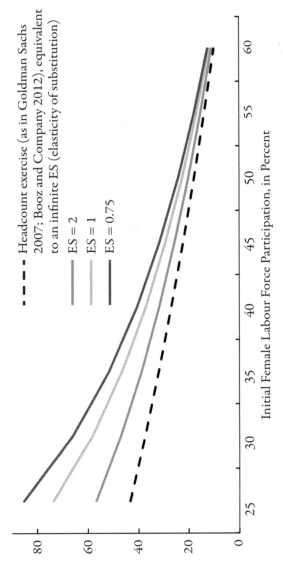

Fig. 2: GDP gains from closing the gap between men's and women's participation in the workforce.

Headcount exercise (as in Goldman Sachs 2007; Booz and Company 2012), equivalent to an infinite ES (elasticity of substitution)

ES = 2
ES = 1
ES = 0.75

Initial Female Labour Force Participation, in Percent

Source: J.D. Ostry, J. Alvarez, R. Espinoza, and C. Papageorgiou, 'Economic Gains from Gender Inclusion: New Mechanisms, New Evidence', IMF staff discussion note 18/06, October 2018.

Fig. 3: Welfare and GDP gains to be made from eliminating the barriers to women's labour force participation (FLFP). The Middle East and North Africa is the region with the most to gain, due to its currently high FLFP barrier.

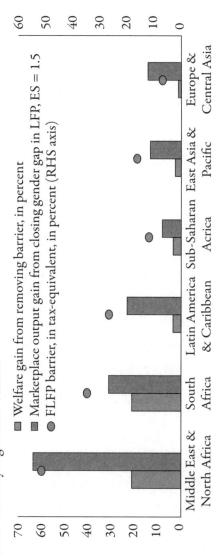

Notes: FLFP = female labour force participation. LFP = least fixed point. ES = elasticity of substitution.

Source: J.D. Ostry, J. Alvarez, R. Espinoza, and C. Papageorgiou, 'Economic Gains from Gender Inclusion: New Mechanisms, New Evidence,' IMF staff discussion note 18/06, October 2018.

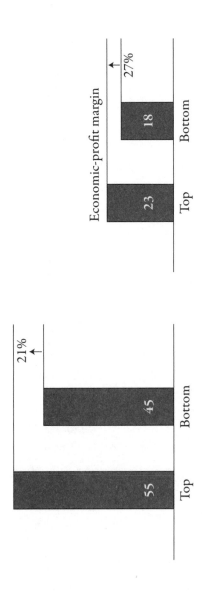

Fig. 4: Greater likelihood of a firm's financial performance being above the national industry median, if there is gender diversity on the executive team. This shows that having women as well as men in leadership is strongly correlated with profitability and value creation.

Notes: Results are statistically significant at p-value <0.05. Measuring EBIT = average earnings before interest and tax.

Source: Vivian Hunt et al., 'Delivering Through Diversity', McKinsey & Company, January 2018.

Fig. 5: Overall, European women's representation on boards has been improving in the twenty-first century.

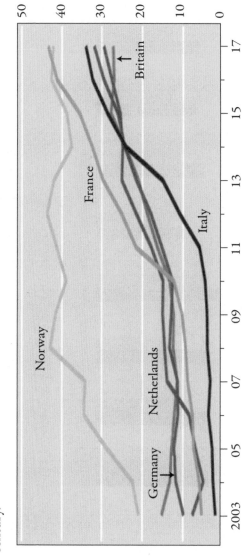

Note: women as a percentage of board membership for large, listed firms.

Source: European Institute for Gender Equality/*The Economist*, 'Ten years on from Norway's quota for women on corporate boards', 17 February 2018.

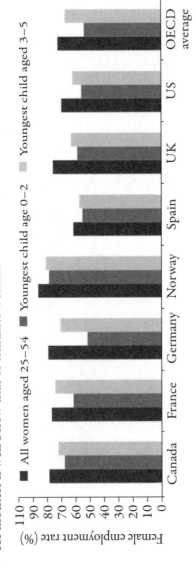

Fig. 6: Women's employment rate in OECD nations, comparing all women with mothers of very young and young children. In most countries, including the ones shown here, the employment rate for mothers is well below that of childless women.

Note: The data for Norway is derived from administrative registries of population, demographics, and income/tax.

Source: Sarah Cattan, 'Can universal preschool increase the labor supply of mothers?', *IZA World of Labor* 2016:312, November 2016; calculations based on data from the OECD Family Database (LMF1.2 Maternal employment).

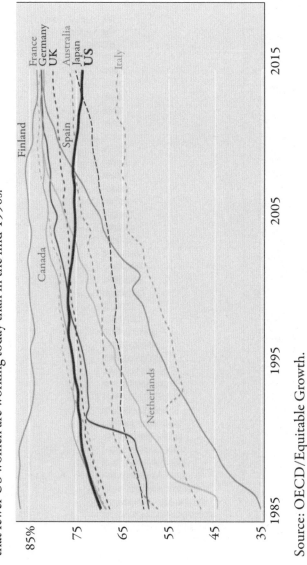

Fig. 7: Women's labour force participation in major OECD countries, from 1985 to 2015, showing that fewer US women are working today than in the mid-1990s.

Source: OECD/Equitable Growth.

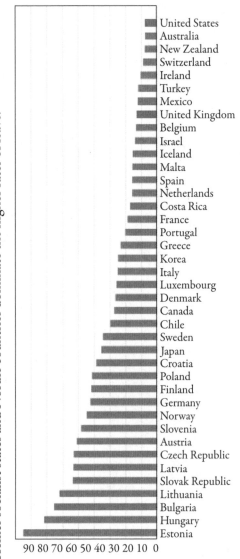

Fig. 8: Generosity of maternity pay in different OECD nations in 2016, measuring total number of weeks on full pay. The UK and US are significantly less generous than their G7 partners, though former socialist states and Nordic countries dominate the higher rates of leave.

Source: OECD Family Database/OECD Social Policy Division—Directorate of Employment, Labour and Social Affairs, updated 26 October 2017.

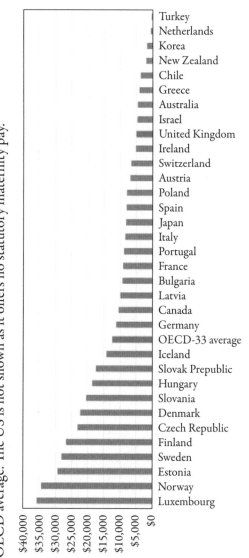

Fig. 9: Public spending, per child born, on all parental leave (both maternity and overall parental leave), in US dollars, across different OECD nations. Again, the UK spends significantly under the OECD average. The US is not shown as it offers no statutory maternity pay.

Source: OECD Family Database/OECD Social Policy Division—Directorate of Employment, Labour and Social Affairs/OECD Social Expenditure Database/OECD Health Statistics, 2013.

NOTES

INTRODUCTION

1. BBC News, '"I was made redundant when I was on maternity leave"', 19 February 2018, https://www.bbc.co.uk/news/business-43107 518; Alexandra Topping, 'UK bosses believe women should say at interview if they are pregnant—report', *The Guardian*, 19 February 2018.

2. Fawcett Society, *The Changing Labour Market 2: Women, low pay and gender equality in the emerging recovery*, August 2014, https://www.fawcettsociety.org.uk/Handlers/Download.ashx?IDMF=0ad02d8e-0445-4b8d-bfc1-1ae54407f139x

3. ONS, *Understanding the gender pay gap in the UK*, 17 January 2018, https://backup.ons.gov.uk/wp-content/uploads/sites/3/2018/01/Understanding-the-gender-pay-gap-in-the-UK.pdf

4. Katie Scott, 'McKinsey and Company reports a 23.8% mean gender pay gap', *Employee Benefits*, 19 February 2018, https://www.employeebenefits.co.uk/issues/february-2018/mckinsey-company-gender-pay-gap/

5. See Homes England website: https://www.gov.uk/government/organisations/homes-england

6. Jack Simpson, 'Homes England boss slams body's lack of progress on gender pay', *Inside Housing*, 1 April 2019, https://www.insidehousing.co.uk/news/homes-england-boss-slams-bodys-lack-of-progress-on-gender-pay-60834

7. Esmee Joinson-Evans, 'Wishing for equality', *24 Housing*, 8 March 2019, https://www.24housing.co.uk/magazine-article/wishing-for-equality/

8. ONS, 'Women shoulder the responsibility of "unpaid work"', 10 November 2016, https://www.ons.gov.uk/employmentandlabourmarket/peopleinwork/earningsandworkinghours/articles/womenshouldertheresponsibilityofunpaidwork/2016-11-10

9. Olivia Goldhill, 'How much is a housewife worth?', *The Daily Telegraph*, 15 October 2014.

10. Royal Society of Edinburgh, *Inequality: Good for the Rich, Bad for the Economy?*, advice paper 16–23, September 2016, https://www.rse.org.uk/cms/files/advice-papers/2016/AP16_23.pdf

11. E.A. Hanushek & L. Woessmann, 'Do Better Schools Lead to More Growth? Cognitive Skills, Economic Outcomes, and Causation', *Journal of Economic Growth* 17 (4), 2012, pp. 267–321.

12. C. Diebolt & F. Perrin (2013), "From Stagnation to Sustained Growth: The Role of Female Empowerment", *American Economic Review: Papers and Proceedings* 103, 2012, pp. 545–49.

13. J. Baten, and A. M. de Pleijt, 'Girl power Generates Superstars in Long-term Development: Female Autonomy and Human Capital Formation in Early Modern Europe', CEPR Discussion Paper no. 13348, 2018.

14. Pedro Carneiro, Costas Meghir, Matthias Parey, 'Maternal Education, Home Environments and the Development of Children and Adolescents', 22 November 2007, https://voxeu.org/article/intergenerational-payoffs-mothers-education

15. Royal Economic Society, 'Education reduces the rates of early marriage: evidence from rural India', summary of paper by Abi Adams & Alison Andrew, 'Preferences and Beliefs in the Marriage Market for Young Brides', RES annual conference, Warwick University, April 2019, https://www.res.org.uk/resources-page/education-reduces-the-rates-of-early-marriage-evidence-from-rural-india.html

16. Forward UK, *National Survey on the Drivers and Consequences of Child Marriage in Tanzania*, February 2017, https://www.forwarduk.org.uk/wp-content/uploads/2019/06/Forward-230-Page-Report-2017-Updated-Branding-WEB.pdf

17. Jon Henley, 'Swiss women strike to demand equal pay', *The Guardian*, 14 June 2019, https://www.theguardian.com/world/2019/jun/14/swiss-women-strike-demand-equal-pay

18. Justin McCurry, 'Women outperform men after Japan medical school stops rigging exam scores', *The Guardian*, 19 June 2019, https://www.theguardian.com/world/2019/jun/19/women-outperform-men-after-japan-medical-school-stops-rigging-exam-scores

19. Victoria Pinoncely & Mario Washington-Ihieme, *Culture Club: Social Mobility in the Creative and Cultural Industries*, Centre for London, February 2019, https://www.centreforlondon.org/wp-content/uploads/2019/02/Report-Culture-Club-Digital.pdf

20. V. Pryce, A. Ross & P. Urwin, *It's the Economy, Stupid: Economics for Voters*, London: Biteback, 2015.

21. 'Does Brexit really mean Brexit?', Annual Change Lecture organised by the Worshipful Company of Management Consultants, Warwick in London, University of Warwick, 11 May 2017.

22. Sharon Mavin & Carole Elliott, 'Gender should be on the agenda of business schools', *LSE Business Review*, 23 January 2018, https://blogs.lse.ac.uk/businessreview/2018/01/23/gender-should-be-on-the-agenda-of-business-schools/

23. Alison Wolf, *The XX Factor: How Working Women are Creating a New Society*, London: Profile, 2013.

24. She took over from Lord Nick Stern, for whom I had worked in government.

25. OMFIF, 'Gender Balance Index 2019', https://www.omfif.org/analysis/gender-balance-index-2018/

26. *The Times*, 19 April 2019, p. 29.

27. Mary Beard, *Women and Power*, London: Profile, 2017.

28. Owen Bowcott & Caelainn Barr, 'Just 1.5% of all rape cases lead to charge or summons, data reveals', *The Guardian*, 26 July 2019.

29. Michael Gyekye, 'Women's leadership and participation in decision-making in the Commonwealth', The Commonwealth, 17 August 2016, http://thecommonwealth.org/media/news/women-leadership-and-participation-tion-decision-making-commonwealth

30. European Parliament Directorate-General for Internal Policies, Policy Dept C: Citizens' Rights and Constitutional Affairs, *Women in decision-making: The role of the new media for increased political participation*, June

2013, http://www.europarl.europa.eu/RegData/etudes/etudes/join/2013/493010/IPOL-FEMM_ET(2013)493010_EN.pdf

31. Lorna Finlayson, 'Travelling in the Wrong Direction', *London Review of Books*, 4 July 2019.

32. Danae Kyriakopoulou, 'Gender balance in central banks', OMFIF, 23 April 2019, https://www.omfif.org/analysis/commentary/2019/april/gender-balance-in-central-banks/; International Finance Corporation, *Moving toward gender balance in private equity and venture capital*, 2019, https://www.ifc.org/wps/wcm/connect/topics_ext_content/ifc_external_corporate_site/gender+at+ifc/resources/gender-balance-in-emerging-markets

33. The OMFIF Podcast, 'GBI Series: Gender Diversity in Central Banks', Ed Sibley in conversation with Danae Kyriakopoulou, 11 February 2019, https://www.omfif.org/meetings/podcasts/2019/february/gbi-series-gender-diversity-in-central-banks/

34. Donato Masciandaro, Paola Profeta, Davide Romelli, 'Why women matter in monetary policymaking', VOX CEPR Policy Portal, 25 September 2018, https://voxeu.org/article/why-women-matter-monetary-policymaking

35. The OMFIF Podcast, 'Gender Diversity in Central Banks'.

36. Christine Lagarde & Jonathan D. Ostry, 'The macroeconomic benefits of gender diversity', VOX CEPR Policy Portal, 5 December 2018, https://voxeu.org/article/macroeconomic-benefits-gender-diversity

PART ONE: WOMEN UNDER CAPITALISM

1. Kristen R. Ghodsee, 'Why Women Had Better Sex Under Socialism', *The New York Times*, 12 August 2017, https://www.nytimes.com/2017/08/12/opinion/why-women-had-better-sex-under-socialism.html

2. J. Kay, *Other People's Money: Masters of the Universe or Servants of the People?*, London: Profile, 2016.

3. World Economic Forum, *The Global Gender Gap Report*, 2017, http://reports.weforum.org/global-gender-gap-report-2017/?doing_wp_cron=1554308998.3283689022064208984375

4. *The Economist*, 'Letters: On equality, Britain, Singapore, judo, airports, business cards', 11 April 2015, https://www.economist.com/letters/2015/04/11/letters

NOTES pp [56–61]

5. Andrew Powell, *Women and the Economy*, House of Commons briefing paper number CBP06838, 8 March 2019, https://researchbriefings.files. parliament.uk/documents/SN06838/SN06838.pdf

6. Alexandra Topping & Caelainn Barr, 'What you need to know about gender pay gap reporting', *The Guardian*, 28 February 2018, https://www. theguardian.com/news/2018/feb/28/what-you-need-to-know-about-gender-pay-gap-reporting

7. ONS, 'Gender pay gap in the UK: 2018', press release, 25 October 2018, https://www.ons.gov.uk/employmentandlabourmarket/peopleinwork/ earningsandworkinghours/bulletins/genderpaygapintheuk/2018

8. Full Fact, 'Do women earn less than men in the UK?', 16 November 2017, https://fullfact.org/economy/UK_gender_pay_gap/

9. *Market Inspector*, 'Women in Top Leadership Positions', 22 November 2017, https://www.market-inspector.co.uk/blog/2017/11/women-in-top-leadership-positions-around-the-world

10. Jean Blaquière & Pierre Zéau, 'Les inégalités femmes–hommes dans le monde', *Le Figaro*, 8 March 2019, http://www.lefigaro.fr/economie/le-scan-eco/2019/03/08/2900120190308ARTFIG00019-les-inegalites-femmes-hommes-dans-le-monde.php

11. Devon Delfino, '12 countries where men earn significantly more than women', *Business Insider*, 17 August 2018, https://www.businessinsider. com/countries-with-the-gender-pay-gap-2018–8?r=US&IR=T

12. June E. O'Neill & Dave M. O'Neill, *The Declining Importance of Race and Gender in the Labor Market: The Role of Federal Employment Policies*, Washington, DC: AEI Press, 2012.

13. Horia Mustafa Douine, 'Les 3 chiffres de l'inégalité salariale entre les hommes et les femmes', *Le Figaro*, 4 March 2019, http://www.lefigaro.fr/ social/2019/03/04/20011-20190304ARTFIG00188-les-3-chiffres-de-l-inegalite-salariale-entre-les-hommes-et-les-femmes.php

14. Blaquière & Zéau, 'Les inégalités femmes–hommes dans le monde'.

15. The People's Pension, *The Gender Pensions Gap: Tackling the motherhood penalty*, 2019, https://thepeoplespension.co.uk/info/wp-content/ uploads/sites/3/2019/05/Gender-pension-gap-report_2019.pdf?_ ga=2.266830215.828085961.1558344839-1994914714.1558344839

16. Data analysis by Dalberg Global Development Advisors using data from UN Women, *Progress of the World's Women, 2015–2016. State of the World's Fathers* report 2017 says: '75 countries included: South Asia (3), Middle East and North Africa (7), Sub-Saharan Africa (12), East Asia and the Pacific (5), Latin America (13), Central and Eastern Europe and Central Asia (16), and Developed Countries (19). Total hours may not add up perfectly due to rounding.' MenCare Advocacy, *State of the World's Fathers 2017: Time for Action*, 2017, https://sowf.men-care.org/wp-content/uploads/sites/4/2017/06/PRO17004_REPORT-Post-print-June9-WEB-3.pdf

17. ONS, 'Women shoulder the responsibility of "unpaid work"', 10 November 2016, https://www.ons.gov.uk/employmentandlabourmarket/peopleinwork/earningsandworkinghours/articles/womenshouldertheresponsibilityofunpaidwork/2016–11–10

18. OECD Statistics & Data Directorate, *Including unpaid household activities: An estimate of its impact on macro-economic indicators in the G7 economies and the way forward*, working paper no. 91, 25 July 2018, http://www.oecd.org/officialdocuments/publicdisplaydocumentpdf/?cote=SDD/DOC(2018)4&docLanguage=En

19. BBC Radio 4, 'The Real Gender Pay Gap', *Analysis*, 16 June 2019, https://www.bbc.co.uk/programmes/m0005t3n

20. ONS, 'Women shoulder the responsibility of "unpaid work"'.

21. OECD, 'Employment: Female share of seats on boards of the largest publicly listed companies', data extracted on 30 July 2019, https://stats.oecd.org/index.aspx?queryid=54753

22. Grant Thornton, *Women in business: beyond policy to progress*, March 2018, https://www.grantthornton.global/en/insights/articles/women-in-business-2018-report-page/

23. Jill Treanor, 'Number of senior women in Britain's boardrooms unchanged in 10 years', *The Guardian*, 9 November 2017, https://www.theguardian.com/business/2017/nov/08/senior-women-britains-boardrooms-unchanged-10-years; Julia Kollewe, 'Number of women in top boardroom positions falls', *The Guardian*, 17 July 2018, https://www.theguardian.com/business/2018/jul/17/number-of-women-in-top-boardroom-posi-

tions-falls-report; *Market Inspector*, 'Women in Top Leadership Positions'. For the FTSE 250, the figure was a slightly lower 24%. See Powell, *Women and the Economy*.

24. *Market Inspector*, 'Women in Top Leadership Positions'.

25. Credit Suisse, 'Credit Suisse Research Institute Releases the CS Gender 3000: The Reward for Change Report Analyzing the impact of Female Representation in Boardrooms and Senior Management', press release, 22 September 2016, https://www.credit-suisse.com/about-us-news/en/articles/media-releases/csri-gender-3000-201609.html

26. Catalyst, 'Quick Take: Women in Management', 30 July 2018, https://www.catalyst.org/research/women-in-management/; Grant Thornton, *Women in Business*.

27. *The Economist*, 'Ten years on from Norway's quota for women on corporate boards', 17 February 2018, https://www.economist.com/business/2018/02/17ten-years-on-from-norways-quota-for-women-on-corporate-boards

28. Vicky Pryce, *Why Women Need Quotas*, London: Biteback, 2015.

29. Kollewe, 'Number of women in top boardroom positions falls, says report'.

30. UK Department for Business, Energy & Industrial Strategy and Andrew Griffiths MP, 'Revealed: The worst explanations for not appointing women to FTSE company boards', 31 May 2018, https://www.gov.uk/government/news/revealed-the-worst-explanations-for-not-appointing-women-to-ftse-company-boards

31. Alison Booth, Elliott Fan, Xin Meng & Dandan Zhang, *Gender Differences in Competitiveness: Evidence from China*, paper presented at the Royal Economic Society conference, University of Sussex, March 2018.

32. Sidney Webb, 'The Alleged Differences in the Wages Paid to Men and to Women for Similar Work', *The Economic Journal* 1(4), 1981, pp. 635–662.

33. Mariana Mazzucato, *The Value of Everything: Making and Taking in the Global Economy*, London: Penguin Economics.

34. Gender Equality in Ireland, 'Women in Decision-Making', n.d., http://www.genderequality.ie/en/GE/Pages/womenindecisionmaking

35. Esther Duflo, 'Women Empowerment and Economic Development', *Journal of Economic Literature*, 50(4), 2012, pp. 1051–1079.

36. Jörg Baten & Alexandra de Pleijt, 'Female autonomy generates superstars in long-term development: Evidence from 15th to 19th century Europe', VOX CEPR Policy Portal, 11 February 2019, https://voxeu.org/article/positive-impact-female-autonomy-economic-gro

37. Lagarde & Ostry, 'The macroeconomic benefits of gender diversity'.

38. Sanchari Roy, *Discriminatory Laws Against Women: A Survey of the Literature*, World Bank Group Development Economics Global Indicators Group, policy research working paper 8719, January 2019, http://documents.worldbank.org/curated/en/393191548685944435/pdf/WPS8719.pdf

39. Thomas Piketty, trans. A. Goldhammer, *Capital in the Twenty-First Century*, Boston, MA: HBS Press, 2014.

40. G.B. Eggertsson & P. Krugman, 'Debt, Deleveraging, and the Liquidity Trap: A Fisher-Minsky-Koo Approach', *The Quarterly Journal of Economics*, 127(3), 2015, pp. 1469–1513.

41. Ilyana Kuziemko, Jessica Pan, Jenny Shen & Ebonya Washington, 'Women's anticipation of the employment effects of motherhood: Evidence and implications', VOX CEPR Policy Portal, 22 September 2018, https://voxeu.org/article/do-women-anticipate-employment-effects-motherhood-evidence-and-implications

42. European Commission, 'European employment strategy', n.d., https://ec.europa.eu/social/main.jsp?catId=101&langId=en

43. Sam Smethers, 'Fat Cat Friday Shows How Little Is Being Done to Close the Gender Pay Gap', *The Metro*, 4 January 2019, available at https://www.fawcettsociety.org.uk/blog/fat-cat-friday-shows-how-little-is-being-done-to-close-the-gender-pay-gap

44. Larry Elliott, 'More women in the workplace could boost economy by 35%, says Christine Lagarde', *The Guardian*, https://www.theguardian.com/world/2019/mar/01/more-women-in-the-workplace-could-boost-economy-by-35-says-christine-lagarde

45. Roy, *Discriminatory Laws Against Women*; Gonzales et al., 'Fair Play: More Equal Laws Boost Female Labor Force Participation', IMF Staff Discussion Note SDN/15/02, 2015; Islam et al., 'Unequal Laws and the Disempowerment of Women in the Labour Market: Evidence from Firm-Level Data', *Journal of Development Studies*, 55(318), 2018, pp. 1–23.

46. Stéphanie Thomson, '18 countries where women need their husband's permission to work', World Economic Forum, 10 November 2015, https://www.weforum.org/agenda/2015/11/18-countries-where-women-need-their-husbands-permission-to-get-a-job/

47. Lucy Lamble, 'Only six countries in the world give women and men equal legal work rights', *The Guardian*, 1 March 2019, https://www.theguardian.com/global-development/2019/mar/01/only-six-countries-in-the-world-give-women-and-men-equal-legal-rights-

48. World Bank Group, *Women, Business and the Law 2019: A Decade of Reform*, 2019, https://openknowledge.worldbank.org/bitstream/handle/10986/31327/WBL2019.pdf?sequence=4&isAllowed=y

49. Roy, *Discriminatory Laws Against Women*.

50. M. Hallward-Driemeier & O. Gajigo, *Strengthening Economic Rights and Women's Occupational Choice: The Impact of Reforming Ethiopia's Family Law*, World Bank, Policy Research Working Paper no. 6695, 2013, https://openknowledge.worldbank.org/handle/10986/16919

51. M. Hallward-Driemeier, M, T. Hasan & A. B. Rusu, *Women's Legal Rights over 50 Years: What Is the Impact of Reform?*, World Bank, Policy Research Working Paper no. 6617, 2013, http://documents.worldbank.org/curated/en/340791468151787181/pdf/WPS6617.pdf.

52. Susan L. Averett & Julie L. Hotchkiss, 'Female Labor Supply with a Discontinuous Nonconvex Budget Constraint: Incorporation of a Part-Time/Full-Time Wage Differential', *The Review of Economics and Statistics*, 79(3), 1997, https://dspace.lafayette.edu/bitstream/handle/10385/986/Averett-ReviewofEconomicsandStatistics-vol79-no3-1997.pdf?sequence=1

PART TWO: MOTHERHOOD AND CARING

1. Josie Cox, 'Women earn on average £223,000 less than men over a lifetime, study shows', *The Independent*, 30 March 2018, https://www.independent.co.uk/news/business/news/gender-pay-gap-wages-young-womens-trust-reporting-deadline-discrimination-a8279186.html

2. James Knight, 'The "gender pay gap" is a non-issue', Institute of Economic Affairs, 12 February 2016, https://iea.org.uk/blog/the-gender-pay-gap-is-a-non-issue

3. Monica Costa Dias, William Elming & Robert Joyce, 'Gender wage gap grows year on year after childbirth as mothers in low-hours jobs see no wage progression', Institute for Fiscal Studies press release, 23 August 2016, https://www.ifs.org.uk/publications/8429

4. Monica Costa Dias, Robert Joyce & Francesca Parodi, 'Mothers suffer big long-term pay penalty from part-time working', Institute for Fiscal Studies press release, 5 February 2018, https://www.ifs.org.uk/publications/10364

5. Paul Johnson, 'The first step to tackling the gender pay gap is to understand it', *The Times*, 23 August 2016, https://www.ifs.org.uk/publications/8435

6. UK Equality & Human Rights Commission, 'Three in four working mothers say they've experienced pregnancy and maternity discrimination', 5 April 2016, https://www.equalityhumanrights.com/en/our-work/news/three-four-working-mothers-say-they%E2%80%99ve-experienced-pregnancy-and-maternity

7. UK Equality & Human Rights Commission, 'Managing pregnancy and maternity in the workplace', n.d., https://www.equalityhumanrights.com/en/our-work/managing-pregnancy-and-maternity-workplace

8. Alexandra Topping, 'Maternity leave discrimination means 54,000 women lose their jobs each year', *The Guardian*, 24 July 2015, https://www.theguardian.com/money/2015/jul/24/maternity-leave-discrimination-54000-women-lose-jobs-each-year-ehrc-report

9. Press Association, '40% of managers avoid hiring younger women to get around maternity leave', *The Guardian*, 12 August 2014, https://www.theguardian.com/money/2014/aug/12/managers-avoid-hiring-younger-women-maternity-leave

10. Francois Béguin, 'A l'hopital, les carrières des femmes sont semées d'obstacles', *Le Monde*, 7 March 2019, https://www.lemonde.fr/societe/article/2019/03/07/a-l-hopital-les-carrieres-des-femmesrestent-des-parcours-semes-d-obstacles_5432707_3224.html

11. Bridget Ansel, 'Is the cost of childcare driving women out of the U.S. workforce?', Equitable Growth, 29 November 2016, https://equitablegrowth.org/is-the-cost-of-childcare-driving-women-out-of-the-u-s-workforce/

12. Claudia Goldin, *The Quiet Revolution That Transformed Women's*

Employment, Education, and Family, NBER Working Paper 11953, 2006 Ely Lecture to the American Economic Association, https://core.ac.uk/download/pdf/6853411.pdf

13. Claudia Goldin et al., 'The Expanding Gender Earnings Gap: Evidence from the LEHD-2000 Census', *American Economic Review: Papers and Proceedings*, 107(5), 2017, pp. 110–114, https://scholar.harvard.edu/files/goldin/files/gkob_longerversion.pdf

14. Goldin (1991a).

15. Vera E. Troeger, *Which way now? Economic policy after a decade of upheaval*, Social Market Foundation, CAGE Policy Report, February 2019, pp. 107–123.

16. Despite the heavy dominance of women in book publishing, for example, the industry still has a substantial gender pay gap, as revealed in the UK's Pay Reviews since 2018.

17. Danny Dorling, *Peak Inequality*, Bristol: Bristol University Press, 2018.

18. European Parliament, 'Work-life balance for parents and carers', European Parliament legislative resolution of 4 April 2019 on the proposal for a directive of the European Parliament and of the Council on work-life balance for parents and carers and repealing Council Directive 2010/18/EU (COM(2017)0253-C8-0137/2017-2017/0085(COD)), http://www.europarl.europa.eu/sides/getDoc.do?pubRef=-//EP//NON-SGML+TA+P8-TA-2019–0348+0+DOC+PDF+V0//EN

19. ScienceDirect, 'Maternity Protection', n.d., https://www.sciencedirect.com/topics/economics-econometrics-and-finance/maternity-protection. Practice for general parental leave was also inconsistent across Europe in the mid-2000s, with the former socialist countries of Poland, the Czech Republic and Slovakia being particularly generous. France was, too, being a country that has traditionally encouraged large families and which still offers substantial financial incentives for mothers. Italy and Belgium, on the other hand, were at the bottom of the scale.

20. This was the rate in the first year of the act's application; it has been adjusted annually since.

21. Wrigleys Solicitors, 'UK: Is Enhanced Maternity Pay Discriminatory On The Ground of Sex?', Mondaq, 22 January 2019, http://www.mondaq.

com/uk/x/773442/Employee+Benefits+Compensation/Hours+Spent+Sleeping+By+SleepIn+Care+Workers+Should+Not+Be+Taken+Into+Account+When+Calculating+NMW; Maternity Action, 'Shared parental leave and pay', information sheet, May 2018, https://maternity-action.org.uk/advice/shared-parental-leave-and-pay/

22. Libertad Gonzalez & Lidia Farré, 'Does paternity leave reduce fertility?', *Journal of Public Economics*, 172, 2019, pp. 52–66; Dream McClinton, 'Men who receive paid paternity leave want fewer children, study finds', *The Guardian*, 20 May 2019, https://www.theguardian.com/world/2019/may/20/paid-paternity-leave-study-spain-men-fewer-children

23. Quoted by *Alice de Jonge*, 'International comparisons and the political context of women on boards', in Alice de Jonge, *The Glass Ceiling in Chinese and Indian Boardrooms: Women Directors in Listed Firms in China and India*, Chandos Asian Studies Series, Cambridge: Chandos, 2015; and Emma Saragossi, *Mothers on Boards: Comparing the Level of Support for Working Mothers to the Proportion of Women in Senior Management in Eight OECD Countries*, 30% Club, August 2013, https://30percentclub.org/wp-content/uploads/2011/06/Mothers-on-boards.pdf

24. European Parliament, 'Work-life balance for parents and carers'.

25. Ibid.

26. Aviva, 'Equal parental leave: why it's good for employers too', 4 February 2019, https://www.aviva.co.uk/business/business-perspectives/featured-articles-hub/equal-parental-leave/

27. S.L. Averett et al., 'Tax Credits, Labor Supply, and Child Care', *Review of Economics and Statistics*, 79(1), 1997, pp. 125–135; P. Fisher, British Tax Credit Simplification, the Intra-household Distribution of Income and Family Consumption", *Oxford Economic Papers*, 68(2), 2016, pp. 444–464. Quoted in Sanchari Roy, *Discriminatory Laws Against Women: A Survey of the Literature*, World Bank Group Development Economics Global Indicators Group, policy research working apper 8719, January 2019, http://documents.worldbank.org/curated/en/393191548685944435/pdf/WPS8719.pdf

28. Darren Jones MP, 'Free Childcare Costs and Benefits,—[Geraint Davies in the Chair], speech in Westminster Hall, 9:30am, 19 February 2019,

available at https://www.theyworkforyou.com/whall/?id=2019–02–19a.467.0

29. OECD, *Society at a Glance 2016: OECD Social Indicators*, OECD Publishing, Paris.

30. Aparna Mathur & Abby McCloskey, 'How to improve economic opportunity for women', American Enterprise Institute, 27 June 2014, http://www.aei.org/publication/how-to-improve-economic-opportunity-for-women/

31. Richard V. Reeves & Joanna Venator, 'Gender Gaps in Relative Mobility', Brookings Institution, 12 November 2013, www.brookings.edu/blogs/social-mobility-memos/posts/2013/11/12-gender-gaps-relative-mobility-reeves.

32. David Blau & Erdal Tekin, 'The determinants and consequences of child care subsidies for single mothers in the USA', *Journal of Population Economics*, 20(4), 2007, pp. 719–741.

33. M. Baker, J. Gruber & K. Milligan, 'Universal Child Care, Maternal Labor Supply, and Family Well-Being', *Journal of Political Economy*, 116(4), 2008, pp. 709–745.

34. M. Berger & D. Black, 'Child Care Subsidies, Quality of Care, and the Labor Supply of Low-Income, Single Mothers', *The Review of Economics and Statistics*, 74(4), 1992, pp. 635–642.

35. Sarah Cattan et al., 'The health effects of Sure Start', IFS report, 3 June 2019, https://www.ifs.org.uk/publications/14139

36. See, for example, M.A. Russell et al., 'Antisocial Behavior among Children in Poverty: Understanding Environmental Effects in Daily Life', in C.A. Pietz & C.A. Mattson (eds), *Violent Offenders: Understanding and Assessment*, Oxford: OUP, 2014, available at https://adaptlab.org/wp-content/uploads/2016/10/RussellEnvEffChp5.30.13R_corr.pdf

37. Ecorys, 'Pillar 4: The Impact of subsidized children's day care on gender equality and economic growth', *Impact Assessments and Industrial Competitiveness*, https://www.ecorys.com/sites/default/files/files/Pillar-4-CD17500-childcare-gender-equality-economic-growth.pdf

38. Mathur & McCloskey, 'How to improve economic opportunity for women'.

39. Jean Kimmel, 'Child Care Costs As A Barrier To Employment For Single And Married Mothers', *The Review of Economics and Statistics*, 80(2), 1998, pp. 287–299.

40. D. Meyer and D. T. Rosenbaum, 'Welfare, the Earned Income Tax Credit, and the Labor Supply of Single Mothers', *Quarterly Journal of Economics* 116, 2001, pp. 1063–114; and B. D. Meyer and D. T. Rosenbaum, 'Making Single Mothers Work: Recent Tax and Welfare Policy and Its Effects', *National Tax Journal* 53, 2000), pp. 1027–62.

41. Vidhi Chhaochharia, 'Childcare policies boost women's wages and careers: Evidence from Germany', Royal Economic Society annual conference, University of Sussex, March 2018.

42. Enrica Maria Martino, 'The labour cost of motherhood: Evidence from Italy', Royal Economic Society annual conference, University of Sussex, March 2018.

43. David C. Ribar, 'Child Care and the Labor Supply of Married Women: Reduced Form Evidence', *The Journal of Human Resources*, 27(1), Special Issue on Child Care, 1992, pp. 134–165.

44. For Sweden, see D. Lundin et al., 'How Far can Reduced Child Care Prices Push Female Labour Supply?', *Labour Economics*, 15(4), 2008, pp. 647–659. For Norway, see T. Havnes & M. Mogstad, 'Money for Nothing? Universal Child Care and Maternal Employment', *Journal of Public Economics*, 95, 2011, pp. 1455–1465; and S. Black et al., 'Cash or Care? The Effect of Child Care Subsidies on Academic Outcomes', *Review of Economics and Statistics*, 96(5), 2014, pp. 824–837. For France, see P. Givort & C. Marbot, 'Does the Cost of Child Care Affect Female Labor Market Participation? An Evaluation of a French Reform of Child Care Subsidies', *Labour Economics*, 36, 2015, pp. 99–111. For the Netherlands, see L.J.H. Bettendorf et al., 'Child Care Subsidies and Labour Supply—Evidence from a Dutch Reform', *Labour Economics*, 36, 2015, pp. 112–123. For Canada, see M. Baker et al., 'Universal Child Care, Maternal Labor Supply, and Family Well-being'. For the US, see J.B. Gelbach, 'Public schooling for young children and maternal labor supply', *American Economic Review*, 92(1), pp. 307–322; and S.L. Averett et al., 'Tax Credits, Labor Supply, and Child Care'.

45. Mike Brewer et al., 'Does free childcare help parents work?', IFS briefing note, 1 December 2016, https://www.ifs.org.uk/publications/8792; Tara Breathnach, '30 hours of free childcare—will my child get it and is it REALLY free?', 1 October 2018, https://www.madeformums.com/news/30-hours-of-free-childcare-will-my-child-get-it/

46. Sarah Cattan, 'Can universal preschool increase the labor supply of mothers?', *IZA World of Labor*, 312, 2016, https://www.ifs.org.uk/publications/8743

47. Ibid.

48. Reeves & Venator, *Gender Gaps in Relative Mobility*.

49. Under exceptional circumstances, two children were allowed, albeit with severe financial penalties.

50. Mark Zandi & Sophia Koropeckyj, 'Universal Child Care and Early Learning Act: Helping Families and the Economy', Moody's analysis, February 2019, https://www.warren.senate.gov/imo/media/doc/Moody's%20Analysis_Child_Care_Act.pdf

51. European Parliament, 'Work-life balance for parents and carers'.

52. Robert Joyce & Agnes Norris Keiller, 'The "gender commuting gap" widens considerably in the first decade after childbirth', IFS observation, 7 November 2018, https://www.ifs.org.uk/publications/13673; Cassie Werber, 'Women have shorter commutes than men—and could be hurting their careers', *Quartz at Work*, 12 November 2018, https://qz.com/work/1460103/the-gender-commuting-gap-could-be-linked-to-the-pay-gap-between-men-and-women/

53. For example, see Jennifer Roberts et al., '"It's driving her mad": Gender differences in the effects of commuting on psychological health', *Journal of Health Economics*, 30(5), 2011, pp. 1064–1076.

54. Data from BHPS 1991–2008 and Understanding Society 2009–15.

55. UK Data Service, 'International Women's Day and the gender pay gap', 8 March 2018, https://ukdataservice.ac.uk/news-and-eventsnewsitem/?id=5284

56. Mandy Garner, 'Mums forced out due to lack of flexible jobs', Working Mums, 18 October 2016, https://www.workingmums.co.uk/mums-forced-due-lack-flexible-jobs/

57. Holly O'Mahony, 'Why now's the time to embrace flexible working', *The Guardian* Jobs, 31 January 2017, https://jobs.theguardian.com/article/why-now-s-the-time-to-embrace-flexible-working/

58. Amna Silim & Alfie Stirling, *Women and Flexible Working: Improving Female Employment Outcomes in Europe*, IPPR, December 2014, https://www.ippr.org/files/publications/pdf/women-and-flexible-working_Dec2014.pdf

59. 2,515 employees in organisations with over 250 members of staff were surveyed.

60. BBC Radio 4, *Today*, 18 March 2019, 7.20 am.

PART THREE: BIAS

1. OECD & Scottish Government, 'Programme for International Student Assessment (PISA) 2009, Highlights from Scotland's Results', Statistics Publication Notice, 7 December 2010, https://www.webarchive.org.uk/wayback/archive/20180517052911/http://www.gov.scot/Publications/2010/12/10141122/28

2. An interactive map of gender inequality in European countries is available at *Market Inspector*, 'How to Decrease Gender Pay Gap in 7 Steps', last updated 13 November 2018, https://www.market-inspector.co.uk/blog/2017/06/decrease-gender-pay-gap

3. Institute for New Economic Thinking CORE project, *The Economy* version 1.7.0, n.d., '19.2. Accidents of birth: Another lens to study inequality', available at https://core-econ.org/the-economy/book/text/19.html#192-accidents-of-birth-another-lens-to-study-inequality

4. Alexandra Topping et al., 'Gender pay gap figures reveal eight in 10 UK firms pay men more', *The Guardian*, 4 April 2018, https://www.theguardian.com/uk/commentisfree https://www.theguardian.com/money/2018/apr/04/gender-pay-gap-figures-reveal-eight-in-10-uk-firms-pay-men-more

5. Prof. Wendy Olsen, Dr. Vanessa Gash, Sook Kim, Dr Min Zhang, *The gender pay gap in the UK: evidence from the UKHLS* [UK Household Longitudinal Survey], UK Government Equalities Office, research report, May 2018, https://assets.publishing.service.gov.uk/government/uploads/system/uploads/attachment_data/file/706030/Gender_pay_gap_in_the_UK_evidence_from_the_UKHLS.pdf

6. ONS, 'Understanding the gender pay gap in the UK', 17 January 2018, https://backup.ons.gov.uk/wp-content/uploads/sites/3/2018/01/Understanding-the-gender-pay-gap-in-the-UK.pdf

7. Nick Curtis, 'Who's afraid of Fiona Woolf?', *Evening Standard*, 11 July 2014.

8. ONS, 'Understanding the gender pay gap in the UK'.

9. UK Department for Education, 'School workforce in England: November 2016', 22 June 2017, https://www.gov.uk/government/statistics/school-workforce-in-england-november-2016

10. UK Department for Education, 'School workforce in England: November 2017', 28 June 2018, https://assets.publishing.service.gov.uk/government/uploads/system/uploads/attachment_data/file/719772/SWFC_MainText.pdf

11. Department for Business, Energy and Industrial Strategy & Andrew Griffiths MP, 'Revealed: The worst explanations for not appointing women to FTSE company boards', 31 May 2018, https://www.gov.uk/government/news/revealed-the-worst-explanations-for-not-appointing-women-to-ftse-company-boards

12. Stefanie K. Johnson et al., 'If There's Only One Woman in Your Candidate Pool, There's Statistically No Chance She'll Be Hired', *Harvard Business Review*, 26 April 2016, https://hbr.org/2016/04/if-theres-only-one-woman-in-your-candidate-pool-theres-statistically-no-chance-shell-be-hired

13. *Sunday Times* style magazine, 28 April 2019, p. 30.

14. Rosabeth Moss Kanter, *Men and Women of the Corporation*, New York: Basic, 1977.

15. Melissa A. Wheeler & Victor Sojo, 'Unconscious bias is keeping women out of senior roles, but we can get around it', *The Conversation*, 7 March 2017, http://theconversation.com/unconscious-bias-is-keeping-women-out-of-senior-roles-but-we-can-get-around-it-73518

16. Pilar Domingo et al., *Women's voice and leadership in decision-making: Assessing the evidence*, ODI, March 2015, https://assets.publishing.service.gov.uk/media/57a08977e5274a31e00000c4/Womens_Voice.pdf

17. Dr K. Bhavani Shankar, 'Women's Empowerment and Their Decision

Making Positions: A Sociological View', *International Research Journal of Interdisciplinary & Multidisciplinary Studies*, II(IV), 2016, pp. 29–38, http://oaji.net/articles/2016/1707-1464945343.pdf

18. Ambrose & Schminke 2015; Siri Terjesen et al., 'Women Directors on Corporate Boards: A Review and Research Agenda', *Corporate Governance, An International Review*, 17(3), 2009, pp. 320–337; C. Wolbrecht & D.E. Campbell, 'Leading By Example: Female Members of Parliament as Political Role Models', *American Journal of Political Science*, 51(4), 2007, pp. 921–939.

19. https://www.library.wisc.edu/gwslibrarian/wp-content/uploads/sites/28/2016/07/FC_3712_Lean-In-Out.pdf

20. *Evening Standard* Comment, 'The head of the SFO shows diversity at work; Farewell, Smithfield; Marathon effort', 26 April 2019, https://www.standard.co.uk/comment/comment/evening-standard-comment-the-head-of-the-sfo-shows-diversity-at-work-farewell-smithfield-marathon-a4127366.html

21. Rosamund Urwin, 'Don't hire the confident one—he'll become a bullying manager', *The Sunday Times*, 24 March 2019, https://www.thetimes.co.uk/article/dont-hire-the-confident-one-hell-become-a-bullying-manager-26t3sb89d

22. Sue Shepherd, 'Why are there so few female leaders in higher education: A case of structure or agency?', *Management in Education*, 31(2), 2017, pp. 82–87.

23. Vivian Hunt et al., *Delivering through diversity*, McKinsey & Company report, January 2018, https://www.mckinsey.com/business-functions/organization/our-insights/delivering-through-diversity

24. Martin Bentham, 'Top judge calls for rules which force women to take off veils when giving evidence in court', *Evening Standard*, 12 December 2014, https://www.standard.co.uk/news/uk/top-judge-calls-for-rules-which-force-women-to-take-off-veils-when-giving-evidence-in-court-9920224.html

25. Louisa Peacock, 'Britain's most senior female judge, Baroness Hale: "My biggest fear … When am I going to be found out?"', *The Telegraph*, 18 April 2014, http://www.telegraph.co.uk/women/womens-business/10773941/

Britains-most-senior-female-judge-Baroness-Hale-My-biggest-fear-...-When-am-I-going-to-be-found-out.html

26. Suzanne Bearne et al., 'Lady Hale: courts and judiciary should reflect diversity of UK', *The Guadian*, 15 February 2018, https://www.theguardian.com/law/2018/feb/15/lady-hale-courts-and-judiciary-should-reflect-diversity-of-uk

27. CityAM.com, Letters, Opinion, 15 March 2019, p. 20.

28. Andrew Grice, 'Labour Wants More Women on Top', *i*, 23 July 2014.

29. Denis Campbell, 'NHS drive for diversity in key roles is "going backwards"', *The Guardian*, 7 June 2019.

30. OMFIF, *Gender Balance Index 2019*, https://thinktank.omfif.org/gbi19#utm_source=omfifupdate

31. Larry Elliott, 'More women in the workplace could boost economy by 35%, says Christine Lagarde', *The Guardian*, https://www.theguardian.com/world/2019/mar/01/more-women-in-the-workplace-could-boost-economy-by-35-says-christine-lagarde

32. Carolyn Cohn & Lawrence White, 'Major UK financial firms make little progress on gender pay gap', Reuters, 5 April 2019, https://uk.reuters.com/article/us-britain-gender-pay-finance-analysis/major-uk-financial-firms-make-little-progress-on-gender-pay-gap-idUKKCN1RH0Z5

33. Ibid.

34. UK Treasury Select Committee, *Women in Finance* (HC 477), 13 June 2018, https://publications.parliament.uk/pa/cm201719/cmselect/cmtreasy/477/47702.htm

35. UK Government response to Treasury Select Committee, *Women in Finance* (HC 477), 10 August 2018, https://publications.parliament.uk/pa/cm201719/cmselect/cmtreasy/1567/156702.htm

36. David Hellier, 'Banks Face U.K. Grilling in Probe Over Big Gender Pay Gaps', Bloomberg, 16 May 2019, https://www.bloomberg.com/news/articles/2019–05–16/banks-face-u-k-grilling-in-probe-over-big-gender-pay-gaps?srnd=premium-europe

37. Tortoise, 'Gender in the city', June 2019.

38. Shepherd, 'Why are there so few female leaders in higher education'.

39. Ibid.

40. Sue Shepherd, *Appointing deputy and pro vice chancellors in pre-1992 English universities: Managers, management and managerialism*, PhD thesis, University of Kent, 2015.

41. M. Davison & R. Burke, *Women in Management World-Wide: Facts, Figures & Analysis*, Aldershot: Ashgate, 2004; H. Savigny, 'Women, Know Your Limits: Cultural Sexism in Academia', *Gender & Education*, 26(7), 2014, pp. 794–809.

42. European Commission, *She Figures 2012: Gender in Research and Innovation, Statistics and Indicators*, 2012, http://ec.europa.eu/research/science-society/document_library/pdf_06/she-figures-2012_en.pdf

43. World Bank, 'Primary education, teachers (% female)', taken from UNESCO Institute for Statistics, https://data.worldbank.org/indicator/SE.PRM.TCHR.FE.ZS

44. Charlotte Avery, 'Women remain under-represented in senior leadership roles in schools—but mentoring can help', Tes, 30 June 2017, https://www.tes.com/news/women-remain-under-represented-senior-leadership-roles-schools-mentoring-can-help; R. Chard, 'A study of current male educational leaders, their careers and next steps', *Management in Education*, 27(4), 2013, pp. 170–175.

45. L. Morley, 'The rules of the game: Women and the leaderist turn in higher education', *Gender and Education*, 25(1), L 2013, pp. 116–131.

46. St Hilda's College, Oxford went co-educational in 2007, following St Hugh's in 1985, St Anne's and Lady Margaret Hall in 1979 and Somerville in 1995.

47. BBC News, 'St Hilda's College to admit men', 7 June 2006, http://news.bbc.co.uk/1/hi/england/oxfordshire/5054126.stm

48. BBC News, 'Katie Bouman: The woman behind the first black hole image', 11 April 2019, https://www.bbc.co.uk/news/science-environment-47891902

49. *The Guardian* weekend magazine, 2 March 2019, p. 27.

50. *New Statesman*, 'Rose McGowan Q&A: "I will always look up to a woman in a man's world"', 15–21 March 2019, p. 62, https://www.newstatesman.com/culture/2019/03/rose-mcgowan-qa-i-will-always-look-woman-mans-world

51. Leonie Cooper, 'Girls to the front: why gender is still a headline issue at

festivals', *The Guardian*, 3 May 2019, https://www.theguardian.com/music/2019/may/03/girls-to-the-front-why-gender-is-still-a-headline-issue-at-festivals

52. Amelia Hill, 'Sexist stereotypes dominate front pages of British newspapers, research finds', *The Guardian*, 14 October 2012, https://www.theguardian.com/media/2012/oct/14/sexist-stereotypes-front-pages-newspapers

53. Abigail Pesta, 'Men Rule Media Coverage of Women's News', *The Daily Beast*, 13 July 2017, https://www.thedailybeast.com/men-rule-media-coverage-of-womens-news

54. Women's Media Center, *The Status of Women in U.S. Media*, February 2019, http://www.womensmediacenter.com/reports/the-status-of-women-in-u-s-media-2019

55. Rob McGibbon, 'A life in the Day: Labour peer Joan Bakewell on Pilates aged 85, *The Times*, 24 March 2019, https://www.thetimes.co.uk/article/a-life-in-the-day-labour-peer-joan-bakewell-on-pilates-aged-85-h53vl3dck

56. Karen Ross, 'Women at Work: journalism a en-gendered practice', *Journalism Studies* 2(4), 2001, pp. 431–544.

57. Kirsty Wark, *New Statesman*, 29 March–4 April 2019, p. 19.

58. Hugh Montgomery, 'Is Ella Road the most promising young playwright in Britain?', *The Telegraph*, 19 March 2019, available at https://www.hampsteadtheatre.com/news/2019/april/the-telegraph-interviews-ella-road/

59. Sonia Elks, 'The bitch is back? UK film festival sparks debate over use of term', Reuters, 5 May 2019, https://in.reuters.com/article/britain-women-film/the-bitch-is-back-uk-film-festival-sparks-debate-over-use-of-term-idINL5N22F513

60. *The Times* magazine, 23 February 2019, p. 6.

61. Gabriel Pogrund, 'Roseanne Barr turns her ire on #MeToo "hos"', *The Sunday Times* magazine, 10 March 2019, https://www.thetimes.co.uk/article/roseanne-barr-turns-her-ire-on-metoo-hos-b8p79zrwd

62. D. Hesmondhalgh & S. Baker, 'Sex, Gender and Work Segregation in the Cultural Industries, *The Sociological Review*, 63(1), 2015, pp. 23–36.

63. Culture Action Europe, *Gender Inequalities in the Cultural Sector*, 2016, https://cultureactioneurope.org/files/2016/05/Gender-Inequalities-in-the-Cultural-Sector.pdf

64. UNESCO, *Gender Equality; Heritage and Creativity*, Paris, Unesco/CLD, 2014.

65. *Evening Standard*, Comment, 18 April 2019, p. 15.

66. UNESCO, *Gender Equality; Heritage and Creativity*, p. 81.

67. *The Sunday Times* magazine, 3 March 2019, p. 21.

68. Sophie Densham, '10,300 now employed in games in UK; 19% are women', Association for UK Interactive Entertainment, 27 April 2016, https://ukie.org.uk/news/2016/04/10300-now-employed-games-uk-19-are-women

69. Rosamund Urwin, 'Male Wikipedia editors are deleting women, says Sandi Toksvig', *The Sunday Times*, 9 June 2019, p. 10.

70. Lucy Pavia, 'Stars call for gender equality at Cannes as debate on quotas continues', *Evening Standard* insider newsletter, 16 May 2019, https://www.standard.co.uk/insider/alist/stars-call-for-gender-equality-at-cannes-as-debate-on-quotas-continues-a4143596.html

71. L.J. Burton & S. Leberman (eds), *Women in Sport Leadership: Research and practice for change*, Abingdon: Routledge, 2017.

72. *The Times*, 27 May 2019, p. 49.

73. Ella Braidwood, 'When the FA Banned Women's Football', Rights Info, 4 June 2019, https://rightsinfo.org/when-the-fa-banned-womens-football/

74. Martha Kelner, 'Salary survey reveals football's staggering gender paygap', *Irish Times*, 27 November 2018, https://www.irishtimes.com/sport/soccer/english-soccer/salary-survey-reveals-football-s-staggering-gender-pay-gap-1.3306764

75. Elise Johnson, 'Who are the 5 best-paid women footballers in the world?', *It's Round & It's White*, 19 April 2018, https://www.itsroundanditswhite.co.uk/articles/who-are-the-5-best-paid-women-footballers-in-the-world

76. Alexandra Topping, 'Gender pay gap: companies under pressure to act in 2019', *The Guardian*, 1 January 2019, https://www.theguardian.com/world/2019/jan/01/gender-pay-gap-2018-brought-transparency-will-2019-bring-change

77. PricewaterhouseCoopers, 'UK Management Board', n.d., https://www.pwc.co.uk/who-we-are/executive-board.html

78. Deloitte, 'About us: The Executive Group', n.d., https://www2.deloitte. com/uk/en/pages/about-deloitte-uk/articles/the-executive-group.html; Ernst & Young, 'EY UK & Ireland leadership team', n.d., https://www. ey.com/uk/en/about-us/our-global-approach/our-leaders/ernst-and-youngs-uki-leadership-team

79. BBC News, 'David Cameron criticised for "calm down dear" jibe', 27 April 2011, https://www.bbc.co.uk/news/uk-politics-13211577

80. James Elfer, 'FTSE100 gender balance: Why "best practices" may be counter-productive', *LSE Business Review*, 17 November 2017, https://blogs. lse.ac.uk/businessreview/2017/11/17/ftse100-gender-balance-why-best-practices-may-be-counter-productive/

81. Frank Dobbin et al., 'Rage against the iron cage: The varied effects of bureaucratic personnel reforms on diversity', *American Sociological Review*, 80(5), 2015, pp. 1014–1044.

PART FOUR: SOLUTIONS

1. European Bank for Reconstruction & Development, 'The EBRD's Strategy for the Promotion of Gender Equality 2016–2020', n.d., https://www.ebrd. com/gender-strategy.html

2. Islam, A., S. Muzi and M. Amin, 'Unequal Laws and the Disempowerment of Women in the Labour Market: Evidence from Firm-Level Data', *Journal of Development Studies*, 55(318), 2018, pp. 1–23.

3. Abortion Rights, 'Closure of the Women's National Commission', 26 October 2010, http://www.abortionrights.org.uk/closure-of-the-womens-national-commission/

4. FSB, *Women in Enterprise: The Untapped Potential*, April 2016, https:// www.fsb.org.uk/docs/default-source/fsb-org-uk/fsb-women-in-enterprise-the-untapped-potential

5. *The Sunday Times*, Business & Money, 3 March 2019, p. 9.

6. UK Government Equalities Office, Women's Business Council, *Maximising women's contribution to future economic growth—Five years on*, Progress Report, 2018, https://assets.publishing.service.gov.uk/government/ uploads/system/uploads/attachment_data/file/758874/Womens-Business-Council-Progress-Report2018.pdf

7. Andrew Powell, *Women and the Economy*, House of Commons Briefing Paper Number CBP06838, 8 March 2019, https://researchbriefings.parliament.uk/ResearchBriefing/Summary/SN06838#fullreport

8. HM Treasury, *The Alison Rose Review of Female Entrepreneurship*, 8 March 2019, https://assets.publishing.service.gov.uk/government/uploads/system/uploads/attachment_data/file/784324/RoseReview_Digital_FINAL.PDF

9. Pam Alexander et al., *Greater return on women's enterprise (GROWE): The UK, women's enterprise task force's final report and recommendations*, 2009, https://strathprints.strath.ac.uk/42203/

10. Michael Searles, 'Time to ditch the tech bros? Women-led fintechs are better investments, says KPMG', *City A.M.*, 4 May 2019, http://www.cityam.com/277181/time-ditch-tech-bros-women-led-fintechs-better-investments

11. HM Treasury, *The Alison Rose Review of Female Entrpreneurship: Government Response*, March 2019, https://assets.publishing.service.gov.uk/government/uploads/system/uploads/attachment_data/file/784336/Government_Response_to_Alison_Rose_Review_of_Female_Entrepreneurship_PDF_1.2_final.pdf

12. NatWest Business Hub, 'The Alison Rose Review', updated 22 July 2019, https://www.natwestbusinesshub.com/content/rosereview

13. *The Economist*, 16 March 2019, p. 28.

14. Sheryl Sandberg, *Lean In: Women, Work and the Will to Lead*, London: Allen Lane.

15. Dawn Foster, *Lean Out*, London: Repeater Books, 2016.

16. UK Government Equalities Office Behavioural Insights Team, *Reducing the gender pay gap and improving gender equality in organisations: Evidence-based actions for employers*, 1 August 2018, https://www.bi.team/wp-content/uploads/2018/06/GEO_BIT_INSIGHT_A4_WEB.pdf

17. Vicky Pryce, 'We need legislation to get more women into top jobs', *The Guardian*, 6 January 2014, https://www.theguardian.com/public-leaders-network/women-leadership-blog/2014/jan/06/vicky-pryce-legislation-women-top-jobs

18. Belle Derks et al., 'The queen bee phenomenon: Why women leaders dis-

tance themselves from junior women', *The Leadership Quarterly*, 27, 2016, pp. 456–469.

19. Rosabeth Moss Kanter, *Men and Women of the Corporation*, New York: Basic, 1977.

20. Astrid Kunze & Amalia R. Miller, 'Women Helping Women? Evidence from Private Sector Data on Workplace Hierarchies', *The Review of Economics & Statistics*, 99(5), 2017, pp. 769–775.

21. *Evening Standard* magazine, 22 March 2019, p. 33.

22. R.H. Kitterød & M. Teigen, 'Bringing Managers Back in: Support for Gender-Equality Measures in the Business Sector', *Nordic Journal of Working Life Studies*, 8(3), 2018.

23. Credit Suisse, 'Credit Suisse Research Institute Releases the CS Gender 3000: The Reward for Change Report Analyzing the impact of Female Representation in Boardrooms and Senior Management', press release, 22 September 2016, https://www.credit-suisse.com/about-us-news/en/articles/media-releases/csri-gender-3000-201609.html

24. M. Teigen & L. Wängnerud, 'Tracing Gender Equality Cultures: Elite Perceptions of Gender Equality in Norway and Sweden', *Politics and Gender* (5), 2009, pp. 21–44.

25. Vicky Pryce with Stefan Stern, *Why Women Need Quotas*, London: Biteback, 2015.

26. The OMFIF Podcast, 'GBI Series: Gender Diversity in Central Banks', Ed Sibley in conversation with Danae Kyriakopoulou, 11 February 2019, https://www.omfif.org/meetings/podcasts/2019/february/gbi-series-gender-diversity-in-central-banks/

27. Michael Gyekye, 'Women's leadership and participation in decision-making in the Commonwealth', The Commonwealth, 17 August 2016, http://thecommonwealth.org/media/news/women-leadership-and-participation-decision-making-commonwealth

28. *Metro*, 10 May 2019, p. 22.

29. UK Government, 'The Equality Act 2010 (Gender Pay Gap Information) Regulations 2017', draft statutory instrument, came into force 6 April 2017, https://www.legislation.gov.uk/ukdsi/2017/9780111152010

30. Clara Guibourg, 'Gender pay gap: Six things we've learnt', BBC News, 7 April 2018, https://www.bbc.co.uk/news/business-43668187

31. Lucy Meakin et al., 'Finance Companies Show Little Progress in Cutting Gender Pay Gap', Bloomberg, 4 April 2019, https://www.bloomberg.com/news/articles/2019-04-04/finance-companies-show-little-progress-in-cutting-gender-pay-gap

32. Cranfield School of Management, 'Professor Sue Vinnicombe' profile, n.d., https://www.cranfield.ac.uk/som/people/professor-sue-vinnicombe-756915

33. Reuters, 'Goldman Sachs UK unit reports gender pay gap of 51 percent', 25 March 2019, https://uk.reuters.com/article/uk-goldman-sachs-gender/goldman-sachs-uk-unit-reports-gender-pay-gap-of-51-percent-idUK-KCN1R61A2

34. Richard Partington, 'UK workers would back pay transparency to fight inequality—poll', *The Guardian*, 3 June 2019, https://www.theguardian.com/inequality/2019/jun/03/uk-workers-back-pay-transparency-fight-inequality-labour

35. Claire Morris, 'Women in law: towards equality', UK Civil Service blog, 30 April 2019, https://civilservice.blog.gov.uk/2019/04/30/women-in-law-towards-equality/

36. UBS, 'Women in Economics', n.d., ubs.com/womenineconomics

37. Vera E. Troeger, *Which way now? Economic policy after a decade of upheaval*, Social Market Foundation, CAGE Policy Report, February 2019.

38. Katie Law, 'Steven Pinker's book claims people are happier and healthier than ever before', *Evening Standard*, 21 March 2019, https://www.standard.co.uk/lifestyle/books/enlightenment-now-steven-pinker-review-a4097561.html

39. *The Economist*, 'A dispiriting survey of women's lot in university economics', 23 March 2019, https://www.economist.com/finance-and-economics/2019/03/23/a-dispiriting-survey-of-womens-lot-in-university-economics

40. Ibid.

41. Further Mathematics Support Programme, *Girls' participation in A level Mathematics and Further Mathematics*, Edition No. 3, 2016, http://furthermaths.org.uk/files/FMSP-Girls-in-Maths.pdf; Cathy Smith & Jennie Golding, *Gender and Participation in Mathematics and Further Mathematics: Final Report for the Further Mathematics Support Programme*,

UCL Institute of Education, March 2017, http://furthermaths.org.uk/ docs/Gender-Participation-Casestudy-final2017.pdf; Chinelo Nkechi Ikem, 'The Importance of Female Role Models in the Classroom', *Pacific Standard*, 30 January 2018, https://psmag.com/education/the-importance-of-female-role-models-in-the-classroom; *The Economist*, 'Women and economics: insufficient equilibrium', 19 December 2017, https://www. economist.com/news/christmas-specials/21732699-professions-problem-women-could-be-problem-economics-itself-women-and; Frances Weetman, 'Where are all the women economists?', *New Statesman*, 3 February 2017, https://www.newstatesman.com/politics/feminism/2017/02/where-are-all-women-economists

42. Vicky Pryce, 'How long until another woman wins the top economics prize?', *Prospect*, 10 October 2018, https://www.prospectmagazine.co.uk/ economics-and-finance/how-long-until-another-woman-wins-the-top-economics-prize

43. Catherine Porter & Danila Serra, 'Gender differences in the choice of major: The importance of female role models', Southern Methodist University Departmental Working Paper No. 1705, 5 December 2017.

44. Leah Boustan & Andrew Langan, 'Variation in Women's Success across PhD Programs in Economics', *Journal of Economic Perspectives*, 33(1), 2019, pp. 23–42.

45. Diane Hofkins, 'Understanding Participation Rates in Post-16 Mathematics and Physics (UPMAP)', UCL Institute of Education, 19 June 2017, http:// www.ucl.ac.uk/ioe/research/featured-research/upmap

46. Amit Roy, '£500 bounty for an A in math, howzat!—British bait to lure students to science', *The Telegraph India*, 4 September 2006, https://www. telegraphindia.com/india/500-bounty-for-an-a-in-math-howzatt-british-bait-to-lure-students-to-science/cid/769995

47. Dame Sue Ion, 'What She Said: Nuclear Engineer Dame Sue Ion Answers Your Workplace Dilemma', *The Sunday Times*, 6 May 2018, https://www. thetimes.co.uk/article/what-she-said-nuclear-engineer-dame-sue-ion-answers-your-workplace-dilemma-8t7qxjdpc

48. Rachel Cassidy et al., 'How can we increase girls' uptake of maths and physics A-level?', IFS report, 22 August 2018, https://www.ifs.org.uk/publications/13277

49. Ibid.

50. Matthew Ballew et al., 'Gender Differences in Public Understanding of Climate Change', Yale Program on Climate Change Communication, 20 November 2018, https://climatecommunication.yale.edu/publications/gender-differences-in-public-understanding-of-climate-change/

51. Suzanne Franks, *Having None Of It: Women, Men and the Future of Work*, London: Granta, 2000, p. 189.

52. Caroline Criado-Perez, *Invisible Women: Exposing Data Bias in a World Designed for Men*, London: Chatto & Windus, 2019.

53. Andrew Powell, *Women and the Economy*, House of Commons briefing paper number CBP06838, 8 March 2019, https://researchbriefings.files.parliament.uk/documents/SN06838/SN06838.pdf

54. Mariya Brussevich et al., *Gender, Technology, and the Future of Work*, IMF staff discussion notes SDN/18/07, 8 October 2018, https://www.imf.org/en/Publications/Staff-Discussion-Notes/Issues/2018/10/09/Gender-Technology-and-the-Future-of-Work-46236

55. Era Dabla-Norris & Kalpana Kochhar, 'Women, Technology, and the Future of Work', IMF Blog, 16 November 2018, https://blogs.imf.org/2018/11/16/women-technology-and-the-future-of-work/

56. Skillset, sector skills council for the creative industries, as part of *The Guardian*'s 2009 Employment Census: Dinah Caine, 'Skillset launches 2010 survey of media workforce', *The Guardian*, 1 June 2010, https://www.theguardian.com/media/organgrinder/2010/jun/01/skillset-survey-media-workforce

57. A. Grice, 'Women bear 85% of burden after Coalition's tax and benefit tweaks', *The Independent*, 4 December 2014, http://ind. pn/1nxth5x

58. Danny Dorling, *A Better Politics: How Government Can Make Us Happier*, London: London Publishing Partnership, 2016.

59. Douglas McWilliams, *The Inequality Paradox: How Capitalism Can Work for Everyone*, New York: Abrams Press, 2019.

CONCLUSIONS

1. Ray Dalio, 'Why and How Capitalism Needs to Be Reformed (Part 1)', LinkedIn, 4 April 2019, https://www.linkedin.com/pulse/why-how-capitalism-needs-reformed-ray-dalio/

2. Alexandra Topping, 'Gender pay gap: companies under pressure to act in 2019', *The Guardian*, 1 January 2019, https://www.theguardian.com/world/2019/jan/01/gender-pay-gap-2018-brought-transparency-will-2019-bring-change

3. GoodCorporation, 'GoodCorporation Announces Revised Business Ethics Standards', n.d., https://www.goodcorporation.com/press-statements/goodcorporation-announces-revised-business-ethics-standard/

4. UK Equality & Human Rights Commission, 'Gender pay gap determines women's choice of employer', 10 October 2018, https://www.equalityhumanrights.com/en/our-work/news/gender-pay-gap-determines-women%E2%80%99s-choice-employer

5. Aleksandra Wisniewska et al., 'Gender Pay Gap: women still short-changed in the UK', *Financial Times*, 23 April 2019, https://ig.ft.com/gender-pay-gap-UK-2019/

6. C.G. Ogloblin, 'The Gender Earnings Differential in the Russian Transition Economy', *ILR Review*, 52(4), 1999, pp. 602–627; C.G. Ogloblin, 'The Gender Earnings Differential in Russia after a Decade of Economic Transition', *Applied Econometrics and International Development*, 5(3), 2005, pp. 5–26.

7. For Taiwan, see J.E. Zveglich and Y.M. Rodgers, 'The Impact of Protective Measures for Female Workers', *Journal of Labor Economics*, 21(3), pp. 533–555, 2003; for a cross-country study, see A. Islam, S. Muzi and M. Amin, 'Unequal Laws and the Disempowerment of Women in the Labour Market: Evidence from Firm-Level Data', *Journal of Development Studies*, 55(318), 2018, pp. 1–23. Cited in Sanchari Roy, *Discriminatory Laws Against Women: A Survey of the Literature*, World Bank Group Development Economics Global Indicators Group, policy research working paper 8719, January 2019, http://documents.worldbank.org/curated/en/393191548685944435/pdf/WPS8719.pdf

8. An organisation performs better the more women executives it has. M. Noland et al., *Is Gender Diversity Profitable? Evidence from a Global Survey*, Washington, DC: Peterson Institute for International Economics, 2016.

INDEX